Personal Meanings

Personal Meanings

The First Guy's Hospital Symposium on the Individual Frame of Reference

Edited by

ERIC SHEPHERD
and
J. P. WATSON
Guy's Hospital Medical School

1807 175 YEARS OF PUBLISHING 1982

JOHN WILEY & SONS

Chichester · New York · Brisbane · Toronto · Singapore

Library of Congress Cataloging in Publication Data:

Guy's Hospital Symposium on the Individual Frame
    of Reference (1st: 1980)
    Personal meanings.

    Includes index.
    1. Meaning (Psychology) — Congresses.   2. Self-
perception — Congresses.   3. Counseling — Congresses.
I. Shepherd, Eric.   II. Watson, J. P. (James
Patrick)   III. Title.
BF778.G85   1980   155.2   82-1986
                                         AACR2
ISBN 0 471 10220 2

British Library Cataloguing in Publication Data:

First Guy's Hospital Symposium on the Individual Frame
    of Reference (*1st: 1980*)
    Personal meanings.
    1. Interpersonal communication — Congresses
    I. Title   II. Shepherd, Eric   III. Watson, J. P.
    158'.2   BF637.C45

    ISBN 0 471 10220 2

Phototypeset by Dobbie Typesetting Service, Plymouth, Devon
Printed and bound in Great Britain at The Pitman Press, Bath

List of contributors

JENNIFER M. BROWN   *Department of Psychology, University of Surrey, Guildford.*

DAVID A. CURSON   *St Andrew's Hospital, Northampton, and Department of Psychiatry, Guy's Hospital Medical School, London.*

J. M. FOSKETT   *Bethlem Hospital, Beckenham.*

F. FRANSELLA   *Royal Free Hospital Medical School, London.*

ROSALIND C. S. FURLONG   *Friern Hospital, Barnet.*

ROM HARRÉ   *Sub-Faculty of Philosophy, University of Oxford.*

KEITH HAWTON   *Department of Psychiatry, University of Oxford.*

GLORIA K. LITMAN   *Addiction Research Unit, Institute of Psychiatry, London.*

R. M. ROSSER   *Department of Psychiatry, Charing Cross Hospital Medical School, London.*

MILDRED L. G. SHAW   *Educational Studies, Middlesex Polytechnic, Enfield.*

ERIC SHEPHERD   *Department of Psychology, City of London Polytechnic, and Department of Psychiatry, Guy's Hospital Medical School, London.*

JOHN SHOTTER   *Department of Psychology, University of Nottingham.*

JONATHAN D. SIME   *Department of Psychology, University of Surrey, Guildford.*

J. P. WATSON   *Department of Psychiatry, Guy's Hospital Medical School, London.*

Contents

Overview and prospect 1
Eric Shepherd and J. P. Watson

Personal meanings: semantic relations of the fourth kind 9
Rom Harré

Understanding how to be a person: an ecological approach 23
John Shotter

Coping with the first person singular 33
Eric Shepherd

Personal meanings and personal constructs 47
F. Fransella

The extraction of personal meaning from a repertory grid 59
Mildred L. G. Shaw

Multidimensional scaling analysis of qualitative data 71
Jennifer M. Brown and Jonathan D. Sime

'To be or not to be' 91
J. H. Foskett

How patients and psychiatrists account for overdoses 103
Keith Hawton

Alcoholics, drinkers, and drunks 115
David A. Curson

**Personal meanings and alcoholism survival: translating subjective
experience into empirical data** 129
Gloria K. Litman

Personal meanings in cancer 141
Rosalind C. S. Furlong

Life with artificial organs: renal dialysis and transplantation 159
R. M. Rosser

Aspects of personal meaning in schizophrenia 175
J. P. Watson

Index of names 191

Subject index 197

Personal Meanings
Edited by Eric Shepherd and J. P. Watson
© 1982 John Wiley & Sons Ltd.

Overview and prospect

Eric Shepherd and J. P. Watson

In 1964, Phenix observed, 'Human beings are essentially creatures who have the power to experience meanings. Distinctively human existence consists in a pattern of meaning.' However, he went on to indicate that the expression of these experiences is far from easy: 'Unfortunately, the pathway to the fulfilment of meaning is never smooth . . . Values, purposes and understandings are fragile achievements and give way all too easily to attitudes of futility, frustration and doubt.'

This volume is concerned with problems in the genesis, expression, and comprehension of personal meanings. Personal meanings arise from events and relationships which a person interprets within his most basic frame of reference—his awareness of being an individual, conscious of personal agency and personal biography. In our efforts to identify another's personal meanings we may find ourselves regarding the other as we might an inanimate object and conceiving personal meaning as if it were a thing. Such an approach, observed Whitehurst (1979),

is like catching rain in a bucket for later display. What you end up with is water, which is only a little like rain.

We may remind ourselves that personal meaning is dynamic—a process, not a thing. Furthermore, much, if not most, of this process occurs outside the envelope of linguistic expression, but as Scharfetter (1980) noted: 'In the absence of speech it is difficult to form any idea of man's thinking.' A social encounter is thus an exercise in improvisation and imprecision, in which participants interact, using and construing creatively conventions in language, intonation, para-language, posture and movement, mindful of self, other, and the shared situation.

It seems to us that everyone who aspires personally and professionally to understand others will need to take these processes of personal meaning seriously and to adopt a frame of reference which sustains an

1

awareness of the individual as a person at all times. We therefore decided to convene a symposium to allow theoreticians, methodologists, and practical workers the opportunity to exchange views on what they considered to be the issues involved in the systematic study of the person within the individual frame of reference. This volume is based upon a number of contributions to the first symposium.

In the first contribution, Harré proposes that the familiar uni-dimensional *subjective–objective* distinction can with benefit be replaced by a schema which locates meanings within a two-dimensional *private–public/individual–collective* space. Following Vygotsky, he stresses a theme which pervades many of the other contributions to this volume — personal meanings both make possible and are made possible by a system of public meaning. If the individual is to have any prospect of being at all understood in a social encounter, the public display of his personal meanings cannot be entirely eccentric. As he employs metaphor to describe the nature of his experience an individual must, as Harré puts it, observe the 'toehold principle': he must maintain at least minimal contact with the world of socially shared meaning. Despite this principle, it requires considerable effort on behalf of a listener–observer to read and see beyond the metaphor. It demands a commitment to work at the problem of gaining access to another's meanings, especially in speech or text which initially appears unintelligible or alien, with all that such communication suggests about the mind of the communicator.

Shotter in the following chapter concentrates upon the interactive origins of personal meanings. He suggests that an individual in interaction is concerned with moral and social being. Encounters can be understood in terms of participants whose actions occur in a self-conscious context of joint action. Individual interpretations of a shared ritual, such as a kiss, confirm separate and shared roles as social rule followers and rule makers, with capacity for rule breaking. He argues strongly for the uniqueness of personal meanings, reflective as they are of an individual's idiosyncratic construction of encounters which can also be interpreted in taken-for-granted terms. Hence, the overtly 'dutiful' kiss as seen by the everyday observer may be quite differently viewed by both concerned. Shotter clearly has doubts as to the extent to which the 'sieve' of taken-for-granted meanings of social and scientific convention can contribute to the comprehension of a singular person's private meanings.

In the next chapter, Shepherd examines the issue of *control of meaning*. He sees assumptions about the professional helper's role and status as an expert in a specific 'field' as exercising a distracting and potentially distorting effect upon the conduct, content, comprehension and, therefore, outcome of the encounter. He suggests that the helper overcome this distancing process by remaining ever aware that he is a first person singular seeking to understand another first person singular. Such recognition brings with it the demand to be aware of personal bias and agency in the focus, form, and content of the individual's account. This implies that the helper must be systematic and examine all first-person statements. Text must be re-examined for missed, misunderstood, and meaningless material as well as for its salient content. Such examinations lead to increasing awareness that text generated by two interacting people is always incomplete and elliptical, an *ex tempore* exemplar of a joint process of tentative definition. The professional's understanding is an intuitive and rational process of reduction and reconstruction. This necessitates a check upon the validity of the helper's understanding—in a setting where feedback is currently not always requested or, indeed, its necessity acknowledged.

It could be argued that necessity for feedback constitutes an additional corollary to Kelly's Fundamental Postulate—a person's processes are psychologically channelized by the ways in which he anticipates events (Kelly, 1955). Fransella's contribution lends weight to such a notion. She points out that the philosophy of constructive alternativism implies accepting that revision and replacement are facts of life. As meaning lies within the person but is not directly accessible, the issue of accessibility takes up much of her paper. She observes that full understanding of personal meanings rests upon rigorous examination of both poles of a construct, particularly with respect to trans-contextual usage and implications. However, even during an explicit search for the meaning of construct poles, as when employing a grid method, it may be hard to identify the negation, or a submerged construct. Awareness is another issue felt to be of importance and Fransella offers an extension of Kelly's views on this. She suggests that Polanyi's (1969) distinction of *focal-subsidiary* awareness can be added to Kelly's *high level–low level* dichotomy and thus permit more adequate description of realms of construing.

Gaining access to constructs and appropriate feedback are core themes in Shaw's paper. Her interactive computer programs seek to make the individual's constructs and their usage more explicit. The properties of the computer in the elicitation and feedback process are seen by her as important since 'an assumption of outside interference is far less tenable' (p.64) for the user. These processes can be felt to be more private and less threatening with the use of a computer. However, her observation about patients' reasons for opting for a computer interview (in order to save professionals' time) needs to be examined against Shotter's observations about the personal realm and Shepherd's comments concerning personally constraining practices amongst professionals. Nonetheless, her programs demonstrably achieve their aims of extending access to constructs and heightening awareness of linkages between these by timely feedback which is in a form comprehensible to the layman.

The researcher who gathers many accounts from individuals faced with the same, or a similar, experience has to cope with vast quantities of qualitative data which challenge his capacity to identify commonalities of experience. The multidimensional scaling techniques described by Brown and Sime lead to the specification of types and taxonomies of perceptions of events. Their account of facet theory raises another theme which recurs in this volume. Researchers, like workaday helping professionals, have to focus upon something. They are obliged to adopt an antecedent, hopefully permeable, frame of reference which leads to the specification of those facets of experience which are observably salient or are important on other grounds. Key issues here are that the rationale for facet selection should be frankly stated and the need for a constant awareness of the conceptual bias which is inevitably introduced to ultimate explanations. The techniques described led to the identification not only of a relatively limited number of commonly occurring profiles —typifications of experience—but also of nontypical experiences.

The next two papers discuss the moral and practical problems raised by the personal meanings of the suicidal. From contrasting yet complementary standpoints, both examine reasons for the behaviour in terms of the essentially personal *expressive* (seeking release) mode of action and the essentially self/other *instrumental* (desire to elicit a response) mode. Foskett comments upon the stark disparity between the perceptions of the suicidal individual and the attitudes of society exemplified by professional helpers and their interventions. The individual who felt misunderstood and misheard continues to feel so. In some hazy way, such a person wants to explore the issue of living and dying. His drama, sensed as isolation and ostracism, is linked to an act, an attempt to change circumstances. The reaction of society is ambivalent and the notion, and act, of self-determination (as demonstrated by an attempt at self-destruction) is anathema to its continued, coherent existence. Society no longer, however, seeks, as it did in the past, to frighten the suicidal; rather it now 'understands and comforts them into living rather than dying' (p.95). Professionals are concerned with a higher, more abstract purpose and their actions are seen as a response to the demand to get the suicidal individual 'to hang on . . . no matter what' (p.95). Foskett feels that these persistent moral imperatives prevent the expression and comprehension of an individual's personal meanings upon which his goal-oriented behaviour is predicated. Akin to others in this volume, Foskett stresses that there is a need to look beyond and beneath the excuses and claims, in this case surrounding the suicidal act, as well as a need to listen more closely and openly to those who seek to speak of suicide.

Foskett comments that 'somewhere in the jungle of behaviour, both that of the suicidal and those who respond to them, there is some flowering of meaning' (p.98). Hawton's paper highlights the task of disentangling the contradictions of both the suicidal and the helpers in their attitudes and statements about self-destructive behaviour. Patients predominantly offer 'state of mind' explanations couched in terms of impulse, rather than instrumental 'bring about change' explanations which reflect a measure of premeditation. The more frequently occurring expressive explanation is known to be more socially acceptable to clinical staff yet, paradoxically, clinicians tend to explain the behaviour in terms of the premeditated and instrumental, characterized by hostility and manipulation. Hawton frankly acknowledges the uncertainty of the 'offered list of possible reasons' method to inform as to the personal meaning before, as opposed to after, the event. 'Thus,' he says, 'the personal meaning of the behaviour prior to taking the overdose may be denied us' (p.112) although post-attempt explanations can in his view be equally important in evaluating effects on others. Hawton's paper points to the continued need to search, as Foskett suggested, for 'ways through the jungle, ways to hold it back from overwhelming the flower, and then ways to encourage the flower's growth' (p.98).

The second pair of joint topic papers addresses the implications of personal meanings in alcoholism — a condition which has been described as chronic suicide. The contributions of Curson and Litman offer extended comments upon the society–individual contrast in a field where moral stance and stereotyping frustrate the expression and comprehension of actors whose destructive acts extend across the longer term.

In an alcohol-consuming social world which invites, cajoles and pressures an individual to join in and associates sociability with moving at least notionally towards intoxication, while at the same time condemning drunkenness in individuals (particularly in public), the personal existence of those who fail to cope is necessarily precarious. Curson describes drinking careers, pointing to social and developmental determinants of patterns of problematic drinking while, like Litman, he seeks to stress the heterogeneity of the condition of alcohol dependence. His paper emerges as a sustained indictment of persistent stereotyping by society and at the level of the professional 'drinking' subculture which includes both professional drinkers and professional helpers. His central thesis, however, turns upon the crucial point in the life of an alcoholic, when he is forced towards self-examination, when he decides to change or when he relapses.

Coping with the relapse is seen by both Curson and Litman as an imperative issue from the vantage point of the customer and from that of the disappointed professional helper—since alcoholism is a chronically relapsing condition. Litman attributes lack of interest in relapse as due to the potency of a 'collective frame of reference' in which the 'causal' constructs of loss of control, dependence and craving are exchanged and embedded in the understandings of alcoholics and helpers alike. She goes on to describe research into this area in which the 'experts', the alcoholics, were given the opportunity for free self-expression in interviews and expansion in their responses to questionnaires. Content analysis of what they said led to the identification of commonly occurring themes. From these a taxonomy of 'risk situations' and 'coping strategies' was derived. These enabled the investigation of the *critical perceptual shift*—that point at which the individual consciously chooses to go no further or, alternatively, to continue along the path to destruction.

The next two papers deal with personal meanings in physical illnesses which are characterized by the ever-present risk of deterioration and death. Both cancer and chronic renal failure present threats to the individual's processes of self-definition. Furlong and Rosser both discuss familiar phenomena of denial, grief, and fear. In both contributions we see patients seeking to exercise a measure of personal influence or control over their lives, even though an external observer would assess their behaviour as irrational.

Furlong points to the taboo which surrounds cancer in our society and inhibits discussion concerning a phenomenon seen to be worse than death itself. She indicates the problems of social isolation inherent in this condition—a situation not helped by the many barriers upon communication arising from hospital life, the medical hierarchy, and medical attitudes. Furlong examines what it can mean in this context for the clinician not to treat the patient as a person. She discusses problems which hinder expression and comprehension of personal meanings, including the ward context, fear of the clinician, fear of what might emerge in the future, and fear of an inability to cope. Counselling may aid resolution of such problems; it is possible to help the sufferer to view the present as a further opportunity for personal growth rather than as simply leading inevitably to general decline and, ultimately, death.

Rosser observes that a 'patient who lives with renal failure, like the patient who lives with cancer, confronts a life-threatening illness' (p.159). These patients pose problems for professionals who have to make both moral and distributive decisions—since transplants are in short supply. Like cancer, dialysis and transplantation are accompanied by problems of psychosocial adjustment covering all aspects of personal and public life. The problems created by transplantation are more dramatic, reflective of the added drama surrounding the decision to act. Rosser's case studies illustrate not only the diversity of meaning amidst denial and deterioration in those who must live with machines, but also the benefit for the sufferer of having a person listen, seek to comprehend, and share in the content of these meanings.

In the last paper Watson examines a theme central to the symposium —the need to integrate expressive and practical orders so as to recognize both the call for help and the request that the content of the communication be respected. He suggests that at present in clinical practice the tendency is to concentrate on practical domains of symptoms and physical intervention. In his discussion he brings together many of the themes which occur and re-occur in the diverse standpoints of contributors to this volume. He concludes that clinicians must go beyond the symptom, to listen and seek an understanding of the individual whose use of metaphor indicates pressing personal experience. For he argues that it may not be that a particular experience, in itself, is a problem, but rather that difficulty arises from the fact that the experience is unremitting.

The symposium has brought together a wide range of views concerning the problems contained within the realm of personal meaning—the dynamic processes of self-definition, self-expression, and comprehension by another in an encounter. Because they are dynamic they provide substantial conceptual and practical problems for the helping professions and researchers seeking to be systematic in the handling of the first person singular. It is, we suggest, entirely scientific for a helper and researcher to expose himself to the complexity of personhood, communication, and the reality of everyday comprehension. This will lead to explicit recognition of what we all tacitly know—that our understanding is born of the application of intuition *and* analysis in order to complete the incomplete, a text which reflects a joint endeavour, an attempt at tentative definition.

Three issues emerge. Firstly, the professional's construing of the individual and his personal meanings is necessarily a reflection of the *professional's* belief-value matrix (Polanyi, 1973). Secondly, this matrix is what renders the emergent expression—the text—intelligible, reducing complexity, identifying saliences, and allowing the construction of a representation of the professional's understanding. Thirdly, encounters with individuals conducted on the basis of greater self-awareness and respect for personhood, with necessarily increased emphasis upon the conversational mode, constitute the *intensive* approach. This is very much more demanding and sobering than more narrowly focused *extensive* designs for data collection and analysis.

For the present we hope that this volume has indicated the scope and importance of personal meanings and that they are the proper material of varied *scientific* enquiries. To ignore their complexity and their implications is impoverishing in all respects—a barrier to personal development and the development of science.

REFERENCES

Kelly, G. A. (1955) *The Psychology of Personal Constructs*. New York: Norton.
Phenix, P. H. (1964) *Realms of Meaning*. New York: McGraw-Hill.
Polanyi, M. (1969) *Knowing and Being*. London: Routledge and Kegan Paul.
Polanyi, M. (1973) *Personal Knowledge*. London: Routledge and Kegan Paul.
Scharfetter, C. (1980) *General Psychopathology* (trans. by H. Marshall). Cambridge: Cambridge University Press.
Whitehurst, G. J. (1979) Meaning and semantics. In G. J. Whitehurst and B. J. Zimmerman (Eds), *The Functions of Language and Cognition*. New York: Academic Press.

Personal Meanings
Edited by Eric Shepherd and J. P. Watson
© 1982 John Wiley & Sons Ltd.

Personal meanings:
semantic relations of the fourth kind

Rom Harré

THE ABSOLUTE PRIORITY OF SOCIAL CONVENTIONS

If, as the philosophers have taught us, meaning can arise only in a world in which conscious agents act in accordance with public and socially sustained conventions (what other kind of conventions could there be?), how can there be any private and personal realms of meaning?

By 'personal meanings' one could, perhaps, be pointing to attempts at meaning by those who have the idea of intentional action according to conventions. A person could know what they intended but be ignorant of or mistaken about the conventions for realizing that intention publicly in the semantic contexts current amongst their friends and associates — the collective in which they exist as social beings. On this view, personal meanings are really nothing but mistakes.

We can go a stage deeper. In what I have just suggested, I have assumed that what the person intended would have made sense if only he or she had known how to realize that intention in speech and for action. But could not their attempt to formulate an intention fail? Somehow the constraints of social intelligibility enter even into our very plans and projects since even what we can intend must come under the discipline of consideration as a possible social act or action.

Should we then conclude that personal meanings are impossible and the whole project of our editors misconceived? I think not, but to reach that happy conclusion some preliminary remarks about the variety of human action are called for.

There is a tendency among lay folk and psychologists to deploy an individualistic conception of the sources of human action so that what people do is thought of as 'put forth', as emerging through the action of dynamic agents that thrust something already fully formed from 'within'. Attention to the kinds of considerations advanced by 'social constructionists' such as Silver and Sabini (1978) in their theory of the

9

emotions suggests that, at least some of the time, it is advisable to look at human action as 'called forth', drawn out by imperatives that reside in the interpretative situations and settings in which people find themselves and which, of course, they may be actively seeking. Silver and Sabini demonstrate that the distinction between envy and jealousy is to be found in the distinctive social relations relative to which each of these 'green' emotions is experienced and in terms of which feelings are construed as particular emotions. But if a situation as interpreted by an actor can call forth the appropriate action to impose a distinctive interpretation on a feeling, that actor must have some form of representation of what it is appropriate there to do, to feel, etc. Intentions, emotions, and even memories, must be embedded in a socially defined semantic lexicon. Further, if we follow a line of thought initiated by G. H. Mead and lately worked up with some precision by Jeff Coulter (1979), we would be inclined to look for the social processes by which such apparent individual attributes and dispositions as the capacity to form the theoretical conception of personhood within which we organize our conception of our own mental and social life, are acquired. Accordingly, we would be inclined to see social relations as lying not only in the moment-by-moment conditions of action, but in the conditions that define its very possibility, and finally in the conditions of the genesis of beings whose actions can have meaning. Even our agency and sense of identity may be 'attributes' with which we are endowed by our *social* environment.

This bouquet of intuitions can be systematized by defining a 'space' in which to locate psychological processes, states, dispositions, and so on, by reference to two orthogonal axes (Figure 1). One axis represents the

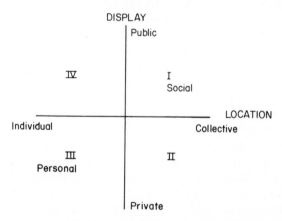

Figure 1   The two-dimensional space of anti-Cartesian psychology

degree of display running from private (displayed only to oneself) to public (displayed to anybody). The other axis represents the domain of existence and runs from individual to collective. I have argued elsewhere that many psychological attributes such as knowledge and rationality have multiple locations in such a space. Our understanding of the nature of psychological phenomena is greatly distorted, I believe, if we try to map them onto a single linear polarized dimension, say inner–subjective to outer–objective—the Cartesian proposal.

With this two-dimensional space we get four quadrants or sub-domains: public–collective, private–collective, public–individual, and private–individual. Ordinary talk as public discourse, using a collectively located system, language, is in the public–collective, or social, domain. Soliloquy, whether *sotto voce* or shouted loud in the empty woods or from an isolated mountain top, though private, is constrained by the sanctions of the socially sustained language system, something essentially collective. Much of our thinking is soliloquy—talking to ourselves. There remain the public–individual and the private–individual domains. Together they constitute the arena in which, I believe, we must seek for personal meaning. It is not just that someone's actions might be mysterious or puzzling, but unless somehow the sayings and other symbolic actions of a person were within the conventions of significant actions admitted by a society, we would not know that these were actions at all. We might not realize that there was something intended and to be interpreted. In extreme cases we might perhaps not know even that it was a person whom we were encountering.

The possibility of there being an idiographic domain of personal meanings intelligible with an interpretative effort by the members of a society requires that the domain be not wholly eccentric. This implies that something must be shared, however minimal. We could call this the 'toehold principle'. How can the unique be constituted out of the shared? The standard view is that what is unique in semiotic objects, say sentences, is their organization; the components (words, say) are the elements of a common stock. A new sentence is a new combination of old words. The problem we might be addressing in this discussion is: Could there be old combinations of new words, so to speak? Could a well known and well tried mode of organization be concretely realized in new matter? An obvious limit to this, and the preceeding possibility, would be the degree to which the organization consists of relations internal to the elements, that is, partly constituting them. In English, part of the meaning, the general grammatical category, is determined by location in the positional grammatical structures of English sentences. But there remains the residual possibility of novelty. Do they appear in and from a realm of personal (private and individual) meanings? But how could anything private and individual have a meaning to it? There seem to be two possibilities. The new semiotic item could be connected up somehow with the existing public–collective semiotic system, say by treating it as *if* it were a figurative extension of that domain. A novel (private–individual) meaning seeking a public–collective expression is rather like an extension of the public–collective linguistic system by an inspired metaphor. Perhaps some of the talk made available to us by the clinical contributors represented as being spoken by their clients a propos their kidney machines, is of this kind. It is intelligible to us just because it *could* have been figurative. Perhaps some of it was. But it might be that someone engaged in conversation with the client could, with the original actor or speaker, who was initially unintelligible, actually construct a new, though restricted, public domain of meaning; that is, build a semantic system to make actual nonsense incipient metaphor, a domain that exists only for them. This could be like the private semiotic world of lovers, but both contribute to fashioning meaning. The case I have in mind is asymmetrical, involving a sympathetic act of integration on the part of one, while the running is made by the other. Access to this restricted semiotic realm would be by establishing toe-holds through a standard lexicon, say English, which would include words like 'mother', 'clean', 'polish', 'nasty', and so on. But the content of the total discourse would be novel in that radical sense that changes would be noticeable through the violation of sub-categorial rules, for a good many but necessarily not for all of the items. The discourse might involve treating thoughts as things, processes as states, inanimate beings as animate, and so on.

These rough-and-ready considerations suggest that there cannot be personal meanings unless these are somehow related to a system of public meaning. But the matter needs much closer analysis since I have been presuming a commonsense understanding of that social meaning as defined, against which my account of personal meaning is still far too simple.

MEANING IN THE PUBLIC–COLLECTIVE REALM

Five different levels of meaning can be identified in public–collective (that is, social) interactions. Each 'level' consists of a network of relations in which the meaningful entity is embedded. The networks are levels, because each presupposes the existence of the levels 'lower' than it, but not vice versa. The lowest level is made up of *action*, distinguished merely as intended, things done rather than happening, separating off a realm of actions from accidents, inadvertencies, and so on. Actions distinguished in this way are related both definitionally and generatively to some intention or other.

When intentions can be identified and specified, two further levels are created. Intentions to act usually involve the social force of actions, or in the practical order their immediate practical effect. It is convenient to call the realization of intentions acts. I may intend to apologize, close the door, etc. But I may also intend, by apologizing, to ingratiate myself with a superior, by closing the door to shut out the noise, and so on: so the *perlocutionary effect* (Austin, 1965) could be thought of as a third level of meaning. But to realize an act, or act-sequence, in the public–social realm, a proper action must be performed. Which action is proper is specified by social rules and conventions for things done to preserve our honour in the expressive order and by the laws of nature for material achievements in the practical order. Acts form networks, as for instance, insults are associated with apologies, hammerings with re-shapings, though insults may also deafen and hammerings be expressions of contempt. Actions form sequences, as for example a wave is usually followed by a waving back, but the elements in the sequence are determined by the social conventions that link actions to act since it is the acts that are the substance of social exchanges.

At a further level we tend to distinguish intended from unintended consequences. *Intended consequences* include future actions and commitments deriving from the action in question. Sometimes these are also referred to as meanings of the action constituting a fourth level of meaning. Since one can intend only the consequence of one's activity, and for most formal, ceremonial action the anticipations are part of the normative aspect of the public understanding of the ritual, normative glosses are often offered as the meaning of ceremonials.

For example, the meaning of marriage is the obligations it creates between the husband and wife. To say that marriage has a different meaning from what it once had is to point to differences in the associated commitments.

From Marx and Durkheim to Habermas, social commentators have insisted that there is yet another sort of meaning, a fifth level, and that some special kind of *hermeneutic* (text interpretative) technique is required to reveal it. Actions and acts have hidden significance. In terms of the analytical scheme I have suggested in my *Social Being* (Harré, 1979), the hidden significance is to be sought through an examination of the force of public–collective actions in the expressive order, that is, how the actions serve to express symbolically the relative worth of human beings. To decode an action would be to show that it expresses a valuation of the people performing it or of those to whom it is directed over and above its practical or intended consequences. For instance, paying out the dole to the unemployed is both a life-support action and an action of ritual contempt, compared, say, with giving out the very same payment, but for dignity-enhancing work. A psychological experiment, particularly in social psychology, is both a realization of a methodological prescription and a degradation of the people taking part who, in being required to act like subjects, have to acknowledge themselves publicly to be mere automata.

We now have a detailed account of levels of meaning in public-collective (social) performances. But we have still not brought out all the presumptions of talking about personal meanings. We have to explain how it is possible for anything to be meaningful at all. It is not just to be the cause of certain kinds of effects. I follow de Saussure (1972) in identifying two conditions necessary for an item to have that mysterious quality — meaning.

(i) The item in question is located at a node in a network of relations to other items in the same semantic system. The network, or semantic field is made up of two kinds of relations:

(a) There are those which realize conventions (for the case of language arbitrary conventions), as to how items of certain kinds are sequentially organized, for example, adjectives precede nouns in English; requests precede takings which are followed by thanks which are not themselves acknowledged in our society.

(b) The sense of meaningful items is partly expressed in non-arbitrary semantic relations of synonymy, antinomy, etc., with other items, as, for example, 'cat' can be substituted by 'pussy' or more rarely, by *'Felix domesticus'*, and in hearing 'cat' we are not hearing *'chat'*, etc. So 'bye-bye' is substitutable by a wave. That 'cat' can sometimes be substituted by 'whip' determines another semantic field.

The totality of such items in relation (field) forms a multi-dimensional network within which an item is located by its relationships. The network defines the 'value' of items and is an intra-systematic aspect of meaning.

(ii) But items also have 'significance', that is, have extra-systematic aspects. In language these include the relation of reference by which some words are conventionally bound public entities, such as things, people, or processes, as well as those extra-systematic connections I have called the social force of action as act in a particular culture. The five levels of meaning I have distinguished above represent the fine structure of extra-systematic aspects of social behaviour.

Significance and value interact. For lexical items such as words, the rules of grammar and conventions of synonomy and antinomy that define the location of an item in a multi-dimensional field of value, are related to the significance of the item. So the fact that in one of the uses, 'horse' is a noun and synonomous with 'steed', is not independent of the normal range of extra-linguistic reference of the term. Rules for the placement of actions, and for what is to count as socially equivalent alternatives (the social value of an action) are intimately linked with the social significance of the action as act, that is with the extra-systematic significance of the act in the social world in which it has significance. Instead of thinking of value and significance as fields of relation, they could be thought of as encapsulated in rules of use, comprehending rules of grammar and sub-categorial rules defining the general semantic category of the item.

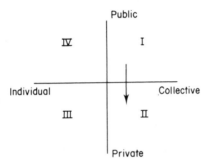

Figure 2   Appropriation

Lev Vygotsky (1963) described learning not as getting what is in teacher's head into my head, but as my appropriating for my personal use practices like speaking which are essentially public and collective (Figure 2). We might say that teacher's role is to ensure the maintenance of an appropriate public world. If this is essentially right, we have a ready-made account of most cognitive processes (sub-vocal speech; mental arithmetic; social interpretation of feelings and emotions, etc.) that treats thought as a privatized version of the public, which remains within the realm of the collective. The conventions of soliloquy are the very same as the conventions of oratory.

Where could anything personal (that is private and individual) emerge in this essentially social process?

I have been talking of public–collective or social meaning of items, but the contrast so far drawn is only between the collective and the individual. If the personal is both individual and private, we need to go further to examine the transition from quadrants 2 to 3 in our psychological space (Figure 3). We must add the contrast between the public and the private. There are two concepts of meaning now to manipulate—value and significance—and two dimensions on which to manipulate them—the individual-collective and the private-public. The normal array of meanings is maintained by public social conventions which stabilize value and significance in ways first sketched out by Wittgenstein.

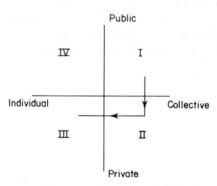

Figure 3   Personalization

What could one make of a *personal* meaning? How could there be value and significance which are both private and individual? Leaving aside Wittgenstein's doubts about the possibility of maintaining the stability of a private meaning in the absence of the constraints of public conventions and practices, it seems obvious that if personal meaning is supposed to be private and truly individual, items that have it cannot interact with the public-social system at all and must remain strictly unintelligible in the public domain and so to other people. Such meanings could exist as a shifting texture of fragile structures, loosely approximating the semantic field of the public language, but in the private-individual quadrant only. They would inform private fantasies and unintelligible dreams of madness.

Fortunately, two weaker cases can be described in principle:

(a) Personal significance is given to an item which maintains its public-collective value. This would seem to be possible only if a trace of social meaning attaches to the personal significance, while the public action is one of those that can be at the heart of more than one semantic field. A case might be that private and personal significance attached to a kiss, which is called for in the public-collective world in a simple greeting, but, say, as planted on a damask cheek by a shy lover who has concealed his passion even from the object of it. It can have a personal significance only because the bashful lover can trade on its having an alternative reading and another semantic field, as a greeting. I shall consider below the more vexing issue of whether there can be personal significance publicly displayed and which thereby becomes socially intelligible. The instance above is not really of the constitution of a public out of a personal meaning, in the sense of 'kiss' unique to that actor. It is simply he alone who is privy to its significance. But its significance is public and collective.

(b) The second case could arise when public–collective significance is maintained while a network of relations that constitute semantic value is modified personally. This case could be possible only at somewhat lower levels of significance than the implicit fifth or hermeneutic level. One might have a case which would be described somewhat as follows: 'Well, that's his queer way of expressing approval', said of someone who growls out an insult to the disconcerted suitor. Here, act-significance (we have the notion of approval) is maintained, but he has his own means of doing it, a way of expressing the approval that no one else uses, but everyone in his circle understands. This requires that the act performed be one recognized as appropriate in that society, e.g. by its location at the point in a structured sequence of actions where an action expressing the act of approval by conventional means would ordinarily have been expected to occur.

If the dimension individual–collective helps us to locate an item of whatever kind in a structure, the dimension private–public differentiates the arenas in which it may be displayed. Obviously it is useless to display something publicly if the whole of its meaning, both value and significance, is personal. It will not be seeable, hearable, or even tasteable, as a meaningful item. We must be concerned, then, with the relation between personal meanings, that is specialized or idiosyncratic, or even inappropriate uses of social meanings, as differentiated above, and public display.

What is it that differentiates an individual in such a way that he or she could construct personal meanings? Now that we have some idea what it might be to have formed personal meanings and how the public possibility of their display might justify it, these questions require us to consider what it is to be a person in a world in which personal meanings can be constructed in an otherwise essentially social *milieu*.

The three psychological attributes that, however much they must be seen to be of social origin are, once established, central to human psychological individuality, are agency, consciousness, and autobiography. The unity of the first two must be taken for granted in this discussion. The key personal attribute that contributes to the possibility of personal meaning is autobiography. It is in relation to his conceived life-course that a person can attribute personal significance of the fifth kind, to some life event, performance, social relation, etc., as providing an opportunity for speech and action to be read as a display of personal value or worth. We have now reached the fourth quadrant of our psychological space (Figure 4). In this quadrant there appears the public display of something individual, the novel things said and done publicly by the kidney machine freak to the kindly neighbourhood psychiatrist, and she understands these *somehow*. My suggestion is that she understands by embedding what is said, and said to have been done, in the framework of a display of autobiography.

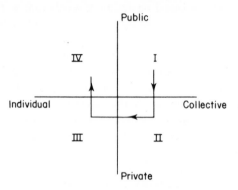

Figure 4   Publication

Let us return to the distinction between expressive and practical orders of society. The practical order is concerned with the social organization of material production of various kinds and in the end, as Marx correctly diagnosed, that organization depends on how the laws of physical nature are being exploited by a particular technology and how those products are appropriated. Undoubtedly, there is an aspect of the practical order in all we do, not least amongst those of us who are in love with our life-support systems. But the expressive order is dominant for more people, the social organization of the means of displaying our moral worth, our dignity, and so on. Now if we ask wherein there may be personal meanings, it is clear that they cannot be defined in the lives we lead in the practical order, dependent as those are on the material laws of nature. They deal with things in general and under types. Practical activities are intelligible to anyone who knows the 'facts of the matter', so actions devoted to a machine's maintenance are intelligible as such since they depend upon laws of nature. The personal meaning must stem from ways of living in the expressive orders of society, contributions to a life form, in which each of us tries to demonstrate our worth and personal value.

How can this be achieved? If lives must be displayed in conventional acts to be meaningful at all, how can any lives be truly personal? We can get a grip on the source of this difficulty by remembering what trouble even the great Goffman (1961) has with this. Consider any role-performance situated within the practical or expressive orders wherein the meanings are part of public knowledge—say a surgeon operating. Now if a certain rising medical star wants to impose a personal stamp on his performance in the theatre, how can it be done? Goffman noted the phenomenon of role-distance displayed in things done by an actor, who while carrying out his officially prescribed task, succeeds in showing that he or she is not fully immersed as a social being in the task in hand, but has another side, a warm human side, say (Himmler distributing chocolate during a Nazi cavalcade). Goffman notices that in 'doing' role-distance, an actor must use another recognizable role as a foil—a rule which is only obliquely disclosed. The surgeon reveals the gambler, the Nazi tyrant reveals the family man, etc.; but what is revealed is just as much a publicly–collectively defined role as that from which the actor is distancing himself.

Role-distancing is not a good model for the public construction of personal meaning. Martin Hollis (1977) in *Models of Man* talks of stamping a role performance with unique qualities, but these must be made out of bits we already know how to interpret. I can think of only two ways in which what is already given can be so transformed that it displays something, at least when first appearing on the public scene, that is unique in terms of autobiography.

In both, the creative actor exploits literal uses of a given lexicon of speech and action. It could be that a role performance is stamped by the fact that it differs from all others in some matter of degree. Calvin Coolidge was the *most inert* of American Presidents. Richard III was the *most bloodthirsty* of English kings, and so on. To stamp one's mark, then, to create an impression of personal being, is to create a kind of efflorescence for the magnifying of the already given. But there is another way to use the already given, a way which leads us into the idea of figurative action. We can construct autobiography which displays unlikely combinations of attributes: the playboy intellectual, the jet-setting coalminer, these are the oxymorons of social action, but each element in the unlikely combination is still to be given literal reading, and as with our examples, in no time at all these once-individual creations become commonplace as conventional life-forms.

How can we return to the public–collective domain with the spoils of novelty acquired during our journey through our own personal and private experience? Finally, there is metaphor, whereby the displacement of an existing form of action or a known word to a new context, a new meaning is created (catachresis) but at the risk of creating no meaning at all (Figure 5). It is this risk that we must be prepared to take in returning our actions finally to the public–collective domain. In metaphor, the sub-categorial rules of meaning are defied, as when concrete things are given properties only properly attributed to abstractions and the inanimate is described in animate terms, and the mechanistic is treated personally, where persons are treated as automata, and so on. In a case-history as discussed in this volume I hear the splintering casements of metaphorical usage as actions and speeches escape from their normal confines to enter other realms of application.

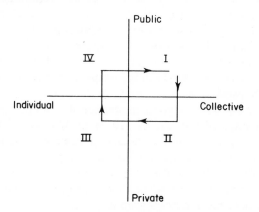

Figure 5   Catachresis

Where does metaphor lead? Richard Boyd has recently (Ortony, 1980) coined the perceptive phrase 'epistemic access' to describe the role of metaphor in scientific language. Metaphorical usage gives us epistemic access since it begins a programme of description and investigation which may become more and more refined, and in that refinement a new range of literal uses is created. Having no way to describe the novel beings science throws up, we can only hang on to intelligibility by drawing on the lexical stock we have. That we can manage to say something new and intelligible is only by breaking some of the original rules of use while hanging on to others. There seems to be no way we can prescribe in advance how the corpus of rules should be partitioned, either to create new meaning or to obtain a foothold in the old.

I think personal meaning, as generated by the people about whose novel lifeways we are talking, in the effort to establish epistemic access both for themselves and potentially for others, to novel realms of feeling and understanding, can be explicated in terms of metaphor. Why do they need metaphor for themselves? Couldn't they just feel and understand theory? No, because they would then have nothing to feel and understand with. Thoughts and feelings are human happenings and must be mediated by some kind of instrument, that with which they are done. Feeling is just funny physiological leakage until it is given some interpretation in some semiotic system, and understanding and necessity require a vehicle. I believe with Vigotsky that in the last analysis thought is a personal appropriation for public activities, using collectively defined semiotic systems. To be able to think this or that we need a concrete vehicle for doing the thinking. That vehicle may be drawn from an existing lexicon and so be understood already in terms of its existing semantic field. The 'tenor' of the metaphor, as I. A. Richards (1965) called it, is that new 'something' to which the vehicle is applied and to which it gives epistemic access by virtue of some, perhaps not fully demarcated fragment, of its existing semantic field. So personal meanings must, in the end, be metaphorical uses of existing semiotic systems. They may have been appropriated for personal use long since by the individual, and there may be a time lag so vast that the person to whom the public display of personal meaning is first addressed may be baffled not only because they are being offered a metaphor, so that the experience is like trying to understand a metaphysical poet on a first reading, but also because the semiotic system which is a vehicle for the metaphor, may itself have come from long ago and far away, that it is not just impenetrable; it is *just* like understanding a poem written in another language from another social world, and even the most oblique of Japanese *haiku* or Persian epics, can become lit-up with meaning for us through the long struggle actually to find the threads of metaphor that link their semiotic system to a literal basis which we all have in common.

But as for the private–individual quadrant, maybe there is not anything but the storage leakages of physiology there, unstable shifting fragments of seeming meaning loosely grasped because for a moment or two some kind of structure shows up, only to dissolve again. The far side of metaphor is real madness.

REFERENCES

Austin, J. L. (1965) *How To Do Things with Words*. New York: Oxford University Press.

Coulter, J. (1979) *The Social Construction of Mind*. London: MacMillan.
Goffman, E. (1961) *Encounters*. Indiana: Bobbs-Merrill.
Harré, R. (1979) *Social Being*. Oxford: Blackwell.
Hollis, M. (1977) *Models of Man*. Cambridge: University Press.
Ortony, M. (1980) *Metaphor and Thought*. Cambridge: University Press.
Richards, I. A. (1965) *The Philosophy of Rhetoric*. London: Oxford University Press.
de Saussure, F. (1922) *Cours de linguistique générale*, 2nd edn. Paris: Payot.
Silver, M. and Sabini, J. (1978) 'The social construction of envy', *J. for the Theory of Social Behaviour*, **8**, 313–32.
Vygotsky, L. (1963) *Thought and Language*. Cambridge, Mass.: MIT Press.

Personal Meanings
Edited by Eric Shepherd and J. P. Watson
© 1982 John Wiley & Sons Ltd.

Understanding how to be a person: an ecological approach

John Shotter

The starting point of this chapter is the notion that our active interaction with others is our most basic mode of common existence. The realm of the personal can be thought of as a product of that interactive process, an artefact produced by human labour, made in the ways human beings actively relate (or attempt to relate) themselves to one another. The personal plays a part in, but is not itself the process of that interaction. Personal meanings function in that ongoing process of people, making themselves and their lives together, in both harmony and conflict.

My interests are thus ones of a broadly 'developmental' kind (Shotter, 1974, 1975, 1978; Shotter and Newson, 1982; Gauld and Shotter, 1977) concerned with the nature of the processes productive of personal existence; with its growth, diminishment, or transformation; with, in short, meanings 'in' action: not with people, already formed as the persons they are, jockeying for different positions within an already well defined social structure, living as if playing a game with pre-established rules. This is of course a fascinating field of study in its own right (Harré and Secord, 1972; Harré, 1980). But human beings are not just rule-followers, they are also rule-makers, and it is essentially in the establishing and stabilizing of a rule-regulated realm of conduct that personal modes of being as such make their appearance; and nowhere else. We are not born as persons; we only come to be so by being treated as such (Richards, 1974). While human beings reproduce themselves in an as yet more or less natural process, persons are made, or 'manufactured' we might say, in a process taking place after birth, a process in which gradually young children understand more and more about how to be persons: they come to think of themselves as *selves*; *as named, unitary individuals*; *as originary sources of action in* a world which assigns them certain rights and duties; as someone with a certain kind of life to live;

23

and above all, as having to apply in the living of that life certain normative and evaluative judgements as to the appropriateness (goodness, badness, stupidity, legitimacy, or otherwise fittingness) of what they and others do, as well as who or what they want to be. Without such post-natal processing, human beings do not attain to a personal mode of being — as the existence of wild boys, wolf-children, and suchlike attests. Learning how to be a person — how to be a responsible and accountable actor, an appreciative or critical spectator, a competent participant, a knowledgeable looker or listener, and above all, a sensible communicator — is just as much to learn a set of skills (ontological skills) as is learning to climb, run, walk, swim, and so on. And the process is never-ending: we have continually to understand what it is to be a person in each new aspect of our lives — as sons and daughters, as parents, as workers, as lecturers, as members of a conference audience; each new context raises a new problem as to what exactly constitutes a properly personal mode of being in each one. Even in dying the problem remains, and different ways of dying (Aries, 1976) are fitting and proper at different times in different places.

But our personal mode of being is more than just a social phenomenon, it is a moral one too, associated with us being good or bad, or with us acting rightly or wrongly. Its moral character arises out of the fact that human beings in groups must act in such a way as to fit themselves and their actions in with the others with whom they share their lives. And although human groups do not seem to possess any innately determined, species-specific way of life, they none the less only exist as groups of *persons*, within the confines of a rational tradition (Macmurray, 1961). In fact, although not biologically determined, personhood is a cultural universal (Geertz, 1973); no human groups exist without some notion as to what constitutes personhood within them. Unique individuals are, paradoxically it seems, necessary for a human social order to exist and to endure. For such an order to endure, as it is not produced or maintained instinctually, it must be maintained by the entities themselves who constitute it. To do this they must be able to recognize transgressions of it, to identify transgressors, and bring them to make restitution and to help reinstitute and maintain the order. Without beings able to be responsible for their action, to be accountable and to relate what they do (and who or what they are) to an established order beyond themselves as individuals; without persons as such, a human social order would fall apart.

In theory, one might propose other 'elements' as basic to the constitution of a social order, other interactive 'unities', pairs such as mother-child, husband–wife, boss–worker, speaker–listener, teacher–pupil, for instance. But such dyadic unities would not do. For in interaction, people act in the context of one another's actions, and quite who is responsible for what in any outcome is essentially unclear. If the source of an action's outcome cannot be precisely identified, then it becomes impossible to discriminate things done by people from things just happening naturally; responsibility and accountability are impossible in such circumstances. Individual persons are the only known entities, it seems, able to sense in their functioning what they are doing and to discriminate it from that which happens outside their agency to control — and we recognize this in assigning people the right or the duty to claim responsibility for what they do: 'I did this but not that.'

No other entities seem able to sense in their functioning the fittedness of themselves or their actions to pre-existing requirements or criteria — to produce in their activity, as Searle (1978) puts it, a *mind-to-world* fit (in their beliefs) or a *world-to-mind* fit (in their desires), or, to extend his terminology, a *mind-to-mind* fit in their communications. In other words, persons act intentionally, they direct themselves in their behaviour and are concerned to behave appropriately. In the realm of cause and effect anything can, in theory, be connected to anything else; we do not find the same relation of appropriateness or fittingness between a cause and its effect that we find between an action and its circumstances, between what is done and a person's reasons for doing it. Human action is thus quite distinct from mere behaviour, from mere physical movement structured by reference to a plan or program. Rather than existing in an already structured world of physical time and geometrical space, human action exists as a natural aspect of the 'intentionality' inherent in the special realm of the personal, and functions to give it its perceived structure; rather than being imposed upon physical reality externally, it is intrinsic to it.

It was Brentano who was essentially responsible for introducing the concept of intentionality into modern philosophy and psychology in an attempt then to clarify the distinction between physical and mental phenomena: 'Every mental phenomenon contains something as an object within itself, although they all do not do so in the same way' (Brentano, 1973, p.88).

In a presentation [any immediate content of experience] something is presented, in a judgment something affirmed or denied, in love loved, in hate hated, in desire desired, and so on.

In its very existence, human action appears to imply or indicate something beyond itself; it is 'directed upon an object', it 'points to', 'contains', 'means', or is 'a means to' something other than itself. Human being 'in' action exhibits an intrinsic interconnectedness to, an interpenetration of, an appropriate fittedness—call it what you will—of itself to its surroundings or its context. Thus, even as an action occurs, more than implying or indicating a structured context into which it is fitted, within which its sense (function or use) can be understood, it posits in effect a whole realm of other possible actions also suited to it. A whole world of meaning or reference is created in a simple action. For instance, just to glance at someone is to posit a world in which recognition of like by like is a possibility, in which (in contradistinction to a merely physical world) 'recognition' is a possible activity, and in which, possibly, those recognizing one another might investigate further other more refined ways of relating themselves to one another, progressively differentiating and articulating in their interaction an implied world of meaning produced between them.

Some of Laing's (1971, p.21) 'knots' illustrate in quintessential form the creation of such 'worlds of meaning' and how people account for their actions in terms of the 'entities' they contain:

Jill: You put me in the wrong.
Jack: I am not putting you in the wrong.
Jill: You put me in the wrong for (me) thinking you put me in the wrong.

The result here is that Jill feels herself 'wrong', in her being, onto-logically. The wrong that she is in, however, is only partly specified, and further activity, which takes account of its nature so far, will be necessary if Jack and Jill are to clarify what is happening between them.

In this respect, we must note that actions do not occur and present their meanings in an instant; they unfold progressively over time, producing a greater and greater degree of specification (or appropriateness to requirements) into their content. Thus an action in progress, while having so far produced a certain degree of specification into its content, can leave that content open to yet further specification, *but only of an already specified kind* (Rommetveit, 1976; Shotter, 1980). What occurs next, if it is to be appropriate, must fit in with the totality specified or determined so far. Thus, just as in the growth of an oak tree from an acorn a point comes when the only appropriate next stage of growth is the production of acorns, so in the progress of human action: at each point only certain further actions fit in and are appropriate. They are not specified by rules but by something much more like the sensed 'shape' or configuration, so far produced by previous action, of the context within which actors find themselves, immersed—where that vague notion of 'shape' may be unpacked in terms of who in the circumstances is who, and what their rights, duties, privileges, obligations, capacities, instrumentalities, beliefs, wishes, motives, desires, and so on, are. Such a totality, articulated for themselves by the participants immersed in it, may be utterly idiosyncratic to them and quite opaque to outsiders. Rules, I believe, come late in the setting up of public arenas of conduct, in the establishment of institutions: they are not crucial in understanding the realm of immediately personal meanings.

The increasing interest in the nature of intentionality reflects, I think, a major reorientation taking place in the social sciences generally: there is a loss, or at least a lessening of interest in the causal connections between things thought of as existing quite independently of one another, and a growth of interest in the necessary interfittedness of things—in their interpenetration into one another, their mutual definition or reciprocal determination; in the self-production of systems rather than their production by external agencies. Thus, rather than being studied as the expression or effect of antecedent causes lying hidden somewhere within the individual, human behaviour is now being studied for its social function, in its social context, for its *use* (Wittgenstein) by people in them coordinating their activities with one another: investigators want to know both towards what people are directing their actions, *and*, towards what their actions are actually leading—for no individual actors hold the meaning of their own actions entirely. We want to know to what further actions their current action can lead in doing what they do.

Such an interest does not preclude an interest in the inner causes operative prior to or during people's expressions. Indeed it is only possible for me to intend a skilled action—like reaching forward to touch a particular point on the furniture before me—if my bones and muscles, neurons, and brain stay constant from one moment to the next, and function in an orderly, stable fashion—according to laws, if you like. Nonetheless, I am the person who moves my limbs, their movements taking place, as required, to fit into the larger context of *my* overall endeavours. But only in a world containing, here and there at least, some causal regularities can intentions be formed and skilfully executed in confident expectation of their usual result. Yet, I think that it is now clear that little of *social* significance is contributed by knowledge of such regularities. For knowing what led up to a person's action, or what sustains it causally, still does not tell us what that action actually *is*, what it achieves socially, what it is appropriate to, what it points to, means, or fits in with. This is a sphere of study in its own right. And it is because I have found it impossible, in my studies of it, to escape a concern with the fittedness of things to one another, that I have called my approach an ecological one.

Let me move on now, more specifically into the realm of personal meanings, and illustrate what further I have to say by reference to an example. Consider the following episode, selected almost at random from Erica Jong's (1978, pp.35–36) *How to Save Your Own Life*:

The door opens and Bennett appears. I continue to stare at my mail. Though we haven't seen each other in three days, I somehow have no desire to get up and face him. I force myself.

'Hi, darling', I say, embracing him . . . He pecks me on the mouth and moves away, unable to give himself to the greeting. He has missed me, but he hasn't yet seen his mail. It must be gotten out of the way like a bowel movement before screwing.

His rigidity angers me. Embracing him is like embracing a tailor's dummy.

'Aren't you really going to kiss me?' I ask.

He returns dutifully and kisses me very wetly (as he has ever since I ran off with a man whose kisses were wetter than his). He presses his pelvis against mine with consummate technique. I feel he is using craft. . . .

It should come as no surprise if I add that the first sentence of the book is: 'I left my husband (Bennett) on Thanksgiving Day', and that the first sentence of the second chapter is: 'I had wanted to leave my marriage for years, had saved it up like a sweet before bedtime. . . .' Though perhaps I can surprise you by asking why you are not surprised.

Normally, implicit in the reunion of lovers (married or otherwise) is the anticipation that they will express a degree of enthusiasm for one another; this is evidenced in their concentration upon one another to the exclusion of outside concerns; it is a part of what it is to be lovers. In the above episode, Bennett enters and Isadora continues to stare at her mail. In a lover's world, this action is inappropriate; and it works to begin the specification of quite a different realm of next possible actions. Isadora draws back from its implications, but (as events depicted later show) too late: Bennett has already perceived her lack of enthusiasm, and attributed it to her hostility towards him. Already, the situation between them is specified as them not, in fact, being true lovers. In such circumstances, her attempt to repair the situation with her forced 'Hi darling' and her embrace jars; it fails to fit the circumstances. Yet they are still civilized, liberal, fair-minded people, aware of the patterns of privileges and obligations such people afford one another. So Bennett reciprocates her embrace. Not to have done so would indicate on his part a definite intention to destroy their relationship (and clearly, he does not want to be the one responsible for any major change in its nature). Yet he reciprocates within the already specified context of them as no longer being true lovers (either *that*, or his stiffness is general, and he is always like it irrespective of his situation): whichever, it angers her. It means that he is withholding from her the right to affect him spontaneously; he has constituted his mode of being such that instead of being open and responsive to her every expression, charitably concerned to interpret them all as directed towards the enhancement of both their personalities, he becomes attentive to her in a much more circumspect way. Both he and Isadora recognize that in general, criteria of appropriateness are socially constructed, and that between them *they make the context within which what they do gets adjudged as being good or bad, as appropriate, or as legitimate or not.* She, so far, has succeeded in constructing those terms. But in this case he tries (while veiling his motive) to get the lion's share of the making; he wants to control the terms in which they both must judge the appropriateness of their actions. Hence his dutiful wet kiss: it has the proper 'outward' form of a passionate embrace (but it is informed, Isadora feels, by self-controlled craft rather than self-abandoned desire); so she must initially at least treat it as sincere.

And so it continues: as a result of such exchanges, people make themselves, in relation to one another, what they are—or are allowed to be. The specification of Bennett's and Isadora's statuses now in relation to one another—the rights they are willing to accord one another and the duties they expect—as a result of the above exchange, are modified. And as their relationship progresses, in the course of them articulating themselves more clearly in relation to one another, what was a vague, global, and unformulated initial mode of relationship is gradually and progressively shaped, specified, formulated, or determined by them in the course of their actual conduct of it.

But how can a 'failure-to-look-up-immediately', a 'stiffness-in-an-embrace' serve to specify the intent in an action? What is involved, practically, in people meaning things to each other in this rather direct and immediate way? Clearly nothing like categorical perception or reasoning from general propositions can be involved: Bennett's and Isadora's own particular and unique personal lives are being lived out here; each moment is unique; it is not a pre-programmed, routine career followed by all more or less identically.

The primary process involved in understanding such unique and momentary meanings is not, I want to argue, anything like inference, or any of the other 'information processing' procedures currently being proposed by cognitive psychologists (Claxton, 1980). A quite different process is required, one in which one's understanding of the precise part played, or function served by a particular expression (or, originally, piece of text) is clarified by constructing (or reconstructing) its proper context, the larger whole into which it is fitted or embedded. Such a process may be termed a hermeneutical one (Taylor, 1971; Gauld and Shotter, 1977). In its operation, if it is to respect the precise and unique meaning in personal expressions, such a process cannot begin with a pre-established general order of things to which particular puzzling expressions are assimilated, with all their uniqueness lost. It must begin with the puzzling expressions in their full individuality, and then proceed in a back-and-forth manner between part and whole to articulate that whole, to fashion a 'world' adapted to the undistorted accommodation of the expressions in question—to create, as Searle puts it, mind-to-world, and world-to-mind fits. Thus rather than inference from a pre-established order, the process involves the creation of its own new order, from within which those conducting the process (and really only those) grasp the part played, function served, or meaning of each of their actions as they perform them—to a limited extent at least.

Till recently, we have struggled with a faulty conception of human being: individuals being thought of as utterly independent unities, with their minds hidden from view inside them, like the clockwork hidden inside the clock. Thinking thus, we have remained sceptical of ever discovering the supposedly private, inner states of mind (or brain) considered to be responsible for our outer, public behaviour. In such circumstances, Skinner's (1972, p.20) strategy of 'turning directly to the relation between behaviour and the environment and neglecting supposed mediating states of mind', would seem to be one of the few methodologies rationally to adopt. But, I suggest, such a conception of human personal existence is wrong in every respect: persons are through and through social entities, utterly dependent for their *status* as unique and independent individuals upon their immersion in a dynamic system of social interrelationships—their status as such dependent upon their place or places in such a system; with the endurance of the system depending, as we have seen, on their uniqueness. So, although people's actions may be shaped and informed by just their own motives and beliefs, the only motives and beliefs open to them to sensibly and legitimately express as responsible members of their society are limited; they cannot be of a completely idiosyncratic kind. They must conform to what one might call the general conception of reality current in their society at the time. And that is not something which can be formed by each individual for himself, nor is it handed down ready-made from on high, but it is something made and remade in the hurly-burly of people relating themselves together in their everyday, practical affairs — with some individuals and groups, clearly, having more influence upon the outcome than others, in this arena of reality construction.

As I now see it, competing in this arena are two distinctly different kinds of psychology and psychological research: one is concerned with discovering the things people themselves can actually *do*; the other is concerned with what people can get done for them, either by (internal or external) mechanisms or by, in fact, other people. In actuality, however, these two kinds of psychology are embedded in one another: like the different aspects of an ambiguous figure, each is implicitly still present when the other is explicitly to the fore; ecologically, they are necessary to one another. However, rather than being interested in constructing mechanisms (or programming a computer) to 'perceive' as people perceive, to 'remember' as people remember, or 'understand' as people understand, I am myself interested in discovering how people *do* perceive, remember, and understand. How do they go about the task of shaping themselves up so that although wholly ignorant of the nature of the processes naturally at work in them, they none the less succeed in setting those processes in motion, thus to provide themselves with the instrumentalities appropriate to their needs? Ecologically, what conditions, what surroundings are necessary for human beings, if embedded in them, to differentiate themselves into such entities: into entities with a self, with an 'inside' and an 'outside', and an ability to relate what they do 'outside' to that self 'inside'? What do they have to do to bring their activities under such self-control? What is the nature of the efforts involved, and how should they compose themselves in order to make them? How, in other words, do we all understand how to be persons?

At the moment, the process is embedded in the ecology of our social world and takes place spontaneously. However, in the more technological quarters of our subject, deliberate rearrangements of that ecology continue apace. Only if we understand more explicitly how to be persons can we be sure that, in such rearrangements, we are not creating a world in which the process by which persons are 'manufactured' no longer exists.

REFERENCES

Aries, P. (1976) *Western Attitudes Toward Death from the Middle Ages to the Present*. London: Boyars.

Brentano, F. (1973) *Psychology from an Empirical Standpoint*. London: Routledge and Kegan Paul (orig. pub. 1874, trans. L. L. McAlister).

Claxton, G. (1980) *Cognitive Psychology: New Directions*. London: Routledge and Kegan Paul.

Gauld, A., and Shotter, J. (1977) *Human Action and its Psychological Investigation*. London: Routledge and Kegan Paul.

Geertz, C. (1973) *The Interpretation of Cultures*. New York: Basic Books.

Harré, R. (1980) *Social Being: a Theory for Social Psychology*. Oxford: Blackwell.

Harré, R., and Secord, P. F. (1972) *The Explanation of Social Behaviour*. Oxford: Blackwell.

Jong, Erica (1978) *How to Save Your Own Life*. London: Panther.

Laing, R. D. (1971) *Knots*. Harmondsworth: Penguin Books.

Macmurray, J. (1961) *Persons in Relation*. London: Faber and Faber.

Richards, M. P. M. (1974) *The Integration of a Child into a Social World*. Cambridge: University Press.

Rommetveit, R. (1976) The architecture of intersubjectivity. In L. Strickland, F. Aboud, and K. J. Gergen (Eds) *Social Psychology in Transition*. New York: Plenum Press.

Searle, J. R. (1978) Sociobiology and the explanation of behaviour. In M. S. Gregory, A. Silvers, and D. Sutch (Eds), *Sociobiology and Human Nature*. San Francisco: Jossey-Bass.

Shotter, J. (1974) The development of personal powers. In M. P. M. Richards (Ed.), *The Integration of the Child into a Social World*. Cambridge: University Press.

Shotter, J. (1975) *Images of Man in Psychological Research*. London: Methuen.

Shotter, J. (1978) The cultural context of communication studies: methodological and theoretical issues. In A. Lock (Ed.), *Action, Gesture and Symbol*. London: Academic Press.

Shotter, J. (1980) Action, joint action and intentionality. In M. Brenner (Ed.), *The Structure of Action*. Oxford: Blackwell.

Shotter, J. (1981) Telling and reporting: prospective and retrospective uses of self-ascriptions. In C. Antaki (Ed.), *The Psychology of Ordinary Explanations of Social Behaviour*. London: Academic Press.

Shotter, J., and Newson, J. (1982) An ecological approach to cognitive development. In G. Butterworth and P. Light (Eds), *Social Cognition: Studies in the Development of Understanding*. Sussex: Harvester Press.

Skinner, B. F. (1972) *Beyond Freedom and Dignity*. London: Jonathan Cape.

Taylor, C. (1971) Interpretation and the sciences of man, *Rev. Metaphysics*, **25**, 3–51.

Personal Meanings
Edited by Eric Shepherd and J. P. Watson
© 1982 John Wiley & Sons Ltd.

Coping with the first person singular

Eric Shepherd

Those who can't see themselves in other people are condemned forever to be strangers to themselves.

(Vaneigem (1979, p.249)

Those who do not reflect on the philosophical foundations of their beliefs and actions will be condemned repeatedly to making fools of themselves, for thoughtless speech is a mark of the child, and wise understanding a sign of maturity.

(Wolff (1971, p.vi)

PERSONAL MEANINGS AND SPEECH EVENTS

Man is the only animal whose consciousness can be directed upon himself. This quality of reflectiveness was seen by Teilhard de Chardin (1959) to be the central phenomenon of man. Distinctively human thinking is circular and centres upon an awareness of primary being, an individual with a concept of self, an *I* with a sense of *me*. Being human implies knowledge of being a first person singular. On this matter Kinget (1975, p.23) observed that only human beings can make first-person statements:

Self reference is something man cannot escape. Whether he speaks about the future of marriage, the trend in politics, a recent discovery, tall buildings and small gains, his statements issue from a point in time and space that is unique to that symbolic locus of reference, the *I*. Near, far, right, left, high, low — all draw their significance from the shifting position of the individual organism and the attending self.

That an individual comprehends and communicates rests upon the fact that (Naess, 1975, p.46):

A person is part of something, and his perseonal identity is relational . . . Man exists in the personal relations, as a changing centre of interactions in a field of relations.

33

Encounters involving the exchange of first-person statements are speech events, the texts of which confirm that an individual lives in a social world of plural minds, each one experiencing the world as meanings. The meanings which constitute an individual's experience as a primitive understanding, a *proto-interpretation* (Taylor, 1971), are telling evidence of his duality of unity. On the one hand, meetings and meanings suggest he is unique, his experience is idiosyncratic. On the other hand, they remind him that he is united with others, who experience, feel, and see things the same way. This duality destines any speech event, as the forum for the expression and social validation of a person's identity (Berger and Luckmann, 1967), to be a fragile and fraught process of meaning exchange. The event emerges (Pride, 1971, p.54) as:

a set of 'ventures in joint orientation', a process of very imperfect sharing, each participant both creatively and conventionally structuring and restructuring his own view of things.

Meaning in a speech event therefore rests, as Rommetveit (1980) suggested, upon *control of what is being meant* and *faith in a shared world*.

DRAMAS AND HELPING ENCOUNTERS

Despite his singular ability to reflect and be conscious of his singularity, the individual copes with day-to-day continuity and change in himself, in events and relationships, unreflectively as *routines* and *rituals* (Morris, 1972). However, circumstances arise from time to time which represent *drama*—when events and relationships point to a process of discontinuity in the person's life space (Hopson and Adams, 1976) which challenges the capacity of the attending self to adapt.

The key attributes of personal dramas are the individual's role in their genesis, their novelty or unfamiliarity, the inherent importance and uncertainty of their outcomes, and their questioning of the individual's ability (or perceived) ability to influence the course of events. Dramas can arise in situations characterized by *physical change*, transitions involving ill-health and accidents, *social change*, transitions involving interpersonal activity and social field composition, and changes in *thought content* and *emotional responsiveness*, which may be either attributed to or independent of environmental transitions. These new experiences, anticipated or unexpected, which the individual perceives as having been wholly or partly brought about by him or thrust upon him, are demands to 'make sense' in the process of personal development. On this note Morris (1972, p.84) commented:

People are at their most individual and personal when they engage in dramas. These are the growing points of their lives, their sources of personal history, the stories of their commitments . . . Perhaps the total truth of the matter is that people strive to shape their most powerful experiences, and the fusing of form and energy is what drama is all about. Where the ability to place a shape on the energy fails, one has the varied forms of breakdown: some so total that they cannot be charted.

In a similar vein, Browne and Freeling (1976) spoke of the variation in level of maturity across the life-span. As they saw it, maturity is:

the ability to integrate new experiences in such a way as to produce the optimum response: in common language the ability to cope. (p.95)

They went on to point out that:

The level of maturity achieved is not something static, but represents a dynamic equilibrium between the subject and the continually changing flow of experience. (p.96)

Moving through a transition notionally involves a behavioural task, an attempt to *manage the strain* generated; and a cognitive task, an attempt to *establish equilibrium* — placing the 'shape' on the experience (Hopson and Adams, 1976). The strain is managed in various ways — through withdrawal, isolation, reducing information, and very often calling upon, or being brought to, the attention of a support system, particularly a helping professional. The cognitive task centres upon the individual's attempts (if any) to reconcile the experiences with his core role constructs (Kelly, 1955). These refer to the individual's *existential self* (Tiryakian, 1966) and circumscribe his conception of self, sense of personal agency, and personal biography.

However, there are substantial individual differences in the performance of these tasks. As Hopson and Adams (1976, pp.19–20) observed:

If the individual is unable to manage the strain he will find the cognitive task exceedingly difficult if not impossible. Some individuals find that managing their strain comes easier than solving their problems. For others the reverse is true. For some, by concentrating on the cognitive task, strain will be managed, while for others strain must be managed before work on the cognitive task can begin.

Those who turn, or are referred, to the helping professional comprise a whole range of coping styles and combination of task enactment. However, life is difficult for the professional since the individual will more often than not present with a request for helping with a *strain* problem rather than an *existential* problem. Helping in these circumstances was defined by Lenrow (1978, p.270) as:

Uncoerced interaction between two or more people that is intended to benefit at least one of the parties and in which the parties are in agreement about who is intended to benefit.

The helping professions, which include medicine, the priesthood, and the 'secular priesthood' (North, 1972) of psychotherapists, counsellors, clinical psychologists, and social workers, have a common core of professional values. These are: impartiality, rationality, empirical knowledge, and ethical commitment to the dignity of the individual and public welfare (Lenrow, 1978, p.268). However, observers such as Lenrow (1978) and Pollak (1976) describe the difficulties involved in implementing these values in the helping encounter. To understand how this situation can arise, with its risks of adding to the individual's distress, we need to understand the pressures upon the professional, which lead many of them to cope through *distancing*.

OBJECTIFICATION: PRESSURES AND PROCESSES

The helping professional is subject to a range of psychological, social, moral, and practical tensions in a series of short-term 'working' relationships with strangers in distress. These encounters are characterized by ambivalence over the fundamental themes of involvement and detachment (Pollak, 1976). For the helper each encounter represents another demand to define, specify, and intervene within the framework of his specialist knowledge of problems and their resolution. His purposive analyses (Vernon, 1963) are for him routine and ritual. This view contrasts with the experience of the individual in distress for whom the encounter is but part of his drama. Vague feelings of disparity, even inequity of personal experience, coexist with folklore notions of self-consciousness and involvement in helping, which in turn contrast with culturally defined perceptions of asymmetry in power, knowledge and status, and culturally defined prescriptions for appropriate behaviour, particularly deference, in the presence of an expert.

Being helped is, in its most basic form, buying the company, the individual attention and therefore the time of another (Pollak, 1976).

Since professions regulate their membership, maintain hierarchies, and negotiate fees commensurate with seniority and experience within the profession, with the exception of the priesthood and the voluntary agencies, access will always be subject to constraint. The law of supply and demand, compounded by career progression and staffing problems, render duration and continuity of access problematic. To cope with the many problems raised by asymmetry, access and the short-lived obligation, some helpers 'gravitate toward being less reflective, others toward being less available or helpful to clients' (Lenrow, 1978, p.279). During and after training they concentrate on narrow technical definition of role and problems. Pollak (1976, p.34) is not alone in seeing professional training as a barrier:

All requirements of special training have produced distance between a helper and the person to be helped and have thereby created new problems in helping.

Lenrow (1978, p.280) also saw the narrowing of role and emphasis on technique as deleterious:

These roles institutionalize a belief that competence in dealing with human problems lies in mastery of specialized techniques considered in isolation from the personal meaning systems and integrity of the people using the techniques or affected by them.

The helper coping in this manner effectively detaches himself from the individual as a self-conscious person. He invokes a *macro plan* for the encounter based on his definition of roles, the nature of possible problems and his powers of intervention. On this basis the encounter becomes a proleptic process — with the helper using asymmetrical status and communication conventions to take the helped on a 'guided tour' of possible options against which the helped is invited to match his experience.

Because of the asymmetrical relationship the professional's statements exercise substantial control over what is meant, what is expressed, and what is to be understood. They can all too easily lead to a definition of the 'problem' which corresponds to the helper's conception of professional commitment and competence to intervene.

Within the framework of the helping encounter it would seem that some helpers are sceptical about the value, or validity, of an individual's responses. They tend to scan the individual's text for gross topics, paying more attention to equally gross aspects of the text-analogue of non-verbal behaviour as a more accurate indicator of affective state (Watts, 1980). The tendency for 'false positives' in problem identification to go undetected, and the tendency to overlook those occasions when heuristics yield an incorrect identification are compounded by the success of the impersonal approach, whose 'objective' style of questioning tends to be considered scientific. The result is a helper who is overconfident and who overvalues the effectiveness of his method.

Coping with a first person singular in an impersonal manner is consistent with what Buber (1958) termed the 'I–it' relationship, in which the other is perceived as an 'object-for-me' (Tiryakian, 1966). 'I–it' relationships are not without their advantages, as we have seen here in the case of the distancing helper. 'I–it' relationships are typical existential defences against a demand to face up to oneself or another. They allow us to embark unreflectively upon the routine and ritual exchanges referred to earlier in this chapter. The appropriateness of such relationships in achieving personal goals stems from the power inherent in defining the other 'in terms of functional specificity (since an object-for-me is determined by specific properties which are instrumental to my ends)' (Tiryakian, 1966, p.78).

'I–it' encounters are a far cry from the ideal encounter which Brenner (1978, p.128) saw as:

enacted in such a way as to achieve the fulfilment of self-expression, and identity, to express models of self to participants.

They are distortions of reality which achieve their own reality since the performance of the professional, as he implements his definition of the situation, is rarely questioned. Indeed the relatively few occasions on which the helped comment upon the helper's performance, together with the frequent interpretation that the 'non-return' is a therapeutic success, contribute to a view that this is the right approach to problem-solving.

Eisenberg has consistently argued that, irrespective of the professional's success in controlling the conduct of the encounter, the helped continues to test the intervention in terms of personal meaning (Eisenberg, 1981, p.168):

It is an intrinsic characteristic of human consciousness to attempt to extract meaning out of the complexity and variety of experience. An adherent to a particular therapeutic school can choose to disregard the meaning a patient imposes on himself and his relationship with his therapist but he does so at the cost of ignoring a continuing process which will go on whether or not he attends to it. The therapist may choose to ignore the patient's history and find it expedient to do so but that does not change its salience for the patient.

Eisenberg concluded that to define the encounter in such a way as to exclude personal meaning jeopardizes the effectiveness of the intervention given. Interventions emerging from *functional definition* of the individual as an object may have practical relevance but they lack personal relevance. It is also disturbing to think that impersonal relationships have implications for the person who invokes them (Tiryakian, 1966, p.77):

If I treat others as objects, as objects-for-me in particular, then unwittingly I also objectify myself: hence all 'I–it' relationships tend to become 'it–it' relationships.

THE ALTERNATIVE: SELF-CONSCIOUS HELPING

The professional helper needs to extend beyond the objectifying, impersonal approach, in which material is examined within a conceptual matrix of typification (Berenson, 1981). Clearly without a frame of reference which subsumes a matrix of typifications, no one could comprehend experience as meanings. No helper can do without a typology. How he uses it matters. For, as Friedman (1965, p.37) noted:

What he must do, however, is throw away as much of his typology as he can and accept the unforeseeable happening in the encounter.

This approach implies a deliberate attempt to achieve a personal grasp of self, the other, and the joint text by adopting a subjective *and* objective attitude. It involves a commitment to the individual as a person and an attempt to comprehend his pressing drama against his existential framework of conception of self, agency, and biography. It involves the helper as a person rather than as an impersonal repairman (Bakan, 1967) or as a machine-minder (Shaw, 1980). This commitment to the self-awareness of both involved lies at the heart of the 'I–Thou' relationship (Buber, 1958). It is a personal acknowledgement of the need to achieve communion in communication so aptly described by Hora (1959, p.237):

To understand himself man needs to be understood by another. To be understood by another he needs to understand the other.

This acknowledgement is fundamental to lay and scientific conceptions of personhood. Only by bearing in mind that I am a first person singular can I know what it is to be a person as a physical, social, and symbolic entity. Margolis (1978, p.23) saw the situation thus:

the concept of a person cannot be introduced at all if not reflexively, that is, to fix our own agency in reporting, experiencing, and performing in whatever way we do. We may be uncertain about the nature of what a person is, but at all costs our theory must accommodate the full range of our first person encounters. Hence, the effort either to 'reconcile' persons with the scientific image or to 'join' them to it must count as such an encounter.

Changing to the personal mode makes a purposive encounter far less programmatic. As Friedman's comment indicated, being a person relative to another person implies acceptance of the value of dialogue which is genuine — spontaneous self-expression emerging from a conversation rather than a remorseless, impersonal interrogation. The result will be information which extends beyond the realms of the conceptually tidy, comfortable, predictable, and economical.

This does not mean that the helping encounter within the personal mode lacks structure. Help without focus is, after all, no help at all (Pollak, 1976). Listening and talking in an unstructured manner is characteristic of the chance encounter. Such conversation communicates little information at the topic progression level. Its importance is at the macro-propositional level: 'Although what I'm saying is trivial, I want to show that I am interested in you as a person. I hope you are interested in me in a like manner.' In the case of the helping encounter, conversation must not only demonstrate this genuine interest but also must be purposive in its pursuit of personal information. The helper does not need to abandon his macro plan for the encounter. He, like the helper who uses the impersonal approach, has a notion of the important items of identification to be covered. The impersonal approach uses the helper's statements to 'gate-keep and filter meaning' (Brenner, 1978) which excludes material disruptive to his definition, that is information germane to the individual as an attending self, an agent with a sense of history. In the personal approach the conversational mode is used as a means of introducing just these aspects of meaning. It requires a mentality of genuine curiosity and a form of questioning which is frankly invitational, of the 'Could you tell me . . .?' genre.

This form of encounter requires the helper to maintain a sense of direction *and* to construct a social, psychological, and communication context which encourages the expression of personal meanings. Its conduct reflects an acceptance that it is indeed 'the social organization of the interview which sets the boundaries for the meanings to emerge' (Brenner, 1978, p.133). These meetings last longer, but not that much longer, and the gains in terms of personal satisfaction and information derived are enormous.

The purposive conversation is harder work than the impersonal approach to information gathering. It requires greater patience and attentiveness. It implies processing a much richer, more extensive field of material. The helper participating in this approach is denied the defence of skimming for gross topics. He cannot deny, or deny himself, the knowledge of the flow of four concurrent channels of communication: language, intonation, para-language, and movement. He has to be scientific about these, unlike the skimmers. He cannot blind himself to the knowledge that only some 60–80 per cent of conversation is usually heard. Neither can he ignore the fact that speakers, in assuming that listeners grasp at the level intended, can be wildly wrong in their assumption. Not for him is the convenient path of not letting on that he has failed to grasp. He cannot hang on in the hope that 'all will fall into place'. However, as part of the confidence-building process with which the encounter commences, he will have prepared the individual to expect interjections of the 'I'm not quite sure what you meant by that, could you tell me . . .?' or 'Could you let me know what . . . means?' Far from viewing such requests for further information as a sign of incompetence or disinterest, the individual will take these to be yet another mark of extreme professional commitment to understand. However, the helper will also have to balance the pursuit of expansion of meaning against the necessity to maintain the conversation flow. Also he will need to recognize that some individuals' 'talk may not be sharp in terms of meaning and cannot be sharpened' (Brenner, 1978, p.123). As a serious student of language, he will know that natural language is logically and expressively imprecise, full of chance metaphor, an *ex tempore* text which is tentative and an implicit invitation to the listener–observer to become a speaker and firm up meaning through conversation (Scheffler, 1978). Because he wishes to be systematic in his approach to text, not just for reasons of identifying the missed and the misheard, the helper employing the personal approach will want to record the text. Succinctly he will wish to examine this recording as stable text for its potential to inform himself about himself and to yield an insight into the individual's personal meaning system.

SELF-KNOWLEDGE THROUGH TEXT

Recording an encounter enables the helper to monitor his social performance and his conversational and interviewing skills. He will be able to seek out the evidence of the 'blind area' unknown to himself but known to others (Luft, 1970). He will be able to examine the exchange for its thematic flow, for the interplay between statement and statement, seeking indications of personal bias, demand characteristics and attempts at social desirability. However, the monitoring of self-performance, whilst an important aspect of text analysis, is subordinate to analysis directed at a representation of the individual's personal meanings.

UNDERSTANDING THE FIRST PERSON SINGULAR

It is not intended in this paper to give an extended account of how a professional helper can effect a useful, reasonably rapid analysis of text. It is sufficient to state here that it does not require the production of transcripts or mindless counting of items in the absence of a theory of analysis. The history of content analysis research is replete with studies which have sought to ignore that meaning is not in one-to-one correspondence with words. For, as Vygotsky (1962, p.150) pointed out:

Thought, unlike speech, does not consist of separate units . . . A speaker often takes several minutes to disclose one thought. In his mind the whole thought is present at once, but in speech it has to be developed successively. A thought may be compared to a cloud shedding a shower of words.

I submit that in the replaying of text, as in the live encounter, the helper is perfectly able to see these clouds. To impose arbitrary units of account, the meaningful definition of which would be impossible, would be meaningless. I recommend that helpers listening to text should follow Vygotsky's maxim for analysis, which Harré (1974, p.248) urged psychologists to observe:

Never analyze a psychological process into units which are below the meaning level of the original phenomenon.

Hence the professional helper being systematic with text will not be in the word-counting business. He will, however, be in the construct-identifying business. He will be on the look-out for constructs which the individual will have woven about the dramatis personae and events in the text. On occasions the cloud of a thought will be suggested, and verbalizable, by a word or series of words actually used by the speaker. On other occasions the cloud will be sensed but no words of the speaker will be to hand. On these occasions the helper has no option but to encapsulate it with a word or words of his own. The important point here is that the helper needs to be explicit about his understanding in either case. He has to be mature about it—he must 'go public' and provide what he thinks is the contrast pole. (Now it can be seen why asking for expansion wherever possible during the encounter is so essential.) In identifying a construct and facing up to the demand to be explicit in his understanding, his task will be personal and far more scientific than those poor content analysts of the solely manifest, slavishly working their way through transcript, counting words at face-value because the 'rules' deny the parallel role of intuition in understanding. He will be free to be scientific in accepting the validity of his own experience presented through intuition and analytical thought (Hammond, 1981), which enables him to cope with the large number of simultaneously and linearly presented cues. In his analysis he will be guided by a frame of reference which seeks both to represent the individual's meanings and also to bring these together as a whole. This is the interpretive outcome of his attempt to be both subjective and objective in his understanding of the individual.

The demand to examine the individual's first-person statements to yield a dual perspective was well described by Buber (1958, p.133) when he suggested that: 'Healing, like education, is only possible to the one who lives over against the other, and is yet detached.' Elsewhere (Buber, 1947) he stressed the need for *inclusion*, to experience the other side of the relationship. But how is the helper to check the validity of his interpretations? Time and motivation to embark upon second-opinion conversations with other professionals is likely to be limited for the helper working on his own. I would suggest that the helper must minimally check out his representation of the other's experience. This can be done again through conversation. Furthermore, his representation will doubtless include material from the individual's own 'blind area'. The individual's invited comments and attempts at expansion or qualification can only lead to greater understanding of him as a person.

With respect to what I term *second-order* interpretations, the effect of the hermeneutical tradition (Kermode, 1979) to which the helper subscribes will be most apparent. In his interpretation he will seek to account for the constructs of contrast, contradiction, change, continuity, and characterization which permeate the entire text. He will attempt to pull together the public, blind, hidden, and unknown areas (Luft, 1970). Like any interpretation, the final arbiter as to its validity is himself (although its acceptance by the individual is also a goal). There is no *best* text (Hudson, 1978) — nor could there ever be.

For the everyday helping encounter conducted in the conversational mode the hermeneutical circle consists of the professional helper and the individual he seeks to help. This is right since they created the context and text through joint action. Some will feel dissatisfied with this arrangement, and consider that these interpretations have the appearance of self-fulfilling prophecies. Absolutely right — in the moral and social sense — since the views of both interpreters, as selves, are respected, that is, fulfilled. Interpretation is unavoidably an act of motivated thought engendered by the listener–observer's desires, needs, interests and emotions—what Vygotsky (1962) termed the affective-volitional tendency. This comprises the sub-text which emerges through meanings and words to become the specifiable representation of a frame of reference. That we see what we want to see, hear what we want to hear, understand what we want to understand, has long been known to laymen and more recently to cognitive science. Like our reflective thought, interpretations are circular: Hirsch (1967, p.237) summed the issue up as follows:

The interpreter posits meanings for the words and word sequences he confronts, and, at the same time, he has to posit a whole meaning or context in reference to which the submeanings cohere with one another. The procedure is thoroughly circular: the context is derived from the submeanings and the submeanings are specified and rendered coherent with reference to the context.

Once two people enter into conversation we are, according to Bleich (1978), p.294):

proposing knowledge, bearing responsibility, and defining a community of common interests. There is no way to reduce the scope of these simple activities, when taken seriously, they become difficult and complex. The only recourse is to increase awareness of them and to establish a vocabulary of subjective initiatives that can command our thoughts and regulate our relationships. Beyond these thoughts and relationships there is no way to authorize knowledge.

This is not the world of solipsism. Far from it. Bleich (p.295) concluded a forceful argument on this issue thus:

When the subjective authorization of knowledge is allowed, the pretence of truth is replaced by inter-subjective negotiation. The responsibility of each knower for his knowledge and to the other party is necessarily an item in the discussion. The consistent influence of mutual responsibility is the opposite of solipsism.

The only thing an interpreter can do is keep an open mind!

THE JUSTIFICATION: STONES OR BREAD?

It seems strange that one has to write a justification for genuine dialogue —the speech event in which two people, here a helper and the helped, recognize each other in all their personhood in order to respect, express, and comprehend personal meanings of the one who needs help to move 'through a breakdown to a breakthrough' (Morris, 1972, p.82). The all-too prevalent alternative, the 'I-it' (or worse 'it-it') relationship, is to respond to a request to be sustained at a time of need with the inanimate and the potentially destructive, in the manner so roundly condemned in St Matthew (Chapter 7, verses 9–10):

Is there a man among you who would hand his son a stone when he asked for bread? Or would hand him a snake when he asked for a fish?

An appropriate attitude and action in helping is subsequently urged (verse 12): 'Always treat others as you yourself would like others to treat you', that is as a first person singular. This is the unavoidable first step in taking personal meanings seriously.

REFERENCES

Bakan, D. (1967) *On Method: Towards a Reconstruction of Psychological Investigation*. San Francisco: Jossey-Bass.

Berenson, F. M. (1981) *Understanding Persons: Personal and Impersonal Relationships*. Brighton: Harvester Press.

Berger, P. L. and Luckmann, T. (1967) *The Social Construction of Reality*. Harmondsworth: Penguin.

Bleich, D. (1978) *Subjective Criticism*. Johns Hopkins University Press.

Brenner, M. (1978) Interviewing: the social phenomenology of a research method. In M. Brenner, P. Marsh, and M. Brenner (Eds), *The Social Context of Method*. London: Croom Helm.

Browne, K. and Freeling, P. (1976) *The Doctor–Patient Relationship*. Edinburgh: Churchill Livingstone.

Buber, M. (1947) *Between Man and Man* (trans. R. G. Smith). London: Routledge and Kegan Paul.

Buber, M. (1958) *I and Thou* (trans. R. G. Smith). New York: Scribner's.

Eisenberg, L. (1981) Critique on the behavioural paradigm. In C. Eisdorfer, D. Cohen, A. Klein, and P. Maxim (Eds), *Models for Clinical Psychopathology*. Lancaster: MTP.

Friedman, M. (1965) Introductory essay. In M. Buber, *The Knowledge of Man* (edited by M. Friedman). London: Allen and Unwin.

Hammond, K. R. (1981) Principles of organization in intuitive and analytical thinking. Centre for Research on Judgement and Policy, *Report No. 231*. Institute for Behavioral Research, University of Colorado.

Harré, R. (1974) Blueprint for a new science. In N. Armistead (Ed.), *Reconstructing Social Psychology*. Harmondsworth: Penguin.

Hirsch, E. D. (1967) Validity in interpretation. Yale University Press.

Hopson, B. and Adams, J. (1976) Towards an understanding of transition: defining some boundaries of transition dynamics. In J. Adams, J. Hayes, and B. Hopson (Eds), *Transition: Understanding and Managing Personal Change*. London: Robertson.

Hora, T. (1959) Tao, Zen and existential psychotherapy. *Psychologia*, 2, 236–42.

Hudson, L. (1978) *Human Beings*. Frogmore, St Albans, Herts: Triad Paladin.

Kelly, G. A. (1955) *The Psychology of Personal Constructs*. New York: Norton.

Kermode, F. (1979) *The Genesis of Secrecy*. Harvard University Press.

Kinget, G. M. (1975) *On Being Human: a Systematic View*. New York: Harcourt Brace Jovanovich.

Lenrow, P. (1978) Dilemmas of professional helping: contradictions and discontinuities with folk helping roles. In L. Wispe (Ed.), *Altruism, Sympathy and Helping*. New York: Academic.

Luft, J. (1970) *Group Processes*. Palo Alto: National.

Margolis, J. (1978) *Persons and Minds*. Dordrecht: Reidel.

Morris, J. (1972) Three aspects of the person in social life. In R. Ruddock (Ed.), *Six Approaches to the Person*. London: Routledge and Kegan Paul.

The Gospel According to St Matthew. In *The New English Bible* (1972). British and Foreign Bible Societies.

Naess, A. (1975) *Freedom, Emotion and Self-Subsistence: The structure of a central part of Spinoza's Ethics*. Oslo University Press.

North, M. (1972) *The Secular Priests*. London: Allen and Unwin.

Pollak, O. (1976) *Human Behaviour and the Helping Professions*. New York: Spectrum.

Pride, J. B. (1971) *The Social Meaning of Language*. Oxford: University Press.

Rommetveit, R. (1980) On meanings of acts and what is meant and made known by what is said in a pluralistic social world. In M. Brenner (Ed.), *The Structure of Action*. Oxford: Blackwell.

Shaw, M. L. G. (1980) *On Becoming a Personal Scientist*. New York: Academic.

Scheffler, I. (1979) *Beyond the Letter*. Harvard University Press.

Taylor, C. (1971) Interpretation and the sciences of man. *Rev. Metaphysics*, **25**, 3–51.

Teilhard de Chardin, P. (1959) *The Phenomenon of Man*. New York: Harper.

Tiryakian, A. A. (1966) The existential self and the person. In C. Gordon and K. J. Gergen (Eds), *The Self in Social Interaction*, Vol.1. New York: Wiley.

Vaneigem, R. (1979) *The Revolution of Everyday Life* (trans. J. Fullerton and P. Siveking). London: Rising Free Collective.

Vernon, P. E. (1963) *Personality Assessment: A Critical Appraisal*. London: Methuen.

Vygotsky, L. S. (1962) *Thought and Language* (ed. and trans. by E. Hanfmann and G. Vakar). MIT Press.

Watts, F. N. (1980) Clinical judgement and clinical training. *Brit. J. Med. Psychol.*, **53**, 95–108.

Wolff, R. P. (1971) *Philosophy: A Modern Encounter*. Englewood-Cliffs, N.J.: Prentice-Hall.

Personal meanings
and personal constructs

F. Fransella

> I know that you believe you understand
> what you think I said,
> But, I am not sure you realize that what
> you heard is not what I meant.
> (Source unknown)

THE MEANING OF A CONSTRUCT

There is no entry for the word 'meaning' or for the word 'understanding' in either of Kelly's two volumes (1955). No entry is needed.

To construe is to impose meaning or interpretations upon something or some things. The meaning is not inherent in the thing itself, it is within the person. So we can start from the position that persons are actively engaged in interpreting the events confronting them. However, we each may impose different interpretations on these events and so disagree about their 'true' nature. For no one has direct access to truth. Kelly's philosophy of constructive alternativism states that 'all of our present interpretations of the universe are subject to revision and replacement'; and this underlies the whole theory, the model of the person and psychological change.

We interpret, or impose meaning upon, events and act accordingly. To a large extent our present actions are based on our past construing of similar events. On the basis of past events we predict that certain things will result from our present behaviour. Our behaviour thus has the characteristic of an experiment conducted to test our hypotheses derived from our past construing. We then look to see whether our predictive system is working reasonably well or whether we have landed ourselves in an unexpected situation. Such invalidation of a prediction has in turn to be construed or interpreted, and hypotheses resulting from the application of a further set of constructs tested by our behaving

47

differently—and so on. *Behaving and construing are thus indivisible.*
The more accurately we can predict the ever-changing world around
us, the better able we are to be in control of it—and of ourselves. The
less meaning we are able to impose on the world or a set of events, the
more likely we are to experience *anxiety*. The more important it is for us
to resist changing a sub-system of constructs, the more likely we are to
become *hostile* and 'make' things turn out the way we predict they
should. The more actively we strive after new experiences and so widen
the range of our system of meanings, the more *aggressive* we are said to
be. The more we find ourselves behaving in ways that are quite contrary
to some essential notion we have about ourselves as persons, the more we
experience *guilt*. And so on. These are some of the ways that the
psychology of personal constructs relates personal meanings to specific
types of behaviour and emotions. *Behaving, construing, and feeling are
indivisible.*

Personal construct psychology is thus about personal meaning and
personal action. It is important to distinguish *meaning* from *meaningfulness* which relates to the measurement of meaning. It was for this
purpose that Kelly developed what has become known as repertory grid
technique (see Fransella and Bannister, 1977). It is, of course, possible to
measure meaningfulness in many other ways, but the grid was specifically designed to help the clinician come to an understanding of the
meanings people and events have for an individual.

Implicit in George Kelly's first principle 'if you don't know what is
wrong with someone, ask them, they may tell you' is a statement of the
nature of personal meaning. Kelly meant that you should listen very
carefully to the underlying meaning of Mary's statement 'Well, the
trouble with me is that no one understands me.' Possibly, Mary *may*, in
fact, be saying 'people always misunderstand what I think I am about as
a person'. Yet again, poor misunderstood Mary *may* be saying that she
understands only too well what *she* is getting at but her ideas are too
loosely hung together for others to follow. Her personal meanings are
private. Kelly was thus saying that if you listen carefully to the tales of
trials and tribulations pouring from Mary you may grasp the essence of
what she is saying.

This dilemma of Mary's exemplifies three important aspects of
meaning. First, by commenting on the perceived misunderstandings of
others, Mary may really be talking about context; saying that there are
some situations in which she is all too readily understood and that it is
only in others that misunderstandings occur. Context is all too often
overlooked in our search for personal meanings. Second, personal
construct theory is a dialectical theory. In talking to this person as a

friend, therapist, counsellor, or priest, we may come to learn the meaning Mary has for herself which is *different from* the meaning she thinks she has for others. Third, Mary is suggesting that there may be aspects of herself that are not fully understood by anyone—including herself, pointing to different levels of awareness.

MEANING AND CONTEXT

It is somewhat naïve to say that we ascribe meaning to events within the context of those events. But it is continually surprising how often we fail to take account of this fact. *Being in control* may be construed somewhat differently in the context of parental behaviour from its use in the context of love-making. Hinkle (1965) considered this when he developed his theory of construct implications. He asked how far could the subordinate and superordinate implications of a construct change from context to context before it lost its identity. How far can one say that *being in control* as a parent and as a lover is the same construct?

Hinkle suggests that we might derive a measure of a construct's *transcontextual identity*. For instance, if in the parental situation A, B, and C imply *being in control* and *being in control* implies 1, 2, and 3, while in the context of love-making A, B, and D imply *being in control* and *being in control* implies 3, 4, and 5, then the transcontextual identity of *being in control* consists of A, B, and 3. No research has yet looked at this way of establishing the meaning of a construct across contexts, but it is worth exploring. For instance, perhaps it would be profitable to study dreaming 'as if' it were an experience in which we used our constructs set free from the ties of context.

THE DIALECTICAL NATURE OF THE CONSTRUCT

Construing is dialectical in nature. Kelly took the philosophical stance that there can be no *up* without a *down*; no *justice* without *injustice*; no *noise* without *silence*. The bi-polarity of meaning is central to the psychology of personal constructs. Kelly (1955, pp.59–60) says:

If we choose an aspect in which A and B are similar, but in contrast to C, it is important to note that it is the same aspect of all three, A, B *and* C, that forms the basis of the construct. It is not that there is one aspect of A and B that makes them similar to each other and another aspect that makes them contrasting to C.

Perhaps this is a modern version of the one-in-many or many-in-one thesis. In the fifth century BC Heraclitus is recorded as saying: 'Things taken together are wholes and not wholes; being brought together is being parted; concord is dissonance; and out of all things, one; and out of one, all things.' (Magill and McGreal, 1963, p.13). This has profound implications for our attempts to understand others' meanings.

For instance, these polar opposites so often cause trouble in communication. Someone may say to me 'I am your friend.' I may not reciprocate and he looks offended. For me, the opposite of *friend* is *acquaintance* and I do not know him well enough to call him a friend. He looks offended because for him the opposite of friend is *enemy* and he is merely making the statement that he is not my enemy. A bystander, whose opposite of *friend* is *stranger* wonders what on earth is going on. Full understanding of what another is trying to convey can only occur when one knows what the other is negating. It may well be that we use different opposites according to the context in which the construct is to be used.

Meaning and behaving

Using the bi-polar nature of constructs, Tschudi (1977) has proposed an ABC model to account for the perpetuation of symptoms. A person expresses the wish to move on construct A from a_1 to a_2, and construct B may give reasons why this should be so. But construct C hinders movement and leads to what Hinkle (1965) has termed an *implicative dilemma*. A is the construct on which the person says they want to move —it describes the problem. To clarify the nature of the dilemma, Tschudi suggests that the person be questioned about the advantages and the disadvantages of being at either pole a_1 or pole a_2. Supposing the construct is *not dominating* as opposed to being *dominating*. The questioning gives rise to a second construct, B; *not dominating* people are *boring* and *submissive*, whereas *dominating* ones are *liberated* and *self-assertive*. Still further questioning may reveal a construct C which gives positive value to the problem (a_1) and negative value to the desired state (a_2): not dominating people have good contact with people and are likely to be loved, whereas self-assertive people may drown others in words. The ABC sequence is thus as follows:

A	a_1	not dominating	a_2	dominating
B	b_1	others define one, submissive, boring, reticent, repulsive	b_2	being forward, liberated, self-assertive, etc.
C	c_2	good contact with people, to be loved	c_1	dominating in condescending way, drown people in words

This person was initially given a programme of treatment to help her to be more self-assertive, but she became increasingly depressed. Then, by working on the constructs themselves, she came to see that 'it is not my nature to be *forward* and *dominating*, that is *not me*'. It transpired that it was her boyfriend who liked girls to be forward. She therefore resolved the implicative dilemma by changing the meaning of constructs A and B so that she could be *direct* yet *not commanding*. By seeking out the advantages and disadvantages of the two poles of the construct relating to a problem, the client is helped to see what it all means, and, hopefully, to reconstrue so that construct C ceases to prevent movement. This can be done by the use of grids, laddering constructs, talking or, very often, a combination of all three.

More complex examples can be found in the construing of some stutterers (Fransella, 1972). People who have had their speech disorder since early childhood may 'know' that they want to be fluent speakers (a_2) rather than stutterers (a_1). But they cannot move across because they see only relative emptiness there, a void—to be sucked into that black hole without preparation would result in a life without personal meaning.

It is argued that this is why many stutterers are unable to make use of speech techniques—these produce fluency but not a fluent speaker. For instance, one person could only construe himself as a fluent speaker along a total of five dimensions of meaning. Most of us need considerably more than this to be viable in interpersonal relations. But, apart from the conceptual vagueness of the desired position, it was possible to obtain some information about how he saw himself and his world from relationships between constructs derived from a bi-polar implications grid (Fransella, 1972).

This type of repertory grid is composed of predictions a person makes about others. For instance, the stutterer who completed the grid from which the information in Figure 1 was obtained, predicted that, if he only knew the other was *hesitant*, the person would also be *quiet*, *keep things to themselves*, and be *wrapped up in their own thoughts*. The *total* network of significant relationships between construct poles for being a *fluent speaker* for this man can be seen in Figure 1. With dashed lines indicating negative relationships, there is a suggestion that being *hesitant* and all that this implies could be desirable. This is particularly so when considering what *not like me* implies. People not like him are shallow, talk a lot of rubbish, and confide in *anyone*. This grid consists of constructs elicited from him in relation to his being a fluent person. It is interesting that none of the constructs in Figure 1 have any significant relationships at all with the construct *stutterers* versus *fluent speakers*.

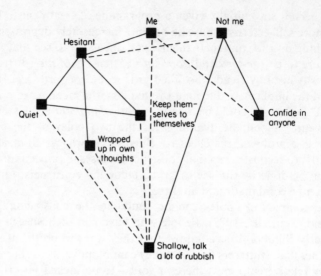

Figure 1   Total number of statistically significant construct poles with the construct ME–NOT ME from a bi-polar implication grid for one stutterer as a 'fluent speaker'

Levels of meaning

For full understanding of personal meaning, we have to look at the implications of both poles of a construct as well as the level at which we are aware of them. Constructs are not discrete entities, but are hierarchically related. In Hinkle's (1965) terms, the meaningfulness of a construct is defined by its immediate range of implications and also in the implications of those other constructs making up its immediate range of implication. The same person completed a second grid with constructs elicited from his perception of himself as a stutterer. Figure 2 shows some of the construct relationships. He sees himself as a stutterer, as being *self-conscious, not able to command a situation, not mentally tough*, and *not able to create his own atmosphere*. But this still does not tell us a great deal about him. We therefore look to see what happens when we go to the next level of meaning, to the implications of the implications of the self. Figure 3 shows the implications of being self-conscious. Nothing very startling again, with further notions of immaturity and passivity in relation to others. But when we treat the construct as a bi-polar unit, we can immediately see that, whatever its limitations, being *self-conscious* is vastly preferable to its opposite pole of *not being aware of one's shortcomings*, with its implications of being *insensitive, uncreative*, and *non-artistic*.

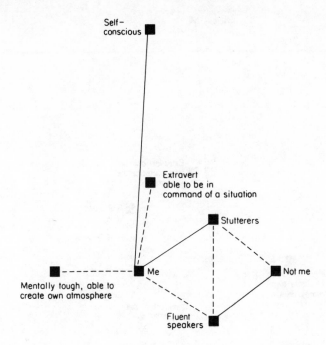

Figure 2 Total number of statistically significant construct poles with the construct pole ME from a bi-polar implication grid for one stutterer as a 'stutterer'

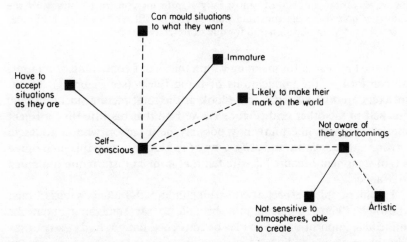

Figure 3 Total number of statistically significant construct poles with the construct SELF-CONSCIOUS–NOT AWARE OF THEIR SHORTCOMINGS from a bi-polar implication grid for one stutterer as a 'stutterer'

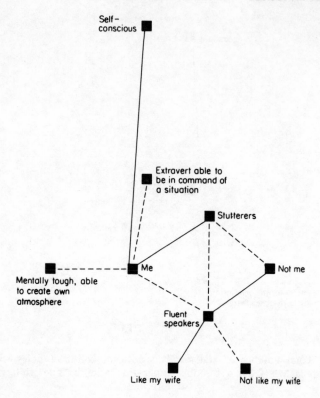

Figure 4   Total number of statistically significant construct poles with the construct poles with the construct pole FLUENT SPEAKERS from a bi-polar implication grid for one stutterer as a 'stutterer'

In one last search for meaning within this man's construing of himself, we can look at the implications of being fluent (see Figure 4). Fluent speakers are *like his wife*. If we look at the total picture, including the non-self in the other grid (Figure 1), we find that his wife (like a fluent speaker and not like him) may possibly be a person who confides in *anyone* and is *shallow* and *talks a lot of rubbish*. In fact, this man opted out of treatment because his wife felt that it might disturb him too much to change.

This hierarchical aspect of construing links with Polanyi's idea of tacit knowing (1969). A person may be able to say something about the immediate implications of an idea or construct, but not find it easy to say what the meaning or lines of implication of these are. But, theoretically at least, we have knowledge of these other levels of meaning and these will have implications for our actions even though we may not be consciously aware of them.

LEVELS OF AWARENESS

If only all our constructs had word symbols neatly attached giving full representation of their meaning, how easy life would be. We could understand what we were all about; we could understand what others were all about; and we could readily understand the meanings others were trying to convey. If this were the case we could, as Kelly says, 'sit in our rocking chair and twiddle our constructs to our endless amusement' (1955, p.460).

But our constructs do *not* all come neatly packaged with verbal labels tied on—in spite of what many seem to think. Constructs are discriminations. They are abstractions derived from similarities and differences we have perceived in our words. We come to give symbolic labels to some, but to a number we do not. Also, for some the verbal labels are very inadequate and fail to represent the full complexity of the construct. It is particularly in these last two cases that personal meaning takes on its idiosyncratic nature.

Kelly chose not to use the construct 'unconscious'. He regarded it as too restricting, and preferred to talk instead of construing as taking place at different levels of awareness. At a very low level of awareness there are *preverbal constructs*. These were originally developed by the infant to organize its world, and they continue to be used even though they have no consistent word symbol. In the clinical setting, 'acting-out' is seen as a preverbal construct in use. For what can you do with a construct that has no verbal label but 'behave' it? Preverbal construing is not equivalent to the 'unconscious' as used in psychoanalytic theory. True, a preverbal construct is not available to consciousness in the sense that we can point to it and discuss it: we are aware of it yet are unable to put a finger on it and nail it down. But there is no 'energy' attached to it. It only 'lives' when used.

Another construct about construing that is not available to conscious awareness is *submergence*. A construct is bi-polar and sometimes one pole is submerged and so is less available to us. To take Kelly's example, the meaning of the statement 'everyone has always been good to me' can *only* be found in its opposite pole. This may be 'but *other* people have been mistreated'; or 'everyone has always been good to me, but I have not always been good to others'; or 'everyone has always been good to me but I don't want to be good to *certain* people'; or 'everyone has always been good to me but some other people go around saying that people are *not* good to them'; and so on. Without knowing what the other is negating, we may well have difficulty in seeing what he or she is driving at.

The construct of submergence can also be helpful in aiding our understanding of the meaning of a dream. For Tom to dream of the buxom, bountiful blonde who distributes all blessings may be little understood by him except at a sexual level, if he takes it literally. But perhaps there is the opposite person in his life at the present time, a svelte, avaricious brunette who is causing difficulties by tempting Tom with sin. Viewed in terms of these submerged opposite poles the dream comes to have more meaning.

Sometimes constructs or elements become *suspended* and so made unavailable to consciousness. In other frameworks, these constructs have been 'forgotten', 'disassociated', or 'repressed'. A construct or element cannot become available to consciousness unless it is supported within a system of constructs. On occasion, when considerable change is going on within a person, some elements in particular may become suspended outside the construct system, because they do not now fit the new pattern. Later, when the person has developed a more comprehensive way of dealing with the change, he or she may reincorporate those temporarily suspended items and make them again available for conscious reflection. Dreaming may serve the function of helping these suspended elements be reconstrued. Roberts (1980) has suggested that in dreaming the self-construct itself is suspended. This then allows the self-as-element, which 'sits' on certain poles of constructs within our personal system, to live a life of its own without the superordinate overseeing self playing its role of reflecting upon its own consciousness. Roberts points out that without this self-construct there can be no anticipation of the future, resulting in all thoughts in the dream becoming immediate reality.

Kelly describes three other constructs relating to construing that is not readily available to consciousness. Each of these may lead to our failing to understand another. For instance, a person may be organizing experiences in a very *subordinate* fashion, using few, if any, abstract or more superordinate constructs to pull events together to form large parcels. If the therapist herself is construing the client's utterances and behaviours in a superordinate way, she will not understand what the client is on about. Alternatively, the client, or you or I, may have made a construct *impermeable*—we will not 'allow' it to incorporate new elements or events. If a person seems to us to have a construct that could readily deal with a new experience and fails to do so, we misunderstand that person. In another psychological model we might accuse the client of 'unconscious resistance'. Or yet again, the therapist may be confronted with marked shifting of thinking which comes with *loosened* construing and might, mistakenly, take this to indicate that some deep-seated construing was taking place simply because he cannot follow it.

So submergence, suspension, together with subordinate, impermeable, preverbal, and loosened construing are all constructs about construing at differing levels of consciousness. These take the place of the construct 'unconscious'.

Kelly's decision not to use that construct 'unconscious' follows directly from his theoretical position. He says (Kelly, 1955, p.467):

This is a psychology of *personal* constructs. We assume that personal constructs exist. If a client does not construe things in the way we do, we assume that he construes them in some other way, not that he really must construe them the way we do but is unaware of it. If later he comes to construe them the way we do, that is a new construction for him, not a revelation of a subsconscious construction which we have helped him to bring to the fore. Our constructs are our own. There is no need to reify them in the client's 'unconscious'.

Much of this seems to tie in with Polanyi's (1969) distinction between focal and subsidiary awareness. Although Kelly wished to argue that awareness might be viewed in scalar fashion, he seems to have got caught up in his own dichotomies. He mostly describes construing at either a fairly high or conscious level of awareness or else at a low or fairly unconscious level. Polanyi may offer us another point on the awareness scale. If we use the idea of focal awareness to indicate the act of applying a construct (or set of constructs) to an event or person, then we may say that not only are we subsidiarily aware of those elements which give those constructs meaning, but also of our submerged construct poles, our preverbal construing, and so forth. It may be that only suspended elements are totally not available to consciousness.

The psychology of personal constructs is a psychology of personal meanings. It provides a framework to help come to an understanding of some of the complexities involved in trying to convey our personal meanings to others and, in turn, in being understood by others.

REFERENCES

Fransella, F. (1972) *Personal Change and Reconstruction*. London: Academic Press.

Fransella, F., and Bannister, D. (1977) *A Manual for Repertory Grid Technique*. London: Academic Press.

Hinkle, D. (1965) The change of personal constructs from the viewpoint of the theory of construct implications. Unpub. PhD thesis, Ohio State University.

Kelly, G. A. (1955) *The Psychology of Personal Constructs*, Vols I & II. New York: Norton.

Magill, F. N., and McGreal, J. P. (eds) (1963) *Masterpieces of World Philosophy in Summary Form*. New York: Allen & Unwin.

Polanyi, M. (1969) *Knowing and Being*. London: Routledge & Kegan Paul.

Roberts, R. (1980) The midnight messages. Unpub. MSc dissertation, University of London.

Tschudi, F. (1977) Loaded and honest questions: a construct theory view of symptoms and therapy. In D. Bannister (Ed.), *New Perspectives in Personal Contruct Theory*. London: Academic Press.

Personal Meanings
Edited by Eric Shepherd and J. P. Watson
© 1982 John Wiley & Sons Ltd.

The extraction of personal meaning from a repertory grid

Mildred L. G. Shaw

INTRODUCTION

One possible approach to the discovery of *personal meaning* is to explore the *personal semantic* space of the individual and to do so with the minimum injection of structure from the process of exploration. A basis for this approach was established in the epistemological theories of the clinical psychologist George Kelly. These are expressed in his seminal work *The Psychology of Personal Constructs* (Kelly, 1955) which provides a remarkably far-reaching and well-structured foundation for the study of human action. His work is anchored very firmly both in its close correspondence to the actual behaviour of people and in its coherent and consistent philosophy. Kelly put forward the model of man as a *personal scientist* who forms hypotheses about the world and, by using *personal constructs* as filters through which he experiences events, reviews and revises his hypotheses in the light of his experiences. In his clinical work Kelly helped people to make their construct usage explicit by defining distinctions between *elements* to which clinically important personal meanings attach such as oneself and one's close family and acquaintances. His *repertory grid* is derived by assigning each element under consideration to one pole or the other of a construct. This usually involves the poles in being labelled in some way but these are treated as memory aids to the person whose 'meaning' is defined by the way in which they are used rather than by the actual labels themselves.

Figure 1 is a repertory grid from Leach (1981) which was completed by a man whose wife had recently died of cancer. The elements he uses are shown as columns—the people he was in contact with during the event, and the construct names are shown on either side of each row. A '1' indicates assignment of the element in that column to the left pole of the construct, and a '2' indicates assignment to the right pole.

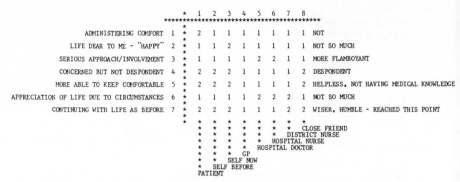

Figure 1   Repertory grid from man whose wife died of cancer (Leach, 1981)

There is an obvious resemblance between Kelly's *repertory grid* and the *semantic differential* methodology of Osgood, Suci, and Tannenbaum (1957). Both techniques eventually produce a matrix of assignments of elements assigned to bipolar rating scales, and both techniques have been applied to similar areas of study. The motivation of the work on semantic differentials has been to provide a psychological theory of meaning in which individual words can be seen to be compounded from relatively few components in a basic semantic space. In itself this is not inconsistent with Kelly's theory but it tends to neglect two features of semantic space that he regarded as epistemologically important: firstly, the *individual* nature of semantic space; and, secondly, the *hierarchical* structure of semantic space. In terms of the practical methodologies, this difference in emphasis shows up in the use of *elicitation* techniques for both constructs and construct hierarchies in work based on Kelly's viewpoint, whereas that deriving from the semantic differential uses consensual constructs over a population.

PEGASUS: A PROGRAM FOR THE EXPLORATION OF PERSONAL SEMANTIC SPACE

PEGASUS (Program Elicits Grids And Sorts Using Similarities) is an interactive computer program which elicits a repertory grid from an individual, simultaneously acting as a psychological reflector for heightening his awareness and deepening his understanding of himself and his processes. This is done by continual real-time feedback commentary on highly related elements or constructs, together with the encouragement to differentiate between them.

The program is divided into six main sections. The first section is the *Basic Grid* in which explanation of grids and the use of the terminal are given, and the first four constructs elicited. Before the user chooses his elements he is asked to think about his purpose which defines the universe of discourse and enables him to choose elements which are relevant and representative of the topic area, since the choice of elements largely determines the depth of interaction which can be achieved. The conventional method is then used to elicit the first few constructs, that is to present a triad of elements to be divided into a pair and a singleton indicating the poles of the construct. After the user has named the poles the computer assigns a 1 to the pair and a 5 to the singleton (assuming a five-point scale is being used), and he has then to assign ratings from 1 to 5 to each of the other elements. These are then retyped in groups to highlight the relative position of each element with respect to the others, and an option to change the ratings is given.

The second section, *Construct Match*, provides feedback when two constructs are highly related.

THE TWO CONSTRUCTS YOU CALLED
2 FLEXIBLE — RIGID
6 VARIABLE CONTENT — SPECIFIC CONTENT
ARE MATCHED AT THE 85 PERCENT LEVEL
THIS MEANS THAT MOST OF THE TIME YOU ARE SAYING
FLEXIBLE YOU ARE ALSO SAYING
VARIABLE CONTENT
AND MOST OF THE TIME YOU ARE SAYING
RIGID YOU ARE ALSO SAYING
SPECIFIC CONTENT
THINK OF ANOTHER ELEMENT WHICH IS EITHER FLEXIBLE
AND SPECIFIC CONTENT OR VARIABLE CONTENT AND RIGID
IF YOU REALLY CANNOT DO THIS THEN JUST PRESS RETURN
AFTER THE FIRST QUESTION MARK, BUT PLEASE TRY. THEN
YOU MUST GIVE THIS ELEMENT A RATING VALUE ON EACH
CONSTRUCT IN TURN.
TYPE A VALUE FROM 1 TO 5 AFTER EACH QUESTION MARK.
WHAT IS YOUR ELEMENT? VIDEO TAPE
RATINGS:
INVOLVEMENT — REMOTENESS? 3
FLEXIBLE — RIGID? 2
....   (Shaw, 1980, pp.61–62)

The user is first asked to add an element which is either at pole 1 on the first construct and pole 5 on the second, or vice versa. If he can add a new element it must be rated on all the constructs so far elicited, but if he cannot split the two constructs this way he is asked if he would like to delete a construct, combine two constructs into one, or just carry on.

When four constructs have been entered, the program moves into the third section, *Element Match*, and begins to calculate matching scores between elements. Each element is matched with every other on the basis of the ratings used, and a comment made on the highest match if it meets the set criterion. In the same way as with matching constructs the first choice offered is to add a new construct on which the two elements are placed at opposite poles, and then all the elements must be rated in the usual way. Alternatively, an element may be deleted, or no action may be taken. The fourth section allows the user to *Finish* at this stage in the cycle; the fifth, *Review*, gives the choice of adjusting or redefining the purpose, and altering the level of match on which feedback commentary is given. There is an opportunity to see a focused version of the grid to date, and to delete any element or construct which is felt to be unsatisfactory in any way. In the sixth section, *Alternative Elicitation*, the user is given the freedom to add an element or to add a construct without using a triad if he so wishes.

When the grid reaches the maximum size allowed, or if the user chooses to finish before that, the results are analysed using the FOCUS procedure. This is a two-way hierarchical cluster analytic technique which systematically reorders the rows of constructs and columns of elements to produce a focused grid which shows the least variation between adjacent constructs and adjacent elements. The printout shows the trees of the elements and constructs as well as the focused grid with the element and construct labels (see Figure 2).

As a PEGASUS elicitation proceeds this FOCUS algorithm is used to offer to the user a possible explanation and interpretation of his meaning system in the terms of the similar patterns he uses in supposedly different circumstances. Cross-references are mapped across the grid and exhibited to the user in such a way as to offer him the facility to reconsider and change anything he feels to be inappropriate, which in turn enables him to be more aware of the links he is implicitly holding in his cognitive model. In this way the participative analysis extracts and displays the essence of the personally meaningful relationships in the grid.

THE SIGNIFICANCE OF THE COMPUTER

It would be easy to assume that interactive programs such as PEGASUS are merely more convenient ways of eliciting construct systems through extensions of Kelly's repertory grid and do not themselves add anything

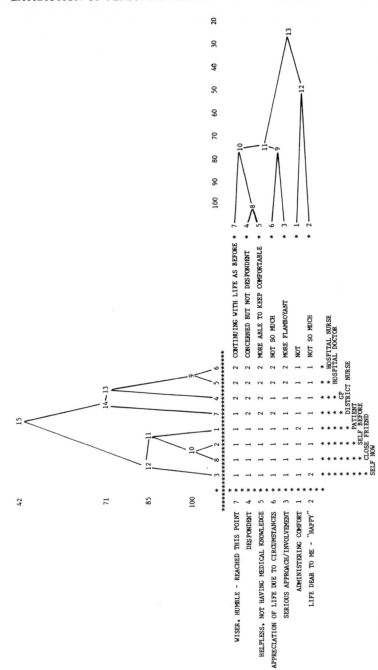

Figure 2   Cluster analysis of the man's grid by FOCUS

qualitatively new to the process. However, such an assumption would be missing certain crucial psychological factors in the person–computer situation and its differences from the person–person situation. It has been observed informally in making PEGASUS available to a wide range of people in a variety of situations that those coming to it for the first time often seem to find it a very dramatic experience. They react to it intensely and become gripped by the interactive process of construct elicitation. They also feel that they are learning something new from the process and are prepared to use this in determining their behaviour.

Probably such involvement is also significant in the elicitation of construct systems by a person rather than computer interaction. However, there are certain quite fundamental differences when the elicitation is done in such a way that interpersonal interaction is clearly absent. In particular, when a *person* is feeding back comments and guidance it is a natural and ready assumption that the constructs are being *injected* rather than elicited. It is easy for the subject to believe that the elicited constructs do not come from himself but that a tutorial or debating situation with another person is taking place. It is necessary to *persuade* him that this is not so and the persuasion has to be stronger the more striking and significant the constructs elicited. However, when a computer is the tool by which his construct structure is being reflected or laid bare then such an assumption of outside injection and interference is far less tenable.

When constructs are being elicited by a computer program then it is more likely to be accepted that it is precisely and only oneself that is being portrayed. We 'trust' a computer program to be doing just what it appears to be doing without deeper motivations and without attempting to persuade us to its point of view. No one is telling the user anything. He is seeing in interacting with PEGASUS, possibly for the first time, the basis for his own thought processes. Very often extreme surprise is the first reaction. If another person were eliciting the construct structure then the surprise would be taken as an indication that he was incorrect and one would ignore him or argue with him. With computer elicitation it is more likely that one will accept the reflected structures as being self-generated and the surprise acts as motivation to know more.

That this knowledge can be totally private to oneself is another important feature of interaction with the computer. We do not like, as Kelly put it, to be 'caught with our constructs down'. When another person is involved we are more reluctant to expose and explore our constructs the more surprising they are; perhaps because the surprise is often the result of a conflict between our ostensive value judgements and the basis of our behaviour. Or it may just be sloppy verbal behaviour:

that we are naming two distinct constructs with the same label. For example, in using PEGASUS a scientist found that he was using the word 'time' to label several different elements and generating confusion in his arguments because of this.

Another reason that we are reluctant to explore construct structures freely in interacting with another person, particularly a professional person, is that we are acutely aware of the possible 'waste' of their time. This phenomenon has been noted (Card *et al.*, 1974) as accounting for a major part of the preferences expressed by patients to be interviewed through an interactive computer program rather than their doctor. There are many pressures and artefacts of interpersonal relationships that can totally obscure and undermine such reflective processes as we require in the elicitation of personal constructs.

A notable technical feature of PEGASUS that profoundly affects human reactions to it is that relationships between constructs may be inferred instantly and queried with the user. This immediate analysis and feedback of personal meaning is a key factor in most applications of interactive computers and can go way beyond what any manual analysis can accomplish. Instant feedback whilst one remembers one's line of reasoning is very different from delayed analyses that are delivered at a later time when the entire context of the replies one has been giving may have been forgotten. Construct structures in particular have a high degree of context-dependence.

REPERTORY GRID ANALYSIS

The analysis of repertory grids has attracted much technical literature and it is worth emphasizing here the role of such analysis. It is to extract possible structure in the personal meanings of an individual and reflect it back to him in such a way that it aids his coming to terms with his problems. The words *possible* and *reflect* are significant since it is the essence of Kelly's approach that one is indeed dealing with *personal* meaning and that any analysis is subject to debate; it is the basis of a conversation rather than some form of absolute model. Clinicians using the repertory grid elicit it through such a direct conversation. In operationalizing Kelly's work through a computer the aim (Gaines and Shaw, 1981) is to develop a *conversational, dialectical* system of computer programs for the *self-reflective* study of one's role as a personal scientist.

For any given construct we may regard the numbers in the grid as a *vector of values* giving the assignment of each element in turn to one or other of the poles of the construct. From this point of view each construct becomes represented as a point in a multi-dimensional space whose dimension is the number of elements involved. A natural relation to examine between constructs is then the *distance* between them in this space. Two constructs which are zero distance apart are such that all elements are construed in the same way in relation to them and hence we might infer that they are being used in the same way—in some way they are *equivalent* constructs. For constructs which are not equivalent we may analyse the entire constellation in space to determine a set of axes such that the projection of each construct onto the first axis accounts for most of the distance between them, the projection on the second axis accounts for most of the remaining distance, and so on. This is a *principal components analysis* of the construct space, and it is related to the *factor analysis* of semantic space used in the study of semantic differentials. We may also group constructs together that are close together in space using some form of *cluster analysis*.

Shaw's (1980) FOCUS algorithm has already been shown in action in Figure 2. It is a distance-based hierarchical cluster analysis technique that sorts the constructs into a linear order such that constructs closest together in the space are also closest together in the order. It has the advantage in presentation that the sorting is used only to re-present the original grid reorganized by the 'neighbourness' of constructs and elements. It is left to the user to construe his own personal meaning into the result and confirm this directly in terms of the original data. Figure 2 shows the grid of Figure 1 as processed by FOCUS. In reorganizing the grid, FOCUS has reversed constructs 4, 5, and 7. Concentrating on the construct analysis, it can be seen that constructs 4 and 5 are equivalent and close neighbours of 7, and that this cluster is itself a close neighbour of the cluster formed by 3 and 6. Constructs 1 and 2 are not linked into the other constructs at a meaningful level. Now looking at the elements there are two main clusters: 5 and 6 being construed identically—the hospital doctor and the hospital nurse—joining at a lower level is 4 and then 7—the GP and the district nurse. The other cluster is much tighter having a centre of 2 and 8—self before and close friend—being construed identically, and linking either side with 1 and 3—the patient and self now.

The grid of Figure 1 has also been analysed using a form of Slater's (1977) INGRID program for determining the principal components. Figure 3 shows the eight elements and the two poles of each of the seven constructs plotted against the first two principal components. In this case the first component accounted for 68.5 per cent of the variance in the data, and the second, third, and fourth components accounted for 9 per cent each. This indicates the almost linear nature of this construct system

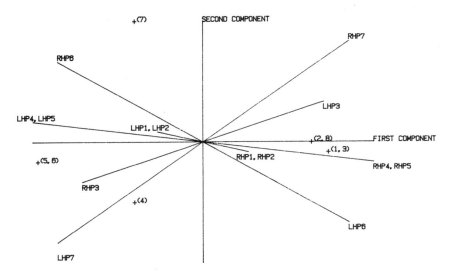

Figure 3   Principal components analysis of the man's grid

as can be seen from the elliptical shape of the clusters. It can be seen that the left-hand poles of constructs 6 and 3 are fairly close to the right-hand poles of constructs 4, 5, and 7. There is a mirror image of the right-hand poles of constructs 6 and 3, together with the left-hand poles of constructs 4, 5, and 7. Because the assignment of elements to poles is such that the vector of assignments to the left-hand pole is the reverse of that to the right-hand pole, such a mirror image is bound to occur with conventionally elicited grids. Although one can see from Figure 1 that constructs 1 and 2 are not identical, they are shown to be the same in their first two principal components. One can also see from its short length that the line denoting constructs 1 and 2 is not fully represented on these two axes, but clearly has components in other dimensions. Again, elements 2 and 8 are shown to be identical, and closely associated with elements 1 and 3. On the other side of the diagram elements 5 and 6 are identical, and cluster more loosely with elements 4 and 7. Thus, for this example at least, the actual clusters produced by FOCUS and INGRID do not differ in any meaningful way.

ENTAIL: A PROGRAM TO
DERIVE ENTAILMENTS BETWEEN CONSTRUCTS

The alternative to distance-based methods of grid analysis is a logical analysis, looking at the poles of constructs as predicates applying to

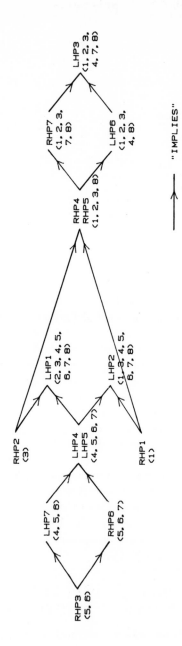

Figure 4   Entailment analysis of the man's grid by ENTAIL

elements (Shaw and Gaines, 1981). The program ENTAIL derives entailment relations between these predicates where a pole of one construct is said to *entail* a pole of another if all the elements assigned to the first pole are also all assigned to the second. Figure 4 shows the directed graph of entailment relations between the poles of the constructs derived by ENTAIL from the grid of Figure 1. There are effectively two main sub-graphs which are mirror images of one another, here connected by weak entailments involving constructs 1 and 2. One of the graphs shows the entailments for one set of poles, and the other the entailments for the opposite poles. Note that the 'reversal' of constructs 4, 5, and 7 apparent in the INGRID and FOCUS analyses shows up as LHP4, LHP5, and LHP7 appearing in the graph of the right-hand poles of the other constructs and vice versa. Because of the essential bipolarity assumed in the elicitation of the grid, the two graphs are essentially the same with the arrows and poles reversed in one relative to the other.

It is very interesting to compare Figure 4 with the results of the INGRID clustering in Figure 3 and the FOCUS clustering in Figure 2. We can see that the same hierarchy of construct clusters has turned up: ((3,6,7,(4,5),1,2). Thus the ENTAIL analysis gives rise to the same basic clustering as did INGRID and FOCUS. Both the fundamental and empirical similarities are important in their own right since two of these programs are widely used for grid analysis and one would hope that any new technique would continue to provide at least the same basic analysis.

However, there is additional information in Figure 4 that goes beyond that available in Figures 2 and 3. This comes from the directed nature of the entailment links shown. There is equivalence only between LHP4 and LHP5—all the other relations are one-way only. To show the significance of this we have indicated the elements assigned to each pole. The asymmetry of the entailment relation may be seen by considering that from LHP6 to LHP3, for example. We see from the descriptions of the poles that he is saying that people who have an appreciation of life due to the circumstances of his wife's death also have a serious approach. However, the converse does not hold. From the element data in Figure 4 we can see the reason for this asymmetry. For example, from the elements assigned to LHP6 and LHP3 we can see that the reason for the entailment between them not being mutual is that element 7—the district nurse—is seen as having a serious approach to life but not so much related to the circumstances of his wife's death. In this case, only one element breaks down the equivalence. Thus the construct analysis produced by ENTAIL has reproduced the clusters shown by INGRID and FOCUS but it has also shown up new features of the data not evident in those distance-based and essentially symmetric forms of analysis.

It has thus been indicated that personal meanings can be extracted from the manner in which an individual orders elements in the world, that is observations, events, or objects. The repertory grid is a way of making explicit an individual's personal models of the world, and the analysis should be judged subjectively as to how it helps in this process. The methods of analysis are not merely mechanized ways to exhibit personal meaning in any static way, but rather must be used in an interactive, conversational mode to outline particular topics for consideration and discussion. This may be carried out either internally with oneself, with oneself through a computer program such as PEGASUS, or with another individual such as the therapist. This methodology has also been extended to explore how one can extract personal and community meaning in a group, either real using SOCIOGRIDS, or perceived using ARGUS (Shaw, 1980).

REFERENCES

Card, W. I., Nicholson, M., Crean, G. P., Watkinson, G., Evans, C. R., Wilson, J., and Russell, D. (1974) A comparison of doctor and computer interrogation of patients. *International Journal Biomedical Computing*, **5**, 175–187.

Gaines, B. R. and Shaw, M. L. G. (1981) New directions in the analysis and interactive elicitation of personal construct systems. In Shaw, M. L. G. (Ed.), *Recent Advances in Personal Construct Technology*. London: Academic Press.

Kelly, G. A. (1955) *The Psychology of Personal Constructs*. New York: Norton.

Leach, C. (1981) Direct analysis of a repertory grid. In Shaw, M. L. G. (Ed.), *Recent Advances in Personal Construct Technology*. London: Academic Press.

Osgood, C. E., Suci, G. J., and Tannenbaum, P. H. (1957) *The Measurement of Meaning*. Urbana: University of Illinois Press.

Shaw, M. L. G. (1980) *On Becoming a Personal Scientist*. London: Academic Press.

Shaw, M. L. G., and Gaines, B. R. (1981) Recent advances in the analysis of a repertory grid. *British Journal of Medical Psychology*, **54**, 307–318.

Slater, P. (Ed.) (1977) *Dimensions of Intrapersonal Space*, Vol. 2. London: John Wiley.

Personal Meanings
Edited by Eric Shepherd and J. P. Watson
© 1982 John Wiley & Sons Ltd.

Multidimensional scaling analysis of qualitative data

Jennifer M. Brown and Jonathan D. Sime

INTRODUCTION

The present volume witnesses that personal meanings are making a comeback to psychology. A spate of other recent books, similarly committed, brings together the major arguments and proponents of new ways of conceiving and conducting research (Brenner *et al.*, 1978; Ginsburg, 1979; Gilmour and Duck, 1980; Antaki, 1981; Brenner, 1981). Contributors to these collections not only chart current dilemmas in social psychology but also propose new strategies for undertaking empirical investigations. Thus Duck (1980) reviews 'crises' of method, of relevance, of theory; Shotter (1981) discusses the 'crisis' inherent in empirical and conceptual modes of analysis; De Waele and Harré (1979) and Brown and Sime (1981) describe methods for the collection of accounts, and Forgas (1979b) innovatory ways of analysing qualitative data by multidimensional scaling (MDS) techniques.

Shifts of thinking are not seen as simply harking back to previous fashions in psychology but represent real steps forward in the collection and analysis of the explanations given by ordinary folk and presented in such a way that the results are communicable and have potential practical applications. The aim of this chapter is to focus upon the analytical and interpretational implications when dealing with the complex content of peoples' accounts of their experiences. Within the context of this volume the studies described illustrate methods with a potential to be applied to the examination of personal meanings across an infinite range of possible contexts.

MULTIDIMENSIONAL SCALING

The issues addressed in this chapter are concerned with the collation and interpretation of verbal reports of experiences that allow the underlying

71

patterns to be revealed, yet preserve the integrity of the personal theme in meanings embedded within individual accounts. Ginsburg (1979, p.9), commenting upon the important work of Forgas in the analysis of such data, wrote:

Forgas argues that the emerging recognition of the person as an active agent and of the importance of personal meanings to an understanding of action carries with it journalistic and anecdotal methods. However more rigorous descriptive techniques are readily available. Forgas suggests that multidimensional scaling (MDS) is eminently suited to the complex tasks of naturalistic descriptions called for by the emerging conceptions.

The use and advantages of MDS procedures are outlined by Forgas (1979a, 1979b), Shye (1978), Lingoes (1977), Bloombaum (1970), and McGrath (1967). In summary, MDS techniques represent the degree of similarity amongst items in terms of Euclidean geometry. The association between items, say responses to questions, are plotted as points in an array such that the greater the similarity, the shorter the distance between any two points. The great advantage of these procedures is that they facilitate the discovery of patterns in data that may not be of the more traditional dimensional kind. Lingoes (1979) comments:

Of all the possible ways of looking at an MDS solution, perhaps the most widely used and certainly most abused procedure, is that of looking for 'dimensions' (i.e. linear orderings usually coextensive with direction in the space, as obtained typically by an orthogonal rotation of the reference axes). Much of this practice is a carry-over from factor analytic training and lore (bordering on mythology). Indeed, the habit seems so deeply ingrained and pervasive that it is very difficult for students with even a modicum of exposure to this 'discipline' to shift gears and address other features of the configuration.

Another advantage lies in the visual representation of data. Typically, MDS procedures have output plots as part of their library of routines and Bloombaum (1970) points out that such maps display data in a visually communicable way that is easily comprehensible.

The search for types and taxonomies is a major thrust of the new orientation in social psychology and these have been carried out with detailed and time-consuming content analyses (see for example Cohen and Taylor, 1972; Toch, 1972). MDS offers a way to construct classificatory schemes in a systematic way by exploring the similarities and differences amongst items. The use of MDS for data reduction is particularly relevant to the search for types. The important issue arising from the two research investigations elaborated below is that experiences, whilst conceptually encompassing an infinite number of individual patterns, in fact emerge as falling within a relatively limited range of profiles.

Summarizing the actual and potential contribution of MDS to the study of social phenomena, Forgas (1979b, p.284) noted that:

the common feature of new strategies in social psychology is their espousal of descriptive analyses of everyday social behaviour. Statistical techniques such as MDS are capable of opening up new avenues of research merely be enabling investigators to represent quantitatively otherwise inaccessible phenomena.

As with any serious investigation, the data input to analyses must be reliable. McGrath (1967) pointed out a major limitation to factor analysis in that

It is mute about the more critical question for classification, namely, what things should be put in, in the first place.

Moreover, Lingoes (1979) commented that:

the geometric representation is but a reflection of a pattern of interrelationships among variables and that one must seek outside the representation for meaning. Furthermore, if an investigator is unable to interpret the coefficients or measures used before the analysis, a mathematical transformation in terms of distances of angles or whatever other spatial element relation is not going to be of much help after the analysis.

Lingoes (1977) and McGrath (1967) recommend the use of a prior input logic in interpreting an MDS solution, pointing to one such approach, facet theory, developed by Guttman and his associates. The particular advantage here is that facet theory techniques may be used in conjunction with a family of MDS procedures developed by Guttman and Lingoes (Lingoes, 1973).

Such a choice is particularly apt in the present context since Guttman's work arose out of critiques of statistical methods deriving from agricultural data (such as those of Fisher). Harré (1980) observed on this note:

no longer can we be content with sloppy investigations using larger samples and statistical operations to yield correlative factors. This is the method of agriculture.

Harré's contribution towards developing an understanding of personal meanings lies in his concern that human beings both understand and can comment on their actions. However Forgas (1979a) suggested that Harré overly relies on the journalistic and the anecdotal. A facet theory approach utilizing the Guttman–Lingoes programs provides a systematic way of handling and interpreting complex verbal data as represented within individual accounts.

FACET THEORY

A thorough exposition of Facet Theory and its associated MDS procedures is given in Shye (1978) and Borg (1977). What follows is an attempt to describe these in as non-technical a way as possible.

Within a facet design, items such as questionnaire responses or observational categories are defined in terms of *facets*. A facet is a conceptual dimension whose constituents, termed *elements*, define the values on the dimension. Hence the facet *sex* is defined by two elements —male and female.

As mentioned earlier, the essence of MDS lies in the mapping of similarities. In facet theory terminology, the principle of contiguity states that the more similar items are in their facet specification, the more similar they will be empirically.

The contents and relationships amongst the facets are stated in a *mapping sentence*. This represents the formal specification of the conceptual structure of the data. The empirical structure may be elaborated as a set of correlation coefficients. The Guttman–Lingoes smallest space analysis (SSA) presents the data in a geometric map such that the higher the correlations, the smaller the distance between the points representing the items. Examples of structures habitually found in investigations using the approach are the Radex (Lingoes and Borg, 1977) and the Cylindrex (Shapira and Zvelun, 1978).

THE HOUSING RESEARCH

The first phases of this study by the Housing Research Unit at the University of Surrey involved the collection of detailed accounts from 142 buyers and the various practitioners with whom they dealt. One set of aims related to the analysis of these accounts was to define a *typology* of movers. Once movers had been classified into types, a coherent account of their experience in terms of housing aspirations, search strategies, and housing outcomes could be derived.

In order to undertake this classification of movers a decision had to be made about the basis on which to define them. Their motives for moving constituted the conceptual dimensions, or facet, selected. Briefly, it is argued that explanations come in various guises. Pettit (1976) discusses four kinds of explanation—intention, policy, motive, and character. Intention refers to a goal-seeking state of mind; policy is also a state of mind—the institution of a number of actions to achieve a goal; motive is a state of desire in view of which it is likely that an agent will form an intention; character refers to disposition. Thus in a population of house buyers their intention, i.e. the purchase of a home, is common to them all. It is their motive for moving that distinguishes them and may be used as the basis for describing their actions in pursuit of their goal.

This usage of 'motives' may be illustrated by reference to the law, where motive and intention are conceptually distinguished in order to facilitate investigation of a crime:

The motive for a crime is the condition of mind which leads the criminal to commit the crime. Motive is not intention, for a person's intention is connected with the results or consequences of the act he intends to do. Thus a man may intend to go to an inn his motive being to get a drink. Motive from the police point of view is of greatest importance. If the motive of a criminal be known, it will throw much light on the case and materially assist in the elucidation of the facts. (Williams, 1976, pp.6–7)

Analysis of motives for moving

Sixty-seven different motives for moving were elicited from the 142 house-buyers. Details of the methods of data coding and transformation are available in Brown and Sime (1981). A smallest space analysis (SSA-1) examined the pattern of association amongst the different motives. A data matrix was prepared for submission to the SSA-1 program. The rows consisted of the 142 buyers and the columns the 67 reasons for moving. Against each buyer a string of 1s and 0s indicated the presence or absence of the column (reason) as being significant or not in that person's move.

Reference to the vast literature on residential mobility suggested three major reasons for moving—those to do with changes in family composition; changes of job; and housing values (Michelson, 1978; Weinstein, 1975; Ineichen, 1973). This preliminary SSA was geared towards honing precise definitions of the elements of these potential facets.

The resulting SSA-1 plots can be most easily partitioned in three-dimensional space. For present purposes only the plot of vectors 1 and 2 is given (Figure 1) as it adequately demonstrates the major partitions. In addition, a schematic representation of the plot illustrates the labels assigned to the major partitions in the space. The SSA shows a

SSA1 three-dimensional solution (numbers in
circles represent family-related motives)

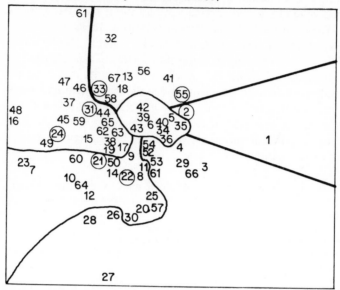

Schematic representation of the SSA plot

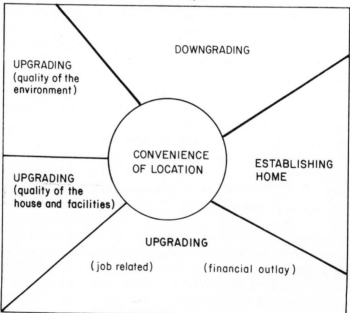

KEY			
1	To buy	36	Nearer friends
2	1st marital home	37	Away from neighbours
3	Price rise	38	Near countryside
4	Up-market	39	Less isolated
5	Quality of home	40	Near schools
6	Better/nicer home	41	Near shops
7	More comfortable	42	Transport
8	More facilities	43	Near work
9	Larger house	44	Escape town
10	More bedrooms	45	Traffic
11	More receps	46	Noise (in general)
12	Sep. lounge/din. room	47	No. of vehicles
13	Smaller house	48	Aircraft noise
14	Garden	49	New building
15	Larger garden	50	Cannot extend
16	Secluded garden	51	Tax relief
17	Garden for children	52	More money available
18	Smaller garden	53	More salary
19	More space	54	Inheritance
20	Space for guests	55	Retirement
21	Space for teenagers	56	Retrenching
22	Space for baby	57	Central heating (in general)
23	Hobby space	58	Easier house to manage
24	Elderly parents	57	Gas central heating wanted
25	Storage space	59	Off an estate
26	Job change (within same firm)	60	No hallway in present house
27	Job promotion (within same firm)	61	Character wanted
28	Job horizontal move	62	Nicer area
29	Job (different firm)	63	Want change (of lifestyle)
30	Back to country	64	Change area
31	Unhappy	65	Change neighbourhood
32	Divorce	66	Forced move
33	Spouse died	67	Near family
34	Location (in general)		
35	Location (spec.)		

Figure 1   Motives for moving house

developmental sequence around the plot in a clockwise direction, indicating an initiating stage in establishing home, incrementing stages to upgrade the quality of house and environment, and finally a decremental stage when size of house and garden are reduced. Interestingly, those items referring to the convenience of the location are positioned in the centre of the plot. This can be interpreted to mean that location is as important to those moving to buy for the first time, as it is to those upgrading and downgrading movers.

It is perhaps unsurprising that the family-related motives are dispersed throughout the plot and tend to be associated with the stage in house buying. This is akin to what has been called the 'family mobility cycle' by Michelson. This partitioning forms the basis for refining the definition of the motive facets which now may be formally specified in the *mapping sentence* (Figure 2). This forms the basis for a typology of movers that

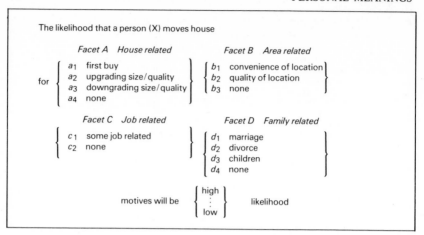

The likelihood that a person (X) moves house

for

Facet A   House related

- a_1 first buy
- a_2 upgrading size/quality
- a_3 downgrading size/quality
- a_4 none

Facet B   Area related

- b_1 convenience of location
- b_2 quality of location
- b_3 none

Facet C   Job related

- c_1 some job related
- c_2 none

Facet D   Family related

- d_1 marriage
- d_2 divorce
- d_3 children
- d_4 none

motives will be   { high : low }   likelihood

Figure 2   Mapping sentence for a typology of house movers

can be empirically verified through a second Guttman–Lingoes procedure termed multidimensional scalogram analysis (MSA-1).

Multidimensional scalogram analysis (MSA-1)

Facet design requires all individuals to be coded in terms of one element from each facet. Thus the elements themselves must be mutually exclusive, and also allow for the possibility of a void response. Such a system permits profiles of single or multiple reasons to be specified.

Once coded, a data matrix may be analysed through the MSA-1 procedure (Zvelun, 1978). This achieves two objectives. Firstly, it determines the number of unique profiles, and secondly, it verifies the facet structure as defined in the mapping sentence. It aims to create a geometric representation of a multivariate distribution (a scalogram) taking into account interrelationships among the items. There are no prior demands on the distribution characteristics of the items or relationships among them. A scalogram is a rectangular matrix in which the variables are coded in the columns, and subjects or types in the rows.

MSA-1 provides a plot of subjects or types as points in a multidimensional space, such that those having the most similar profiles are closest together. The program also gives separate plots for each variable or facet in terms of which the individuals have been coded.

At present there is a program size limitation to MSA-1, i.e. matrices are confined to 99 individuals, 50 variables, and 20 categories. Thus 99 individuals from the 142 buyers were chosen at random and coded in the manner described above. The MSA-1 program compares all profiles and reduces them to unique types indicating the number of exemplars. Take the following examples:

Respondents	Facets	A	B	C	D
Case 1		1	3	2	4
Case 2		3	3	2	2
Case 3		1	3	2	4

The mover exemplified in Case 1 is moving to buy for the first time. This profile is exactly the same as case number three. The MSA-1 program treats these as one unique type comprising two exemplars. Case 2 represents a downgrading, divorced mover for which there is just one exemplar. The number of profiles that could be generated from the mapping sentence is 96 (i.e. $4 \times 3 \times 2 \times 4$). The actual analysis revealed 9 as presented in Table 1. In addition, the separate plots demonstrate the

Table 1   Type of house mover

	Definition of profile	Facet A	B	C	D	Number of exemplars for each profile
1	First-time buyer	1	3	2	4	11
2	First-time buyer/marriage	1	3	2	1	5
3	First-time buyer/job	1	3	1	4	2
4	Job	4	3	1	4	3
5	Job/upgrade house/ upgrade area	2	2	1	4	2
6	Upgrade location	4	1	2	4	15
7	Upgrade area	4	2	2	4	13
8	Upgrade house	2	3	2	3	44
9	Downgrade/divorce	3	3	2	2	4
						99

reconstruction of the facets and their elements in the MSA space. This provides empirical verification for the definitions of the facets. These plots (given in Brown, 1980) will not be illustrated here, as another example of MSA-1 is provided in a later section with respect to the fire study.

This typology provided the groundwork for a further study of a national sample of 1052 recent house movers by means of a question-naire survey. The typology was partially confirmed but some adjust-ments were made with respect to the area facet. This refined classification of the types of mover acted as the basis for the definition of search strategies and housing outcomes and are reported elsewhere (Brown, 1980; Alliance Building Society House Research Unit, 1980).

The facet approach allows for the specification of every possible combination of profiles. By categorizing individuals in this manner a great range of potential profiles may be generated from as many facets as are deemed necessary. That relatively few emerged in the empirical data is evidence of the strength of reoccurring patterns rather than forceful data reduction. This is not just a phenomenon noted in the housing research study.

THE FIRE RESEARCH

The general brief of the Fire Research Unit at the University of Surrey was to discover what people do when involved in a fire and to relate their behaviour to aspects of building design (Canter, Breaux, and Sime, 1980). The work reviewed here followed the official inquiry into the Isle of Man's Summerland fire disaster (Summerland Fire Commission, 1974). A number of police witness statements were made available. This provided a unique opportunity to analyse a large number of accounts relating to a shared experience, a significant fire, a form of data normally difficult or impossible to obtain. For further discussion of this fire and related issues in the analysis of police witness statements, see Brown and Sime (1981) and Sime (1979a, b).

Through the application of Guttman–Lingoes analytical procedures, descriptions from the statements yielded insight into the routes chosen by people from the Marquee Showbar area of the Summerland Complex. The range of information contained in the statements was extremely wide. There was a choice of exits in either corner of the Bar: the entrance used by members of the public to enter and leave, or the fire exit leading to a rear staircase and back exits from the building. This staircase was used regularly by members of staff as their route to work. The Marquee Showbar itself contained a series of bars on one side, a stage and dance floor, tables, and chairs. Furthermore, there was information on the age, sex, and occupation of the witnesses, indicating whether the witness was a member of the public or staff, details where the witness was located in the bar, size of the group the witness was with, the type of 'cue' the individual responded to as the first indication something was wrong, whether all members of the group were with them at the time of being alerted by a cue, the outcome of their behaviour (e.g. safe escape or sustained injury), and the ability of the group to stay together.

A preliminary content analysis of the types of information given in the statements resulted in the omission of descriptions or actions that were

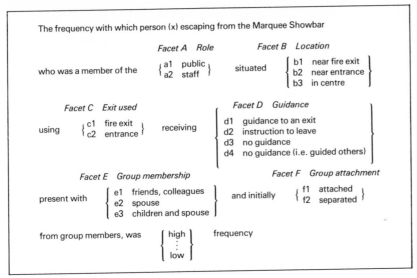

Figure 3   Provisional mapping sentence for choice of exit route

unrelated to exit choice and aggregation of categories of *low frequency of occurrence*. As a result, six facets were identified and specified in a provisional mapping sentence (Figure 3). The 75 individuals in the Marquee Showbar were then coded in terms of these six facets and the data matrix analysed by the MSA-1 procedure.

MSA-1 of exit route taken

The mapping sentence theoretically could provide $2 \times 3 \times 2 \times 4 \times 3 \times 2 = 288$ profiles. The actual data reveal 34, which are illustrated in the MSA-1 plot (Figure 4). The additional plots of each facet are also reproduced to show that these were retrieved from the empirical analysis and reconstructed in the MSA space (Figure 5). By overlaying plots A to F on the overall configuration, the interrelationships amongst the facets can be explored, with regions of overlap reflecting similarities in individual profiles. The regions which overlap with plot C indicate that when individuals were separated from one or more group members, including children, they tended to use the entrance, whereas members of staff and public near to the fire exit used this. Although 'familiarity' with the building was not examined directly, it was assumed to be reflected by the exit route facet. A further clarification and refinement of this scheme of plots was undertaken by use of another of the Guttman procedures — the partial order scalogram analysis (POSA).

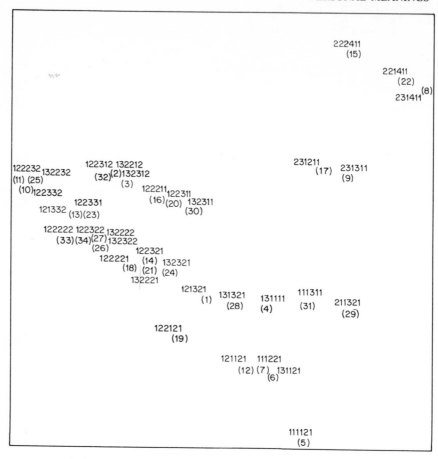

Figure 4   Overall MSA-1 plot of facets related to exits used (34 profiles)

POSA of exit routes

From the MSA-1 presented in Figures 4 and 5, it is evident that the facet plots may be dichotomously partitioned. Separate chi-square analyses for facets A, B, D, E, and F were undertaken in relation to facet C (exit used) in order to assess the degree to which they discriminated between choice of exit. All were statistically significant (at the .001 level) except that of group membership, i.e. family–non family, which was not significant. Since this facet did not discriminate between the exits chosen it was excluded in the subsequent analysis.

It should be noted that a combined analysis of the interrelationships between all of the facets is possible using loglinear analysis (see Fienberg,

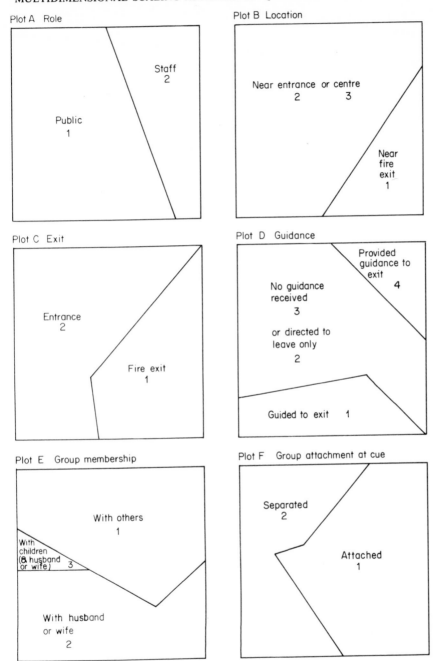

Figure 5   Individual MSA-1 plots for the six facets

1977). This was not undertaken because of the relatively large number of items to be incorporated in the contingency table and the considerable occurrence of zeros in its cells. Whilst the separate chi-square analyses may fail to reveal this more complex set of relationships, they do lend some support for the choice of facets in the subsequent analysis.

A second mapping sentence was generated that reflected the merging or omission of facets. The facets were re-ordered to reflect, firstly, the increasing external constraints of the actual fire and, secondly, the sequence of events in time. Background psychological factors, facet A (role) and B (group attachment) were placed first. The criterion or target facet of primary interest was placed last, making it easier in the subsequent analysis to distinguish between the sets of categories related to the exit chosen. A revised mapping sentence was constructed and is shown in Figure 6. From this specification $2 \times 2 \times 2 \times 2 \times 2 = 32$ profiles

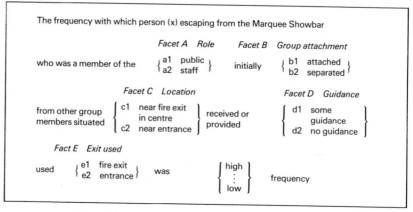

Figure 6   Mapping sentence for choice of exit route

are theoretically possible. Table 2 shows the 14 that actually accounted for the 75 people in the sample. Examining the profiles, it can be seen that there is not a simple linear ordering as might be expected from a Guttman scale. In other words, there is more than one order possible, e.g. profile 21111 could be adjacent to 21121 or 21211 or 21112, indicating the increasing number of categories associated with the use of one or other of the exits.

An extension of the simple Guttman scale has been provided by the partial order scalogram (POSA). Shye and Elizur (1976) describe POSA as a technique for ordering empirical data on more than one dimension simultaneously. It assumes that items are ordered in discrete categories and that there is a common order to the items. Profiles are arranged into

Table 2   Explanatory profiles for choice of exit route

	Definition of profile	A	B	C	D	E	N	%
				Facet				
1	Staff, near fire exit/centre, provided guidance, used fire exit	1	1	1	1	1	5	6.7
2	Staff, near fire exit/centre, no guidance given, used fire exit	1	1	1	2	1	6	8
3	Attached, near fire exit/centre, guided to exit, used fire exit	2	1	1	1	1	13	17.3
4	Attached, near entrance, no guidance, used fire exit	1	1	2	2	1	2	2.7
5	Attached, near fire exit/centre, no guidance, used fire exit	2	1	1	2	1	8	10.7
6	Attached, near entrance, guided to exit, used fire exit	2	1	2	1	1	1	1.3
7	Attached, near fire exit/centre, guided to exit, used entrance	2	1	1	1	2	3	4
8	Staff, near entrance, no guidance given, used entrance	1	1	2	2	2	1	1.3
9	Attached, near entrance, no guidance, used fire exit	2	1	2	2	1	1	1.3
10	Separated, near fire exit/centre, guided to exit, used entrance	2	2	1	1	2	4	5.3
11	Separated, near entrance, no guidance, used fire exit	2	2	2	2	1	1	1.3
12	Attached, near entrance, no guidance, used entrance	2	1	2	2	2	16	21.3
13	Separated, near fire exit/centre, no guidance, used entrance	2	2	1	2	2	2	2.7
14	Separated, near entrance, no guidance, used entrance	2	2	2	2	2	12	16

the most compact geometric space possible which preserves the original order and can account for qualitative differences amongst them.

In the present example, it can be observed that profiles with more 'ones' in the string are associated with use of the fire exit, whilst those consisting of a greater number of 'twos' are associated with the use of the entrance. Figure 7 illustrates the POSA configuration. The profiles are represented at different levels with the frequencies below each profile in brackets. The 'additive index' to the left is the sum of digits in the profiles at each level. A feature of a POSA configuration is that all order relations are represented by lines connecting comparable profiles. Thirteen of the empirical profiles of the logically possible 32 are represented. There is an underlying dimension extending from the top of the configuration to the bottom. Profiles nearest to the top are more likely to represent categories associated with the use of the fire exit. Towards the bottom are profiles associated with use of the entrance.

The lateral spread of profiles reflects variations of a more qualitative nature related to exit use. The configuration is affected partly by profiles with low frequencies. Profiles to the left tend to be those of people who did not offer or receive guidance and who left via the fire exit. Guidance emerged as less important in determining the exit used than a combination of other factors—for example, whether an individual was separated from one or more group members and location.

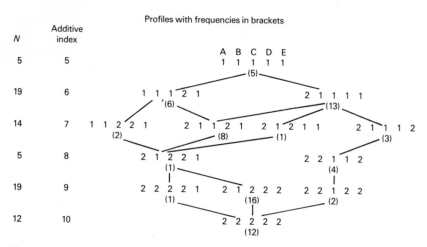

Profiles with frequencies in brackets

Key to facets and category code   N = 74*

A: *Role* 1: staff 2: public
B: *Group attachment at cue* 1: attached 2: separated
C: *Location* 1: near fire exit, in centre 2: near entrance
D: *Guidance* 1: guided to exit, provided guidance 2: no guidance
E: *MSB exit route* 1: fire exit 2: entrance

*Profile 1 1 2 2 2 has been excluded (see text).
    (1)

Figure 7   Partial order scalogram analysis of facets affecting exit route from the Marquee Showbar

The main difference between staff was in whether they actually guided people to the fire exit or not. Five staff members provided guidance of this kind. Profiles 11111 and 11121 account for 11/14 or 78.6 per cent of the staff. The staff tended to be located away from the entrance. The only member of staff to leave via the entrance (the ticket collecter located there) is represented by a profile which has been omitted. Inclusion of his profile led to a 'crossing' of lines in the configuration. This implies that he was an *exception* to the general pattern in the data.

Four profiles account for 80.3 per cent of the 61 members of the public: 21111, 21121, 21222, and 22222. These profiles reflect the important part certain combinations of variables played in the exit behaviour. The majority of the individual members of the public present in 'intact' groups (i.e. attached) and located in the centre or near the fire exit, left via this exit (21 out of 24). While both 'separated' and 'attached' individuals left via the entrance, 28 out of 37 of these were located at the entrance end of the Marquee Showbar and received no guidance to the alternative exit.

When there are exceptions to the general pattern in the data, this is usually because of other mediating factors influencing particular individuals. For example, profile 22221 represents the one separated individual who did not leave via the entrance. Because of his late departure the exit was blocked by the fire itself. In most cases the smoke or fire did not appear to influence the exit chosen. The fire conditions did contribute to the subsequent difficulties individuals experienced once they had left the Marquee Showbar.

What the POSA demonstrates most clearly is the interplay between a number of social-psychological and environmental constraints in the situation. While the individual's original location was important, the choice of location itself was determined in part by the psychological variable of group attachment. Separated individuals tended to sit at the entrance end (13 out of 19). A number of 'separated' individuals stated that they had done so to be nearer their children who could be reached via the entrance. All of the couples with children elsewhere sat at the entrance end. Their physical location meant that they were less likely to receive direct guidance to the fire exit.

It is likely that a person's choice of location was influenced by other factors besides group separation, for example, whether the seats at the entrance were the first empty ones encountered, and the distance from the stage and bar. However, the fact that an individual's location and exit used can be predicted from the social-psychological variables examined suggests their importance in understanding the exit choice behaviour.

CONCLUSION

According to Forgas (1979b), MDS represents an emerging strategy that is applicable to the essentially phenomenological orientation of a psychology committed to personal meaning. The use of facet theory, coupled with the Guttman–Lingoes family of MDS procedures, provides a systematic approach to the definition of items submitted for analysis and their interpretation afterwards. This method of analysis neatly complements the procedures of account analysis described elsewhere (Brown and Sime, 1981). A facet approach does permit the specification of actually existing profiles within a potentially larger number of profiles. Thus, 9 out of a possible 96 types of house-buyer were identified and in the fire research 14 out of a possible 32 action profiles discovered. Hence the potential complexity of the data is reduced to manageable and usable profiles not by 'number crunching' but by the demonstration of the power of *strongly recurring patterns* through the sensible use of MDS techniques. This is not achieved, however, at the expense of the individual's frame of reference. Indeed, whilst the MDS procedures outlined permit the discovery of reoccurring patterns they also highlight those individuals who are the exceptions.

ACKNOWLEDGEMENTS

Both research units were established by David Canter. The Housing Research Unit was initially funded by the Leverhulme Trust and subsequently sponsored by the Alliance Building Society. The Fire Research Unit was funded by the Building Research Establishment Fire Research Station.

REFERENCES

Alliance Building Society Housing Research Unit (1980) Reasons for moving. *Report No. 9*. University of Surrey. Mimeo.

Antaki, C. (1981) *The Psychology of Ordinary Explanations of Social Behaviour*. London: Academic Press.

Bloombaum, M. (1970) Doing smallest space analysis. *J. Conflict Resolution*, **14**, 403–16.

Borg, I. (1977) Some basic concepts of facet theory. In J. C. Lingoes (Ed.), *Geometric Representation of Relational Data*. Ann Arbor: Mathesis.

Brenner, M. (1981) *Social Method and Social Life*. New York: Academic Press.

Brenner, M., Marsh, P., and Brenner, M. (1978) *The Social Context of Method*. New York: St Martin's.

Brown, J. (1980) The role of motivation in moving and buying a house. Unpublished PhD dissertation, University of Surrey.

Brown, J., and Sime, J. O. (1981) A methodology for accounts. In M. Brenner (Ed.), *Social Method and Social Life*. London: Academic Press.

Canter, D., Breaux, J. J., and Sime, J. D. (1980) In D. Canter (Ed.), *Fires and Human Behaviour*. London: Wiley.

Cohen, S., and Taylor, L. (1972) *Psychological Survival*. Harmondsworth: Penguin.

Duck, S. (1980) One of the futures of social psychology. In R. Gilmour and S. Duck (Eds), *The Development of Social Psychology*. London: Academic Press.

Fienberg, S. E. (1977) *The Analysis of Cross-classified Categorical data*. MIT Press.

Forgas, J. P. (1979a) *Social Episodes: the Study of Interaction Routines*. London: Academic Press.

Forgas, J. P. (1979b) Multidimensional scaling: a discovery method in social psychology. In G. P. Ginsburg (Ed.), *Emerging Strategies in Social Psychological Research*. Chichester: Wiley.

Gilmour, R., and Duck, S. (Eds) (1980) *The Development of Social Psychology*. London: Academic Press.

Ginsburg, G. P. (1979) *Emerging Strategies in Social Psychological Research*. Chichester: Wiley.

Harré, R. (1980) Making social psychology scientific. In R. Gilmour and S. Duck (Eds), *The Development of Social Psychology*. London: Academic Press.

Ineichen, B. (1973) Housing classes and housing careers. *Social and Administration Quarterly*, **7**, 30–38.

Lingoes, J. C. (1973) *The Guttman–Lingoes Non-metric Program Series*. Ann Arbor: Mathesis.

Lingoes, J. C. (1977) *Geometric Representations of Relational Data*. Ann Arbor: Mathesis.

Lingoes, J. C. (1979) Testing regional hypotheses in multidimensional scaling. Paper presented at the Second International Symposium on Data Analysis and Information, Versailles, 17–19 October.

Lingoes, J. C., and Borg, I. (1977) Identifying regions in space for interpretation. In J. C. Lingoes (Ed.), *Geometric Representations of Relational Data*. Ann Arbor: Mathesis.

McGrath, J. E. (1967) A multifaceted approach to classification of individual group and organization concepts. In B. P. Indik and F. K. Berrien (Eds), *People Groups and Organizations*. Columbia University Press.

Michelson, W. (1978) *Environmental Choice, Human Behaviour and Residential Satisfaction*. Oxford: University Press.

Pettit, P. (1976) Making actions intelligible. In R. Harré (Ed.), *Life Sentences*. Chichester: Wiley.

Shapira, Z., and Zvelun, E. (1978) On the use of facet analysis in organization behaviour research. *Working Paper No. 10-78-79*. Graduate School of Industrial Administration, Carnegie-Mellon University.

Shye, S. (1978) *Theory Construction and Data Analysis in the Behavioural Sciences*. San Francisco: Jossey-Bass.

Shye, S., and Elizur, D. (1976) Worries about deprivation of job rewards following computerization. *Human Relations*, **29**, 63–71.

Shotter, J. (1981) Telling and reporting: prospective and retrospective use of self-ascriptions. In C. Antaki (Ed.), *The Psychology of Ordinary Explanations of Social Behaviour*. London: Academic Press.

Sime, J. D. (1979a) Sequence analysis of people's behaviour in fires. Presented at a one-day workshop on the 'Analysis of open-ended data'. Department of Psychology, University of Surrey, 12 December.

Sime, J. D. (1979b) The use of building exits in a large scale fire. Paper presented at the Internation Conference on Environmental Psychology. University of Surrey.

Summerland Fire Commission (1974) *Report*. Douglas: Isle of Man Government Office.

Toch, H. (1972) *Violent Men*. Harmondsworth: Penguin.

de Waele, J. P., and Harré, R. (1979) Autobiography as a psychological method. In G. P. Ginsburg (Ed.), *Emerging Strategies in Social Psychological Research*. Chichester: Wiley.

Weinstein, E. T. A. (1975) The movement of owner occupier households. *Regional Studies*, **9**, 137–45.

Williams, W. J. (1976) *Moriarty's Police Law* (23rd edn). London: Butterworths.

Zvelun, E. (1978) Multidimensional scalogram analysis. In S. Shye (Ed.), *Theory Construction and Data Analysis in the Behavioural Sciences*. San Francisco: Jossey-Bass.

Personal Meanings
Edited by Eric Shepherd and J. P. Watson
© 1982 John Wiley & Sons Ltd.

'To be or not to be'

J. H. Foskett

To be, or not to be — that is the question —
Whether 'tis nobler, in the mind to suffer
The slings and arrows of outrageous Fortune,
Or to take arms against a sea of troubles,
And by opposing end them?

Hamlet, Act 3, Scene 1

I can think of nothing more personally meaningful than the decision to live or to die, and yet societies have been overwhelmingly reluctant to allow individuals the right to explore and indeed decide upon this question without prejudice. Our lives and our deaths belong in the end not to ourselves but to our Gods, our States, our neighbours, or just to fate. There have of course been exceptions to this rule, but as the present debate on the 'right to die' suggests, the idea that individuals have a fundamental human right to take control over their own living and dying, is something from which society shrinks. It is as though we can not trust ourselves or others with such an awesome responsibility. Is there, I wonder, a connection between our reluctance to face and explore this most personally meaningful of issues, and the phenomena of and responses to suicide and attempted suicide? Before pursuing that question I want to review what we know about the causes which prompt individuals to attempt suicide, and the responses that such action has provoked and continues to provoke in society as a whole.

Lists of the reasons why individuals attempt and often succeed in killing themselves, drawn both from the things that they themselves say or write, and from the observations of those close to them, include the following.

First, a need to escape 'the slings and arrows of outrageous Fortune'. To find some relief and release from the present circumstances, the despair, terror, or depression. Anything is better than going on living, and death is conceived of as peaceful and unencumbered by the trauma of life. 'At times,' a woman recently said to me, 'I feel how good

91

it would be just to slip away, to give up the struggle and let go of life.'

The second is related to fear of the future and of one's inability to cope with that. The news of a long, painful, and terminal illness terrifies individuals not so much to want to be out of the present, but out of the future and of the degradation and suffering that is lurking around the corner. Anticipated personal or professional humiliation carry similar terrors, and encourage the need to make an end of one's life before the worst about that life is made public.

A third reason involves the sense that life has already lost its meaning, that the feeling of existential vacuum makes just existing purposeless, that beliefs once held have evaporated, relationships once sustained dissolved away, or their superficiality confronted for the first time. One lived in hope of finding a meaning, forming a relationship, and neither ever happened.

The fourth is as a response to rejection or loss. The death of a loved one, a separation or a divorce, creates such an intolerable vacuum, that life on one's own cannot be contemplated. Individuals speak of hearing their dead partners calling them to come over and be reunited.

A fifth springs from the need to make a point, to draw attention, to resolve a grudge. To communicate to others in a way that has been impossible hitherto. The message is 'Listen to me, if I die then you will have to take notice, and if I survive do something about it.'

The sixth is the other side of that coin, 'My dying can do something for you.' 'I will lay down my life for the one who matters to me.' Dramatically, in battle or as Captain Oates did on Scott's Antarctic expedition; more privately, by the individual who decides no longer to be a burden to family or friends.

The seventh involves a gamble with Fate or God. 'I can find nothing to live for, but if I survive this attempt to kill myself, then that will prove that there is a reason for my living.' A young man with a long history of depression was transformed by throwing himself in the Thames and surviving.

These reasons overlap one another, appear in different forms, and have greater and lesser importance in the minds of those who consider suicide. Some, like the first three, are essentially personal; external conditions may well have contributed to them but the individuals involved are preoccupied with themselves and how they are to resolve their personal crises. The others involve not only the individual but his relationship to others, the one he has lost, those whose attention he wants, or whose lives he will enhance by his death.

Societies' attitudes to suicide can be traced through the records of how social institutions like Church and State, Law and Medicine have reacted to the suicidal, and how individuals have interpreted societies' behaviour. There were no Roman laws against ordinary citizens taking their lives, but those awaiting criminal proceedings, that is those who conceivably owed the state something, slaves and soldiers, did face penalties. Greek philosophers were divided on the rights of the individual and of society in these matters, Cynic, Stoic, and Epicurean philosophers arguing with different emphases, that individuals should have the liberty to decide whether to live or die. Epictetus provides the example of one who saw the need for man to fulfil his duties to others, to himself, to God, and to his state; but having completed what he could do or could bear, he was free to make his exit from life's stage.

How long shall I stand fast to the post to which God has appointed me? So long as it is profitable — that is to say, so long as I can do what becomes and befits me . . . Doth it smoke in the chamber? If it is not very much I will stay, if too much I will go out, for remember this always, and hold fast to it, that the door is open . . . I will depart whither no man shall hinder me to dwell — for that dwelling stands ever open to all. Only do it not unreasonably, nor cowardly, nor make every common chance an excuse. (1888, II, ix, pp.2-3)

Others, adherents of Pythagoras for instance, claimed that man had no right under any circumstances to leave his place in life, and must endure whatever life brought with humility and resignation. Aristotle, too, saw suicide as an offence, for it deprived the state of one of its citizens, it being the citizen's duty to participate fully in public affairs.

The Christian response to suicide has equally mixed and confused origins. The Bible records eight cases of suicide, but there is no record of any penalty or suggestion that suicide was a sin. Saul's suicide, for instance, provides the opportunity for an act of worship and David's song of praise (1 Samuel). Razis is said 'to die nobly rather than fall into the hands of wicked wretches', when he falls on his sword (2 Maccabees). Samson's destruction of himself along with the Philistines is recorded as an act of extreme heroism (Judges). And Matthew's account of the death of Judas conveys a sense of the appropriateness of this end to his life (Matthew).

Nevertheless, Christians and Jews have both come to regard suicide as bad and sinful; as an offence against God, the taking of life which He alone created, a violation of the sixth commandment, and an act which precludes the possibility of repentance. Like Pythagoras, Jewish and Christian theologians have also emphasized the value implicit in man bearing his sufferings; for the Christian in particular, as his unique opportunity to share in the sufferings of Christ. No doubt it was through the influence of such ideas that suicide came to be regarded as a crime.

The successful suicide was prevented from a Christian burial, and the 1662 Anglican Prayer Book contains a rubric which prevents clergy reading the burial service for any who have laid 'violent hands' on themselves. Until 1823 the bodies of those who committed suicide were pierced with a stake and buried at a crossroads; until 1870 their property was confiscated; until 1961 the law declared them felons; and still of course it is a criminal offence to help anyone to take their own life. The Roman Catholic Church, following the early councils of Nimes (AD 394) and Bruga (AD 563), regards suicide as a mortal sin which is subject to the harshest of punishments. Alongside these official attitudes, individuals have raised questions similar to those of the Greek philosophers. Is suicide always a sin, are there not occasions when it can be justified? Dean W. R. Inge (1930, p.373) writes:

I confess that I cannot resist the arguments for a modification of traditional Christian law, which absolutely prohibits suicide, under all circumstances. I do not think that we can assume that God willed the prolongation of torture for the benefit of the soul of the sufferer.

Earlier John Donne had suggested that suicide was not inherently unchristian, pointing out as others have done that there is no prohibition against it in either Old or New Testaments, and that it has only been dealt with by the declaration of councils and not by Canon Law. Another philosopher and pastor, Peter Green (1931, pp.283–4), has this to say about the argument for accepting suffering as a valuable discipline:

It is often argued that for a man to end a painful illness by his own act, is to avoid a divinely appointed discipline of trial and suffering. But it may be noted that precisely that argument was used by religious people to prove the unlawful nature of anaesthetics.

He goes on to say:

I have found it impossible to discover any really conclusive argument against suicide under due restrictions. I ought to add that though I have discussed the question with many physicians and surgeons, I have not yet found one who would approve the suggested permission. The usual answer I received has been that the medical profession would oppose any change in existing law and custom in this matter, and that the doctor's business is to prolong life to the utmost.

No doubt medical reactions to the suicidal have been affected by the changing of the law and the lessening of rigid attitudes over the last two decades; but it is still the doctor's business to prolong life, and so where the influence of Church has waned and that of the state has changed, now medicine works actively to prevent death. And over the same period we have witnessed the birth and blossoming of agencies like the Samaritans expressly organized to help prevent suicide and to care for those contemplating it. So where society once frightened the suicidal, now it understands and comforts them into living rather than dying.

The foregoing review of why it is that individuals consider suicide and of society's response to them, illustrates all too clearly that each is concerned with something different. Society, be it represented by Church or State or latterly by Medicine, is concerned with its self-preservation. Citizens are the servants of the state, sinners the children of the Church, neither is prepared to lose its life blood without a fight. Medicine's success and worth depends upon the saving and the prolonging of life: death is failure. The notion of self-determination is anathema, for the primary though often unconscious motivation of groups is to preserve themselves and to seek to justify that self-preservation with apparently selfless reasons, so it is always for the good of the individual that he is coerced into living and prevented from dying, no matter what the circumstances. The individual, on the other hand, has only a hazy grasp of this. His desire to end it all springs from his inability to see any value to himself or anyone else in his continued existence. He wants to explore the issue of whether he lives or dies; the struggle of life and death within him demands attention which he can no longer ignore. And instead of meeting a society which affords him the opportunity to explore this issue without prejudice, he hears a voice bullying or begging him to hang on to existence no matter what. Ironically it is this reaction which often pushes the suicidal to make their attempt and to have society take them and their reasons really seriously. A social worker, David Brandon (1978, pp.68–9), records an occasion of when he did take a client's reasons very seriously and found to his surprise that it did not make him more suicidal:

This man wanted a genuine answer from me. I thought deeply about his whole life —the depression, the poverty, his failing health and loss of family. Finally I replied, 'I can see no reason to go on living in your case. I can see clear reasons for wishing to die.' I felt afraid. It seemed an enormous risk to say that to him. What kind of responsibility would I have if he killed himself? . . . Months afterwards when the depression had largely disappeared he told me that my answer had been helpful.

Erwin Stengel's (1968) research into attempted suicide underlines the significance of this cry for help from the misunderstood and misheard individual to the self preoccupied and to deaf society.

Every suicidal act has an appeal effect. If it is fatal it mobilizes guilt feelings, and a temporary upsurge of posthumous love. If it is non-fatal the members of the group or groups to which the survivor belongs tend to behave in such a way as they would have felt they ought to have behaved had the suicidal act been fatal. (p.182)

Stengel and Cook (1958) list the following results of attempted suicide:

1. Temporary hospitalization and treatment was the most common consequence, the attempt being both a symptom of depression which had gone unnoticed, and an alarm signal which demanded attention and provoked appropriate treatment for the illness.

2. For some, the attempt revealed a more chronic mental or physical illness and an inability to survive outside a sheltered environment, and so led to more permanent hospitalization. In a number of cases the physical injuries sustained in the attempt contributed most to this major change in the individual's life style.

3. A great variety of changes in human relations and in modes of life were observed.

An improved adjustment in relationships to spouse, parent or lover etc. was most common. (Stengel, 1968, p.183)

Changes in work or life pattern were also significant both for the individual who had attempted suicide and for those close to him or her.

4. In a number of cases, suicidal attempts appeared to be a regular warning signal of personal crises which were not heralded in other ways.

5. In many cases, attempting suicide led to considerable social changes. Individuals broke out of their state of isolation, and community resources were mobilized to support them.

Considering that social isolation is generally regarded as one of the most important factors in the causation of suicidal behavior, this effect is of particular importance. As the result of the suicidal attempt, the person would come, if only for a brief period, face to face with his fellow men, with whom he had lost contact. (Stengel, 1968, pp.183-4)

6. The punitive reaction of society to those attempting suicide has already emerged in our summary of the history of responses to suicide, and although official attitudes may have changed, helping can still be as punitive and as ineffective a deterrent as ever.

The current epidemic of overdosing with therapeutic substances has not yet peaked, but the liaison psychiatrist seems powerless to halt it. About 15 per cent of acute medical admissions to hospitals in London are for overdose . . . The attitudes of the hospital staff in the face of their therapeutic impotence and the increasing work load it represents have been explored and succinctly denoted as 'counter-transference hate'. (Connelly, 1979, p.612)

The most noticeable theme in this list of the consequences of suicidal behaviour is that of the change in circumstances which the attempts provoke. Isolated individuals are incorporated into a social or community setting, initially through hospitalization, latterly through increased community care. Inadequate or unsatisfactory close relationships are altered or changed, in many cases constructively. Unnoticed and undiagnosed illnesses are discovered and treated. The relationship between the individual and society is renegotiated both positively and negatively, as if the suicidal attempt awakens both to the need for this renegotiation, which has gone unnoticed hitherto. It is this factor which is in keeping with the conclusions that Durkheim (1951) reached concerning suicide. He noted how strongly integrated societies effectively restrained individuals from killing themselves, whereas societies with weaker links, such as Protestant as opposed to Catholic, urban as opposed to rural, industrial as opposed to agricultural, etc., had higher suicide rates. The weaker the integration and links between individuals within a society, the greater the need to renegotiate and re-establish those links. Attempted suicide provides both the alarm and the opportunity for society to regroup around its most vulnerable link.

Hopefully it is now becoming clearer why attempted suicide is an important subject for the application of any symposium on personal meanings. Throughout our review it has been obvious that rarely do individuals encounter the conditions under which they can freely explore the question 'whether to be or not to be', and yet so pressing is that question, particularly for those who feel most isolated or ostracized from society, that it emerges willy nilly in our casualty wards and prisons, on our railway lines, and in our mental hospitals. In part it is then faced, for society reorganizes itself to remove the question from that particular questioner. A weak point in society's flood defences has been detected and must be effectively replugged. In part it is not faced, for the flood tide of death and destruction, despair and meaninglessness remains, battering away at the defences. Holding it back neither removes its threat nor tames its power. On the other hand, a gap in the defences might herald an end to the war, not just a renegotiating of the *status quo*, but a reconciling of opposing forces, a facing and integrating of what it is that frightens us all most. As we have seen, society through its religions and laws, its medical and social sciences has laboured valiantly to maintain those defences and resist that flood. And only the occasional voice has suggested that the battle cannot be won in that way.

Notable individuals from ancient Greece until the present day have suggested that there are conditions under which it is appropriate to end one's life. Others have argued that it is only by taking one's death seriously, including death at one's own hands, that one can take life seriously.

Suicide can be for some an act of unconscious philosophy, an attempt to understand death by joining it. The impulse to death need not be conceived as an anti-life movement; it may be a demand for an encounter with absolute reality, a demand for a fuller life through the death experience . . . Until we can say no to life, we have not really said yes to it, but have been carried along by its collective stream. (Hillman, 1964, pp.63–4)

It is my conviction that somewhere in the jungle of behaviour, both that of the suicidal and of those who respond to them, there is some flowering of meaning. And to continue that metaphor a little further, we need to find ways through the jungle: ways to hold it back from overwhelming the flower, and then ways to encourage the flower's growth. James Diggory (1968), in a paper entitled 'Suicide and value', suggests that one way forward would be to apply value theory to suicidal behaviour. In particular, he explores the works of Pepper and his development of the goal-seeking activities, learning, and consummatory behaviour of the individual organism.

For example in the course of its attempts to find food an organism may perform a sequence of different actions. On subsequent occasions of seeking food its behaviour may be quite different. Analysis of what an organism actually does in such a situation indicates that the successive occasions of food-seeking are characterised by a decrease in the frequency of the actions which had nothing to do with getting the organism closer to the food. (p.11)

Diggory suggests that suicidal behaviour can be examined in this way as purposive or instrumental acts, some of which are inevitably wrong and therefore bad, but some of which may be correct.

No doubt there are actual suicides in which the victims have made mistakes about the hopelessness of their situation but this is not to say that all of them are mistaken. The problem is to distinguish the mistaken from the others while the potential victim is still alive . . . To say that is a difficult distinction is not the same as saying that it is inherently impossible, or that we should not undertake the labour of research required to arm ourselves to make it. (p.15)

Diggory goes on to point out the weakness of the social arguments against suicide, namely that it deprives society of one of its citizens.

If a man can resign public office on grounds of infirmity or derangement in his personal affairs, why can he not terminate his existence with no imputation or harm to society? Suicide would not only be innocent, but laudable in those who have become a burden to society. (p.15)

An important truth lies hidden in these statements, namely that the clarifying of when and why something is appropriate, all be it only rarely, is a most potent force in identifying when and why something is inappropriate. Those who condemn all suicide as bad and inappropriate offer the suicidal a very imprecise and unsatisfactory foundation upon which to try and build their lives. Diggory goes on to raise a number of important questions in which he sees the seeds of a science of value with which it will not only be possible to evaluate suicide but other things as well.

First we will ask whether suicidal behaviour is to be in all circumstances, the object of attempts at suicide prevention? When we say that in attempting to prevent suicide we are attempting to save life, do we know what we mean by life? Do we value life in the sense of continued individual development of skill, knowledge, affiliations and achievements; or do we value it as the prolongation of vegetative metabolism? When we say a reason for preventing suicide is so that children not be 'stigmatized' by having a suicidal ancestor, do we ever call in question the reality and influence of the stigmata to which we point? Do we ever question the value of the state of public opinion which makes such stigmatizing possible? Do we ever ask *whose* values are lost when someone commits suicide? Are we sorry for the value lost to the dead individual himself (supposing there was any such value), or the loss of his possible value to others, or are we sorrowing over the scratch on the image of our omnipotence, a blemish inherent in the supposition that we could have 'prevented' the suicide?
    The road to the answers of these questions is long and arduous . . . But it is inherent in the faith of a scientist that intelligible and objective answers will surely come . . . Because it is the faith of a scientist it declares that we will never achieve answers to these or any other questions without first being profoundly dissatisfied with the present state of our knowledge and techniques. Furthermore, the dissatisfaction must be effective; each of us must do what he can to intrude objective methods of thinking into the study of suicide. (pp.17–18)

This is a helpful statement to me as a pastoral counsellor, for it directs me to look beyond or beneath the alarms and excursions which surround those who attempt suicide, to listen more closely and I hope openly to those who wish to speak of suicide, to be less precipitate in my desire to prevent or avert suicide at all costs. It also leads me to look expectantly towards social and behavioural scientists in the hope that they have or will soon take up some of the questions that Diggory challenges us not to ignore, and that indeed they may begin to test the science of value to which he points.

Finally, it demands an attempt to engage with the perennial question which nags at philosophers and moralists, politicians and economists, as well as theologians and social scientists. How are we to do justice at one and the same time to the rights of individuals and of the group or society of which they are a part? What are the conditions under which an individual's rights are properly subordinated to those of his family or state, 'It is expedient for you that one man die for the people and that the whole nation should not perish' (John), and vice versa. Behavioural scientists have alerted us to the ways in which individuals are uncaringly used by others; the theories of scapegoating, splitting, and projecting all illuminate the destructive and exploitative nature of such using, in which neither individual nor group survive unscathed. On the other hand, the conscious acceptance of a representative function, or doing something for others, can enoble the doer and those for whom he does his deed. 'Never have so many owed so much to so few,' said Churchill. Perhaps it is the consciousness of such activities which makes the difference? The development of a science of value would surely help us here. In the meantime it is sanguine to consider how far those who attempt and those who succeed in taking their own lives are the representatives of a society (or the symptoms of a social disease) which, while it acknowledges the urgency of reconciling the conflicting rights and needs of those who work and those who cannot, those who have and those who have not, the North and South of the Brandt report (1980), is for the most part pessimistic about its capacity to resolve and reconcile, and prefers to put what time and energy it has into the preservation and care of those representatives and of the disease which they herald.

REFERENCES

Brandon, D. (1978) *Zen in the Art of Helping*. London: Routledge & Kegan Paul.

Connelly, J. (1979) *Essentials of Postgraduate Psychiatry* (ed. Hill, Murray, and Thorley). New York: Academic.

Diggory, J. (1968) *Suicide and Value*. In H. L. P. Resnik (Ed.), *Suicidal Behaviours*. London: Churchill.

Durkheim, E. (1951) *Suicide* (trans. J. A. Spalding and G. Simpson). London: Free.

Epictetus (1888) *The Teaching of Epictetus* (II.ix.2–3) (trans. T. W. Rolleston). London: Scott.

Green, P. (1931) *The Problem of Right Conduct*. London: Longman.

Hillman, J. (1964) *Suicide and the Soul*. London: Hodder & Stoughton.

Holy Bible: John 11: 50; Judges 16: 30; 2 Maccabees 14: 41; Matthew 27: 5; I Samuel 31: 4.

Independent Commission on International Development Issues (The Brandt Report) (1980) *North–South: A Programme for Survival*. (Chaired by W. Brandt.) London: Pan.

Inge, W. R. (1930) *Christian Ethics and Modern Problems*. London: Green-wood.

Stengel, E. (1968) Attempted suicide. In H. L. P. Resnik (Ed.), *Suicidal Behaviours*. London: Churchill.

Stengel, E., and Cook, N. G. (1958) *Attempted Suicide: its Social Significance and Effects*. London: Chapman and Hall.

Personal Meanings
Edited by Eric Shepherd and J. P. Watson
© 1982 John Wiley & Sons Ltd.

How patients and psychiatrists account for overdoses

Keith Hawton

INTRODUCTION

Suicidal behaviour is a form of human action that quite understandably demands explanation. Indeed, rarely can a suicidal act occur without explanations being sought by individuals close to the person involved, and by professionals who are subsequently required to deal with the individual or the consequences of his actions. Clearly, in seeking such explanations there is an underlying assumption that suicidal behaviour is 'meaningful'. However, explanations provided by different individuals for the same suicidal act are often at variance. When an individual is asked to explain a suicidal act, his explanation is likely to be shaped by several factors, including his preconceived attitudes to such behaviour in general, and the attitudes to the behaviour he perceives in others. Clearly these factors, especially the latter, might lead to bias in his explanation. Nevertheless, we rely on his explanation as indicating the personal meaning of the behaviour for him. This is understandable because it is the individual's explanation of the behaviour to others that is liable to be a major factor in determining their subsequent behaviour. In this chapter, investigations of the personal meanings of acts of deliberate self-poisoning through study of explanations given by individuals will be described.

Typically such explanations take the form of a description of either the circumstances preceding the act (e.g. he did it because his wife was unfaithful, or he was depressed), or the apparent purposes of the behaviour (e.g. he did it to show his wife how much she had upset him, or, he intended to die). The former type of explanation can be termed 'expressive' (i.e. a reaction to circumstances) and the second 'instrumental' (i.e. goal-orientated). If one asks patients who have taken overdoses for a spontaneous account of why they did it, or if one asks for spontaneous accounts from those involved in helping such patients, the

103

explanations will more often be in expressive than instrumental terms. This is illustrated in Table 1, which presents the results of studies in which 40 psychiatrists and 40 patients who had taken overdoses in the past were asked to give reasons for overdoses taken by four individuals described in case vignettes (see Ramon, Bancroft, and Skrimshire (1975) for details of the cases).

Table 1   Explanations provided by psychiatrists and patients for four cases of deliberate self-poisoning

	Psychiatrists ($N = 40$) (%)	Patients ($N = 40$) (%)
Events/problems	74	78
State of mind	61	33
Goals/outcome	38	46

(More than one type of explanation could be provided in each case)

On approximately three-quarters of occasions the psychiatrists and patients suggested that events or problems were the reasons for the overdoses. In addition, the psychiatrists, perhaps understandably, attributed the behaviour to a disturbed state of mind twice as often as did the patients. However, less than half the explanations of both the patients and psychiatrists included any mention of purposes for the overdoses. This is in accord with Ginsberg's (1971) findings from a population survey that the majority of people view suicidal behaviour as something that happens to a person, rather than something that he intentionally brings about.

Nevertheless, there is a common assumption that those involved in suicidal behaviour have intended the acts, which carries with it the implication that there are goals involved. It is virtually impossible to get directly at the cognitive processes that precede such acts; instead one has to rely on the explanations or reasons provided subsequently. It is hardly surprising that systematic studies intended to cast light on this area have been rare. Most investigations have been confined to descriptions of circumstances and events preceding the behaviour, and personality types of those involved. Yet it is important that efforts should be made to investigate the instrumental aspects of the personal meanings of suicidal behaviour. It seems highly likely, for example, that psychiatrists make important clinical judgements concerning attempted suicide patients partly on the basis of their understanding of the purposes of the acts. It would also help further our understanding of the behaviour if we could have available the instrumental explanations provided by patients themselves.

INVESTIGATION OF THE MEANINGS OF DELIBERATE SELF-POISONING

During the past few years, several investigations aimed at disentangling the nature of instrumental explanations of deliberate self-poisoning have been carried out in Oxford (Ramon, Bancroft, and Skrimshire, 1975; Bancroft, Skrimshire, and Simkin, 1976; Hawton, Bancroft, and Simkin, 1978; Bancroft et al., 1979; Hawton, Marsack, and Fagg, 1981). Self-poisoning was chosen as the focus for these studies for several reasons. Firstly, it is extremely common. The rates of deliberate self-poisoning increased steeply during the 1960s and early 1970s to such an extent that the term 'epidemic' was being used to describe this phenomenon, which became the commonest reason for acute medical admission to hospitals in this country. Secondly, it can be extremely dangerous. Although the official suicide rates for this country were until recently on the decline (Adelstein and Mardon, 1975), self-poisoning is one of the most frequent ways used, especially by females. Moreover, it is clear that in some cases of suicide the individuals do not intend to die. Thirdly, for many people it is a socially unacceptable form of behaviour (Sale et al., 1975) and may evoke extremely negative attitudes.

During the course of the investigations, attention was concentrated particularly on eliciting reasons for overdoses from different people, including the self-poisoners themselves and staff involved in their care. One of these investigations will now be described in detail. It concerns the ways in which patients and psychiatrists attribute instrumental reasons for overdoses. Subsequently the clinical implications of the findings will be discussed.

Method

The investigations of the reasons given for self-poisoning behaviour have involved a method derived from one first introduced by Birtchnell and Alarcon (1971). A list of reasons was drawn up, based partly on those used by Birtchnell and Alarcon, with the addition of others commonly given spontaneously by patients and some which seemed likely on common-sense grounds. In the study to be described here, the ways in which reasons were chosen from the prepared list by patients who had taken overdoses were compared with those selected by psychiatrists who were asked to explain the patients' behaviour.

The patients

Forty-six overdose patients were selected for study. They were randomly selected from referrals to the psychiatric service in the general hospital in

Oxford (95 per cent of admissions for self-poisoning are referred to this service). Five patients were excluded (three because they refused on account of the tape-recording that was used for part of the study, one had hysterical aphonia, and another was very deaf). Thus 41 subjects were left in the study. These included 25 females and 16 males. Comparison of the sample with all attempted suicide patients admitted to the hospital in a one-year period showed the population of this study was representative according to sex, age, marital status, drugs used for self-poisoning, history of previous attempts, and psychiatric history.

Procedure

First, a research assistant interviewed each patient. She obtained an account of what had happened in the day or two leading up to the overdose and asked for spontaneous reasons for the act. She then asked the patient to select from a series of printed cards those which best described the reasons for the overdose and to rank them in order of importance. The patient was then asked to choose whether at the time of the overdose he wanted to die, didn't mind whether he lived or died, or did not want to die. The list of reasons, including those relating to suicidal intent, are shown in Table 2. For the sake of brevity, the reasons shown in full in Table 2 will subsequently be referred to in abbreviated form (e.g. 'situation so unbearable', 'relief from state of mind', 'escape situation', etc.).

Table 2   Reasons used to study explanations for overdoses

1	The situation was so unbearable that you had to do something and didn't know what else to do.
2	Get relief from a terrible state of mind.
3	Escape for a while from an impossible situation.
4	You seemed to lose control of yourself and have no idea why you behaved that way.
5	Show how much you loved someone.
6	Make people understand how desperate you were feeling.
7	Seek help from someone.
8	Find out whether someone really loved you or not.
9	Frighten or get your own back on someone/make people sorry for the way they have treated you.
10	Try to influence some particular person or get them to change their mind.
11	Make things easier for others.

(a) Wanted to die, (b) didn't mind if you lived or died, (c) did not want to die.

The research assistant's interview was tape-recorded and later subjected to content analysis. The result of this part of the study are reported elsewhere (Bancroft *et al.*, 1979).

Following the first interview, each patient was interviewed by either a research psychiatrist or an experienced research nurse. The interview was a detailed clinical assessment during which the interviewer completed a structured interview schedule which particularly focused on the circumstances of the overdose. Other individuals, such as relatives, friends, doctors, and nurses, were contacted and asked their views about the overdose and the patient. Where appropriate, the psychiatrist or nurse continued in a clinical role with the patient and in the process often gained further information relevant to the overdose. By this means a clinical 'dossier' of information concerning each patient's overdose was built up. The dossier was then given to psychiatric 'judges' to attribute likely reasons.

The psychiatrists

Three experienced psychiatrists acted as judges. They had all worked together in a general hospital psychiatric service and therefore shared a number of concepts and attitudes. They read each clinical dossier and then attributed reasons for the overdoses according to probability ('very likely', 'moderately likely', 'slightly likely', or 'not likely'). One item from the list of reasons, 'the situation was so unbearable that you had to do something and didn't know what else to do', is a subjectively 'expressive' reason; the psychiatrists were therefore not asked to rate this. The psychiatrists made their ratings independently. Of course, they did not know the content of the research assistant's interview, particularly the reasons chosen by the patients. They were provided with a series of common-sense criteria for and against each reason (see Bancroft *et al.*, 1979) and were asked to use these as well as any other common-sense factors that seemed appropriate in each case. The following illustrates the use of such common-sense reasoning. High suicidal intent would be more likely if a person had made careful preparations concerning their overdose, or had taken precautions to avoid discovery, than if he had taken the overdose on impulse, or contacted someone immediately after the act.

A small number of pilot cases were discussed among the three psychiatrists to ensure they each carried out the task in a similar fashion.

Results

The proportions of patients choosing the three answers relating to suicidal intent and the judgements concerning suicidal intent made by the psychiatrists are shown in Table 3. As found in a previous investigation (Bancroft, Skrimshire, and Simkin, 1976), a little more than a third of patients indicated that they had wanted to die, a third that they did not mind either way, and just under a third said that they had not wanted to die.

Table 3   Agreement between patients (N = 41) and psychiatrists for suicidal intent

Psychiatrists' choices (at least two in agreement)	Patients' choices		
	Wish to die	Didn't mind	Did not want to die
Suicidal intent (high/mod. probability)	8	4	0
No suicidal intent (low/nil probability)	7	10	12
	15 (37%)	14 (34%)	12 (29%)

The psychiatrists were in agreement with all 12 patients who denied any suicidal intent. However, they only agreed on suicidal intent for 8 of the 15 patients who said they had wanted to die. For 6 of the other 7 patients who said they had wished to die, the psychiatrists chose 'frighten/make sorry'. This will be discussed later.

The patients' and psychiatrists' choices for the other reasons are shown in Table 4 (the expressive reason, 'situation so unbearable', was not included in the psychiatrists' list).

There are a number of interesting features concerning these results. First, the expressive reason ('situation so unbearable') was most often chosen by the patients, thus reflecting the tendency referred to earlier. Second, and perhaps most striking, is the disagreement between the patients and psychiatrists for what may be described as hostile and manipulative reasons ('frighten/make sorry' and 'influence') which were chosen frequently by the psychiatrists but rarely by the patients. The levels of agreement between the psychiatrists for these two reasons were extremely good.

This marked discordance between the psychiatrists and patients clearly deserves further examination. A possible explanation is that patients choose not to give such reasons because they perceive them as being socially unacceptable. Certainly the hostile and manipulative reasons were found to be the least acceptable in a study of general hospital doctors' and nurses' attitudes to self-poisoning (Ramon, Bancroft, and

Table 4   Reasons chosen by the patients (first, second, or third choice) and by the psychiatrists (high and moderate probability; at least two in agreement for each case)

	Reasons	Chosen by patients	Chosen by psychiatrists	Rank order of psychiatrists' choices
1	Situation so unbearable	23 (56%)	—	—
2	Relief from state of mind	18 (44%)	16 (39%)	4
3	Escape situation	13 (32%)	6 (15%)	5 =
4	Loss of control	11 (27%)	0 (0%)	—
5	Show love	10 (24%)	2 (5%)	8
6	Show desperation	8 (20%)	29 (71%)	1 =
7	Seek help	6 (15%)	6 (15%)	5 =
8	Find if loved	4 (10%)	4 (10%)	7
9	Frighten/make sorry	4 (10%)	29 (71%)	1 =
10	Influence	3 (7%)	22 (54%)	3
11	Make easier	3 (7%)	0 (0%)	—

Skrimshire, 1975) and also in a study of junior psychiatrists' attitudes to the behaviour (Hawton, Marsack, and Fagg, 1981). On the other hand, in both of those studies 'wish to die' was the most acceptable reason. The above explanation therefore seems plausible because when the psychiatrists did not agree with the patients concerning suicidal intent they often chose 'frighten/make sorry' instead. Certainly some of the patients for whom there was this disagreement acted in a way to ensure survival. Their choice of reasons may therefore have reflected a need to enhance the social acceptability of their behaviour. At the same time the suicidal message may produce powerful reactions of guilt or concern in others. In other words, if an overdose is not intended to result in death but to have some other effect such as influencing another person's behaviour, the goal is more likely to be achieved if the act is perceived by that other person as having been suicidal. Although such perception presumably depends to a large degree on the nature of the act, the patient's explanation will also be important.

An alternative explanation is that psychiatrists misunderstood the self-poisoner's behaviour in such cases. This is certainly possible. However, their choice of reasons seems to be in keeping with our knowledge that the majority of people who take overdoses have experienced a recent serious row in the setting of chronic relationship difficulties (Bancroft *et al.*, 1977). It seems understandable in such circumstances that a dramatic measure like self-poisoning might be used to modify the situation, either by causing guilt and/or by putting pressure on a partner to change his or her behaviour. In such circumstances death would not be a relevant outcome.

A third finding (Table 4) was that 'relief from state of mind' was chosen fairly frequently by both patients and psychiatrists. However, when individual cases were examined the level of agreement was not better than chance.

Finally, 'seek help' was rarely chosen by either the patients or the psychiatrists. This is surprising in view of the commonly assumed interpretation of self-poisoning as being a 'cry for help' (Stengel and Cook, 1958). This may be explicable for the psychiatrists in that the common-sense criteria suggested for this reason emphasized specific help from external agencies, rather than getting a helpful response from one's family and friends. In addition, the psychiatrists frequently chose 'show desperation', which is perhaps akin to 'seek help'. Nevertheless, as the patients rarely chose this reason either, clearly few saw their behaviour as aimed at getting help. As has been noted elsewhere (Kovacs, Beck, and Weissman, 1976), the common notion that suicidal acts are often motivated by a wish to elicit help may be due to *consequences* being mistakenly equated with *motives*.

APPLICABILITY OF THE FINDINGS FOR PSYCHIATRISTS IN GENERAL

Since the three psychiatrists in the study which has been described worked in the same clinical setting and had been encouraged to use a common approach, it was clearly necessary to determine whether the findings were consistent with the reasons attributed to self-poisoning behaviour by psychiatrists in general. Therefore 50 senior psychiatrists were provided with transcripts of the research assistant's interviews with six of the patients, excluding the final portion in which the patients chose their reasons. Twenty-five psychiatrists received three transcripts and a further 25 the other three transcripts. The cases were chosen to represent different types of story. The psychiatrists were asked to attribute reasons for the cases as in the previous study.

When the three reasons most frequently chosen for each case by the 50 psychiatrists and those given most importance by the three psychiatric judges (using a graded scale according to their ratings of probability) were examined, it was clear that both groups discriminated between the cases in their choice of reasons and also showed very good agreement with each other (Table 5). In all six cases the two groups agreed on the first reason. For five patients the same reasons were included in the first three choices by the two groups of psychiatrists, and in the sixth case the first two reasons were the same.

Table 5   Choice of reasons (first three) by the three psychiatrists and 50 other
psychiatrists (25 rates cases ABC and 25 rated cases DEF)

		Three psychiatrists	50 psychiatrists
Case A	1	influence	influence
	2	make sorry/frighten	make sorry/frighten
	3	find if loved	find if loved
Case B	1	show desperation ⎫	show desperation ⎫
		make sorry/frighten ⎬	relief from state of mind ⎬
	2		
	3	relief from state of mind ⎫	seek help
		seek help ⎬	
Case C	1	to die	to die
	2	make sorry/frighten	relief from state of mind
	3	relief from state of mind ⎫	make sorry/frighten
		influence ⎬	
Case D	1	show desperation ⎫	show desperation
		make sorry/frighten ⎬	
	2		make sorry/frighten
	3	relief from state of mind	relief from state of mind
Case E	1	to die	to die ⎫
			seek help ⎬
	2	seek help	
	3	show desperation	show desperation
Case F	1	influence	influence
	2	make sorry/frighten	make sorry/frighten
	3	seek help	show desperation

CONCLUSION

This has been a description of a method used to investigate the personal
meanings of deliberate self-poisoning, particularly the instrumental
explanations that are given for the behaviour. Before interpreting the
findings it is vital to consider two questions concerning this approach.
Firstly, is the use of lists of reasons as a method of enquiry really tapping
the meaning of the behaviour for each individual? It is clear that in many
cases the reasons chosen from the list were not those given spontaneously
by the subjects. Therefore, perhaps one is simply putting words into their
mouths by providing them with a list of reasons from which to choose,
or, alternatively, this could be helping them to put into words reasons
which they have found difficult to formulate. It does seem likely that this
method is tapping the personal meanings of the behaviour for the
patients to a significant extent because the patients' choices are not

random; patterns of relationships between their choices can be demonstrated (Bancroft, Skrimshire, and Simkin, 1976), and there is reasonable consistency between the choices made initially and at subsequent follow-up (Hawton *et al.*, in preparation). Similarly, it has been possible by the use of multidimensional scaling techniques to demonstrate patterns of relationships between the psychiatrists' choices.

The second question is whether this method helps elucidate the meaning of the behaviour for the self-poisoner as it was *prior* to the overdose. This is very uncertain, particularly when many overdoses are apparently taken impulsively. In fact, two-thirds of patients in this study reported having contemplated the act for less than an hour, and half of these described it as entirely unpremeditated. Clearly the decision to take an overdose may be taken quickly, precipitated by some event such as an argument, but it remains probable that in most such cases the possibility of taking an overdose had been rehearsed in imagination some time previously. As with many kinds of socially unacceptable behaviour, to describe oneself as 'acting on impulse' is to deny any premeditation as a way of making the behaviour more acceptable either to oneself or to others. Thus access to the personal meaning of the behaviour prior to taking an overdose may be denied us. However, as discussed earlier, how a patient explains the behaviour subsequently may be equally important, particularly when considering the effects of the behaviour on others.

There is a strong possibility that the difference between the psychiatrists and patients in their use of the hostile and manipulative reasons is explained by the patients' choices being affected by their perception of the varying social acceptability of the reasons. Now more needs to be known about how relatives and other persons close to self-poisoning patients both attribute reasons and respond to the behaviour. If some overdoses are motivated by a need to communicate anger and to manipulate other people's behaviour it should be possible to observe predictable responses in such people. This is clearly an area for further study.

The infrequent use of some reasons by both patients and psychiatrists, and the similarity between some of the reasons, suggests that in fugure studies the list of reasons could be shortened. The extent to which the reasons cluster together and the nature of clusters are currently being investigated in order to determine how far the list can be reduced and the extent to which some reasons can be condensed together. A brief list will obviously be more practical for clinical purposes.

Finally, what are the clinical implications of this study? First, the fact that the behaviour is infrequently explained by patients as a means of obtaining help from outside agencies needs to be taken into account when trying to engage overdose patients in after-care. Secondly, this also suggests that making professional help more available for people in crises may not be very relevant in prevention. Studies by Kreitman and Chowdhury (1973) and Holding (1974) have shown that agencies such as the Samaritans cater for either a different type of person or for a different type of crisis. It is easy to see that, for many of these cases, taking an overdose may have far greater impact on a tense family or interpersonal situation than going out to a phone box and having a confidential chat with a volunteer. Finally, the possibility that a high proportion of these acts are intended to communicate anger or to influence family members or close friends emphasizes the need to focus on these relationships in trying to provide help for such patients. Conjoint or family therapy will be necessary in many cases.

ACKNOWLEDGEMENTS

The work described here was part of a series of studies concerning the reasons given for and attitudes shown to deliberate self-poisoning. In addition to the author, the following have at various times been involved in these studies: John Bancroft, Clyde Cumming, Joan Fagg, Breda Kingston, Pamela Marsack, Shula Ramon, Susan Simkin, Angela Skrimshire, and David Whitwell.

REFERENCES

Adelstein, A., and Mardon, C. (1975) Suicides 1961–74. In *Population Trends*, No. 2, pp.13–18. London: HMSO.

Bancroft, J., Hawton, K., Simkin, S., Kingston, B., Cumming, C., and Whitwell, D. (1979) The reasons people give for taking overdoses: a further enquiry. *Br. J. Med. Psychol.*, **52**, 353–65.

Bancroft, J. H. J., Skrimshire, A. M., Casson, J., Harvard-Watts, O., and Reynolds, F. (1977) People who deliberately poison or injure themselves: their problems and their contacts with helping agencies. *Psychol. Med.*, **7**, 289–303.

Bancroft, J. H. J., Skrimshire, A. M., and Simkin, S. (1976) The reasons people give for taking overdoses. *Br. J. Psychiatry*, **128**, 538–48.

Birtchnell, J., and Alarcon, J. (1971) The motivation and emotional state of 91 cases of attempted suicide. *Br. J. Med. Psychol.*, **44**, 45–52.

Ginsberg, G. P. (1971) Public conceptions and attitudes about suicide. *J. Health Soc. Behav.*, **12**, 200–7.

Hawton, K., Bancroft, J., and Simkin, S. (1978) Attitudes of psychiatric patients to deliberate self-poisoning. *Br. J. Psychiatry*, **132**, 31–5.

Hawton, K., Marsack, P., and Fagg, J. (1981) The attitudes of psychiatrists to deliberate self-poisoning: comparison with general hospital doctors and nurses. *Br. J. Med. Psychol.* **54**, 341–8.

Hawton, K., Osborne, M., O'Grady, J., and Cole, D. (in preparation). Motivational aspects of self-poisoning in adolescents.

Holding, T. A. (1974) The BBC 'Befrienders' series and its effects. *Br. J. Psychiatry*, **124**, 470–2.

Kovacs, M., Beck, A. T., and Weissman, M. A. (1976) The communication of suicidal intent. *Arch. Gen. Psychiatry*, **53**, 198–201.

Kreitman, N., and Chowdhury, B. (1973) Distress behaviour: a study of selected Samaritan clients and parasuicides ('attempted suicide' patients). *Br. J. Psychiatry*, **123**, 1–8.

Ramon, S., Bancroft, J. H. J., and Skrimshire, A. M. (1975) Attitudes towards self-poisoning among physicians and nurses in a general hospital. *Br. J. Psychiatry*, **127**, 257–64.

Sale, I., Williams, C. O., Clark, J., and Mills, J. (1975) Suicide behaviour: community attitudes and beliefs. *Suicide*, **5**, 158–68.

Stengel, E., and Cook, N. G. (1958) *Attempted Suicide*. London: Oxford University Press.

Personal Meanings
Edited by Eric Shepherd and J. P. Watson
© 1982 John Wiley & Sons Ltd.

Alcoholics, drinkers, and drunks

David A. Curson

The three words alcoholics, drinkers, and drunks provide a suitable focus for a discussion of alcohol and alcoholism which attempts to acknowledge the importance of personal meanings. Our starting point is the drinking behaviour of individuals, for as Lederman (1956) observed, as alcohol consumption increases in a society more and more 'normal' people develop drinking problems. Important causes of alcohol dependence are likely to include the use, availability, and pharmacology of alcohol (Alcohol Education Centre, 1977), even though factors crucial to recovery from alcohol dependence may be different and focus particularly upon the personal qualities of the dependent individual. It is helpful to avoid the perpetuation of inaccurate stereotypes, such as of the wives of alcoholics (Walen, 1953; Futterman, 1953) and of the alcoholic personality (Kessel and Walton, 1969; Kammeier, Hoffman, and Loper, 1973), which have been popular in the past.

CAREER

We begin by looking at the social and cultural attitudes which underpin the use of the drug itself. How do our alcoholics, drinkers, and drunks serve their apprenticeship? What moulds their attitudes, alters their behaviour, and changes their responses over time? The chemical and pharmacological properties of alcohol are clearly important, but the behavioural concomitants of drinking alcohol depend as much on notions of anticipated effect as on the biochemistry of the drug. MacAndrew and Egerton (1970) remind us that:

when man lifts a cup it is not only the kind of drink that is in it, the amount he is likely to take, and the circumstances under which he will do the drinking that are specified in advance for him, but also whether the contents of the cup will cheer or stupify, whether they will induce affection or aggression, guilt or unalloyed pleasure. These and many other cultural definitions attach to the drink even before it touches the lips.

115

In addition, the rules and standards governing the place of drinking become clearly defined within single social or subcultural groups. From the dawn of recorded history drinking has been integrated into social occasions, religious rituals, and various rites from the cradle to the grave. Social anthropological field studies have revealed that drink-related cultural practices vary from total rejection to the most enthusiastic use. Robinson (1977) points out that though the form of drinking is usually explicitly stipulated including the kind of beverage to be used, the social rules governing the amount and the rate of intake, the time and place of drinking, the sex and age of the drinker, and the whole range of behaviours proper to drinking—which comprise the 'meanings' of drinking—though certainly in existence, are almost always implicit and carried informally in the culture.

Within our own (late 20th century British) culture, children appear to discover the custom by heresay, being eye witnesses to drinking behaviour and its consequences, and in some cases experimenting themselves. Three important studies have investigated children's knowledge of alcohol at different ages and how they start to use it themselves. Though two of these studies were performed in Glasgow and one in England, the results are probably applicable to children in Britain generally.

Jahoda and Cramond (1972) found that most children begin learning about alcohol at home and had formed definite impressions about it well before they had started attending primary school. Two-fifths of six-year-olds were able to identify alcoholic drinks by smell, and the proportion had increased to three-fifths by the age of ten years of age. The same researchers found that many children tasted alcohol when quite young, they commonly saw alcohol around and were able to recognize it, and the majority of Glasgow children in the study were able to interpret drunken behaviour depicted in a film as the outcome of drinking. Even before the age of six, most children had encountered drunken adults. Another interesting finding was that from the outset boys were given more encouragement than girls to sample alcoholic drinks. Rearing of the sexes was different and there were major differences in later alcohol use by males and females.

Davies and Stacey (1972) investigated alcohol use amongst children aged 14 to 17 years of age in Glasgow. As children grew up the influence of their home diminished and the influence of the teenage peer group became dominant. By the age of 14 years, 92 per cent of boys and 85 per cent of girls had tasted alcohol. Three years later, only 2 per cent of boys and 4 per cent of girls had not yet tried it. The often extreme and negative pre-pubescent attitudes had changed dramatically; the drinker was now seen as sociable and tough, whilst the abstainer as socially undesirable, weak, and unsociable. Between 13 and 17, the peer group had become the influential reference point for drinking, and drinking regularly occurred because their friends did it and because it was regarded as socially desirable and prestigious.

Another recent survey of over 7000 English schoolchildren aged 13 to 18 years supported the Glasgow findings that most children establish regular drinking habits in their early teens (Hawker, 1978). The desired norm for most teenagers was light or moderate drinking. Like Davies and Stacey, Hawker found that approval did not extend to heavy drinking which was perceived as excessive and unsociable.

Parents who drink moderately appear to provide a useful model for their children and there is evidence that children who in adult life develop drinking problems come from homes where their parents either abused alcohol or were rigid abstainers. O'Connor (1978), in a study of English and Irish families, concluded that Irish children were frequently discouraged from drinking, whilst English children were not. Subsequently the former were more likely than the latter to suffer harmful consequences from drinking, even if their alcohol consumption was low.

The continuing learning process that each of us undergoes is yet another important factor in the development of drinking behaviour. We learn to associate objects or events in our lives with specific results. While there is still much to be discovered about the mechanisms involved, the law of effect suggests, as far as it goes, that if the response to a stimulus (such as alcohol) is pleasant or 'positive', the behaviour will be reinforced or strengthened. So, if drinkers feel that drinking is beneficial they will continue to drink, but if drinking is no longer felt as beneficial, drinkers will be less inclined to drink (Plant, 1979). For the vast majority and for most of the time, imbibing alcohol is construed as pleasant and an aid to social and in some cases sexual intercourse. Low doses are found to induce euphoria, relaxation, and disinhibition in a predictable and acceptable form. High doses produce dysphoria, unacceptable behaviour, and even acute physical illness but in a less predictable way. By a process of trial and error, and influenced by particular assimilated attitudes, our apprentices learn to titrate the dose of the drug against anticipated and often hoped-for responses. They also learn to lesser or greater degree that such behaviour is self-determined (at least initially) until judgement itself is so distorted and disturbed that anticipated responses become more difficult to achieve.

Thus the apprentice drinkers have embarked upon a personal exploration into drinking behaviour from a relatively early age. An admixture of modelling, social expectations, social, personal and group reinforcement, and the pharmacological effects on mood, perception, impulse control, and behaviour moulds their views and attitudes to alcohol, drinking, and drunkenness.

As our apprentices progress towards the status of qualified drinkers, they begin to discover that other factors enter or have already entered the complex equation. For example, drinkers drink for differing reasons at different times, and this is manifested in terms of beverage choice, place of consumption, social pressure to drink, social and financial circumstances, and social role. Even the reasons for the first and last drink may be different. For the young, drinking tends to remain a part of some more general social activity. Plant (1979) has observed that although some young people drink excessively and get into trouble due to drinking, few become physically dependent or 'addicted' to alcohol since this generally follows some years of heavy drinking. Most difficulties encountered by young drinkers are due to high alcohol consumption over a short period of time, e.g. fights and accidents, though the majority escape even these problems.

To a considerable extent, individual drinking is correlated with social class and sex. Few middle-class people get into fights while drunk, and women, who tend to drink less than men, get into trouble with drinking less often. (This gender difference may be diminishing as society evolves.) Most young people who become deeply involved with drinking are young males from socially deprived backgrounds, who generally display a whole range of social and psychological problems. The majority of young alcohol abusers mature out of heavy drinking. This is frequently precipitated or at least facilitated by the development of an enduring personal relationship or a change in occupational status, which serve to disengage them from their heavy drinking peer group (Cahalan, Cissin, and Crossley, 1969). So long as a person is able to enjoy marriage and work, alcohol will tend to play a minor part in life and be consumed in moderation. When a person drinks heavily it is usually for social reasons and linked to types of job, availability of alcohol, and financial resources. Most male heavy drinkers are social animals and they form the nucleus of 'regulars' in pubs and clubs. Drinking is one of the principal social activities of these individuals. Their behaviour may have no adverse social effects, or problems may gradually develop in various areas of their lives.

Internal factors may begin to play a part in drinking behaviour at any time. Alcohol serves to relieve the effects of anxiety, depression, and disappointment (though for brief periods only), to take the edge off premenstrual tension, and to offer oblivion for those faced with boredom or loneliness. Against a background of constitutional factors such as trait anxiety, temperament, predisposition to hangover effect, impulse control, and even possible inherited characteristics which may determine amount consumed (*British Medical Journal*, 1980), each individual develops a baseline of values originating from multiple sources and personal experiences over time. Each source and each experience has a different degree of impact at different times.

THE DEVELOPMENT OF DEPENDENCE AND PROBLEMS

The World Health Organization (1974) defines psychological dependence as a condition in which a drug not only promotes a feeling of satisfaction but also promotes a drive to repeat the consumption of that drug in order to induce pleasure or avoid discomfort. Unfortunately, such dependence is not a clearly defined state, and it is not easy to determine the point at which a drinker has become psychologically dependent. The difficulty is increased by the possibility that mild or even moderate forms of psychological dependence are not necessarily abnormal states (Davies, 1976). Many feel uncomfortable without an evening drink after a very hard day; this virtually defines psychological dependence! So does the acute distress experienced by crossword addicts during a newspaper strike!

At the other end of the scale, however, more severe degrees of alcohol dependence may be identified reliably and accurately. Edwards and Gross (1976) have described what they call the alcohol dependence syndrome, which is characterized by the narrowing of drinking repertoires, salience of drink-seeking behaviour, increasing tolerance, physical withdrawal symptoms, drinking to relieve and allay withdrawal symptoms, a subjective awareness of a compulsion to drink, and reinstatement of the syndrome after a period of abstinence. The utility of such a concept has been explored (Hodgson *et al.*, 1978; Stockwell *et al.*, 1979) and its predictive value in terms of drinking outcome has been described by Hodgson (1980) in a follow-up study. Though the development of the full-blown alcohol dependence syndrome may induce personal dissatisfaction or dissonance in the drinker, aid is often sought only when additional alcohol-related problems arise.

There is no doubt that some drinkers are alerted to potential hazards before drinking can be said to have caused serious problems to themselves or others. In contemporary Britain, the act of drinking tends not to be judged as 'bad', though getting drunk too often is generally viewed with disfavour and this may account for some drinkers curtailing their consumption simply to avoid opprobrium from family, friends, and colleagues. More idiosyncratic responses may result from the belief that certain types or patterns of drinking are unacceptable, e.g. drinking alone rather than with another or others. It is an oddly prevalent assumption even in the literature that social drinking is good and solitary drinking is bad. Though such a belief may be beneficial to some by restricting overall consumption, it may also cause problems in its own right. First, it may drive drinkers (especially male drinkers) into the company of male friends and away from the home and family. Second, it may mislead heavier drinkers and alcoholics into believing that they cannot have a drinking problem at all because they never drink alone. Hayman (1967) has admirably attempted to explode the myth of social drinking when he writes 'We cannot say that all who drink are alcoholics. But can we say that they are all "social drinkers" who, because of drinking, have hurt others by hostile criticism, made unwelcome passes at other men's wives, had unreasonable fights, given their children a model of drunkenness, squandered time needed for constructive pursuits, driven while in a drunken state, had accidents coming home from a cocktail party, impatiently punished their children, or stay detached from wife and children in front of the television set evening after evening in a semi-stuporose state following several "social" drinks before dinner? We need another category "anti-social drinking" to replace much of what we call "social-drinking" '.

Once unhappiness is experienced by self or others, the drinker is under threat. Drinking may become construed as 'bad' and by inference the drinker also as 'bad'. However, drinking may not be a continuous behaviour at this stage, and time spent drinking may still be construed by the drinker as pleasurable.

In time the drinker with alcohol-related problems is faced with a dilemma. To change implies the sacrifice of much of the pleasure and the acknowledgement that some of the consequences have been bad. Moral notions may require an admission that they have themselves been bad at some point and have brought problems upon themselves as a result of irresponsibility. Meanwhile, any associated dependence leads to a reduction in self-control and an over-reliance on a chemical substance. The combined effect is an enormous threat to self-esteem. This threat demands action and that action can only be a major curtailment of or complete abandonment of a pleasure-inducing and frequent activity. When total abstention is given as the only realistic solution it implies a dramatic switch from what is in effect one deviant position to another. It is not perhaps surprising that this is unacceptable to many and for those who choose not to change it is inevitable that ego defence mechanisms such as denial, projection, and rationalization are brought into play and intensify with the level of personal threat. No matter how preposterous such defences may appear to others (and often to the alcoholic in enlightened hindsight), at the time they are essential to defend the self against the invasion by reality and to maintain the drinking position. There remains a powerful reluctance to abandon a source of pleasure (sometimes the only source of immediate pleasure at this stage) which is in turn reinforced by psychological dependence, perhaps chemical dependence, and the fear of unpleasant physical withdrawal symptoms and an unspecified often vague but powerful fear of having to fill the vacuum created by the absence of drinking alcohol. For most this state continues for a considerable time; for some unto death.

For some, the picture is complicated further by brain damage. Though the correlation between neuropsychological deficit and degree of cerebral atrophy in all but the most severe and obvious cases is uncertain (Lishman, 1980) the possibility of previously unrecognized and perhaps irreversible changes in cognitive function cannot be lightly dismissed. The impact on judgement and particularly on new learning ability can be devastating.

THE DECISION TO CHANGE

The decision to change usually follows some sort of personal crisis and is manifested by such privately spoken statements as 'I can't go on like this'.

The core of the decision to change appears to be a recognition by the problem drinker and usually others that the future under these circumstances is intolerable. Defences no longer operate or have substantially disintegrated. The demands to recognize and face up to reality and other people are continuous and unavoidable. The painful consequences now persistently outweigh the pleasures of drinking. Against a background of acute reversible or chronic irreversible impairment of cognitive functioning, a life filled with apparently overwhelming difficulties, and some degree of psychological and chemical dependence, the drinker must choose to reduce the rate of alcohol consumption relatively or absolutely. For the problem drinker, and any assigned helper, this is a moment of maximum potential gain, since attitudes and behaviour are most likely to change at this time.

It is important not to view this event as a once-and-for-all affair. There is a tendency for many problem drinkers and alcoholics to take decisive action, embark on abstinence or controlled drinking, or seek help, only to revert to their former drinking pattern with all its associated problems weeks, months, or even years later. Orford (1980) has suggested a decision model of drinking behaviour change which not only highlights the role of personal crisis and personal dissatisfaction but points to the role of later stressful events or temptations in precipitating relapse. It encapsulates the all-too-familiar cyclical pattern of drinking, crisis, resistance to relapse, and relapse.

THERAPISTS, HELPERS, AND AGENTS OF CHANGE

Whilst some problem drinkers undoubtedly succeed alone, many are forced to seek the aid of some sort of lay or professional help. From a professional viewpoint, the theoretical choice is wide, but this is rarely so from the viewpoint of the problem drinker. With rare and even eccentric exceptions in major conurbations such as radio phone-ins and help-lines, the choice is limited to the family doctor, the Fellowship of Alcoholics Anonymous, and less frequently the Voluntary Counselling Services such as the Local Councils on Alcoholism. Almost every other resource is accessible only via referral from these initial contacts.

The response of the first helper contact may vary enormously according to the perception of the problem drinker by that helper and the problem drinker's perceptions of the helping resource. Though in Britain the 'Primary Care Team' has been deemed to be responsible for the identification and treatment of alcoholism (DHSS, 1978) in practice, many general practitioners and their staff lack knowledge, insight, and even sympathy with such problems. Flat rejection or an equally harmful reluctant referral to a psychiatric outpatient clinic two months hence is common. For many, rejection leads to either a prescription for tranquillizers and/or a return to the bottle; psychiatric referral leads to an implicit label of being mentally disordered, and in any case those critical weeks are too long to wait.

Throughout this period, the drinkers may have highly ambivalent views about their own problem. Many have sought help as a result of direct or indirect coercion. They often see themselves in terms of failure and moral weakness. They are maximally vulnerable yet their defences are necessarily maintained. A potential helper may be viewed as an angel of mercy, but at the same time as a threat to their drinking. Just as a potential helper will respond to the personal attributes of the drinker in a different ways, so the drinker will respond to the perceived attributes of the helper. Yet perceptions and judgements of the drinker may be influenced by actions of the drug itself on brain function, and the drug-distorted behaviour influences the way the drinker is perceived by the helper.

The responses of helpers will also be influenced by their own experiences, mores, values, and knowledge. The construing of the problem itself can be very variable, a composite perhaps of the disease model, moral judgements about the person, and inconsistencies between the construct of 'a typical alcoholic' and the person actually facing them. The likeability of the alcoholic for the helper is also important, though often only acknowledged privately, for to regard clients as differentially attractive runs counter to some traditional professional codes.

The helper's confidence in their own therapeutic skills in dealing with alcoholics may also influence whether they accept or deny the existence of a drinking problem. Denial is frequently exemplified by one of two possible approaches—a denial by the helper of the severity of the problem, or a denial of the existence of any problem at all whilst preferring to focus on what the helper can comprehend and handle. Whilst both of these approaches may reflect non-possessive warmth, empathy, and non-judgemental attitudes, they both leave the major problem undetected, unrecognized, and unresolved (Hunter, 1963).

After an alcohol problem has been recognized, accepted, and viewed as a valid area for concern and help-giving, the helper has to choose a therapeutic focus. The helper also has to survive; some helpers avoid alcoholics through fear that they will not survive. Significant factors for helper survival would seem to include the ability to accept problem drinking in a non-moralistic way; the abandonment of traditional stereotypes; a consistent determination never to ignore or allow the drinker to minimize the drinking no matter how many other problems prevail; an optimistic approach combined with the positive belief that change is possible; the ability to care whilst refusing to accept any responsibility for the person's drinking; and a recognition that alcoholism is a chronic, relapsing condition, so avoiding unrealistic therapeutic expectations.

Curiously, all these elements can be readily acquired, but the outstanding stumbling block is often the last. Reluctance to accept chronicity is manifested in short-term treatment contracts negotiated by helpers, and treatment programmes offered by statutory and private agencies. One outstanding exception is the Fellowship of Alcoholics Anonymous, and they have never waivered in accepting the proposition of chronicity. Perhaps this is not so surprising since the membership comprises the true experts. Unfortunately, there is one major reservation about their approach which has been reviewed by Pattison (1968, 1976), and is shared by many working in the field. One of the foundation stones of the philosophy of Alcoholics Anonymous is that drinking alcoholically is triggered off by physiological craving and continued drinking occurs as a result of the 'loss of control' phenomenon which is part and parcel of the alcoholic disease process. In practice there is an expressed belief that to take one drink will inevitably lead to addictive drinking, and to tell patients that they are only one drink away from becoming a drunk, may constitute a self-fulfilling prophecy. An alcoholic imbued with this philosophy who takes one drink may proceed to 'binge' drinking because he believed that it would inevitably occur, and the notion that alcoholism is a disease, undermines self-determination and self-control as prerequisites to alcoholism recovery. This credo presumably survives because it works for some or even many alcoholics, but it may retard the progress of others.

HELPING AND TREATMENT

'Treatment' is a word borrowed from medicine and has to do with arresting or changing the course of a disease process.

Current medical models of 'treatment' may have to be examined critically when applied to alcoholism and especially to the earlier stages of problem drinking. Thus it can be argued that alcohol education coupled with the destruction of myths and stereotypes, and linked to early recognition and intervention with timely and sensible advice should all be subsumed by the term alcoholism treatment, even though not applied to any established 'disease'. This preventive approach could increase the ability and willingness of individuals to recognize problems earlier, inform them that something can be done, and that they may be able to largely help themselves provided dependence is not fully established. The disease model and its influence on treatment philosophy and practice sometimes tend to undermine this approach.

Current research into the efficacy of alcoholism treatment makes somewhat gloomy reading. Orford and Edwards (1977) failed to demonstrate a difference between traditional in-patient treatment in a specialized unit and half a day's intensive out-patient counselling and education with monthly visits by social workers to review progress. The more publicized and criticized *Rand Report* produced discouraging figures on the effects of different treatment styles and equally depressing results in terms of outcome at four years (Armor, Polich, and Stambul, 1978; Polich, Armor, and Braiker, 1979). Costello's sophisticated attempts at assessing the variance of different factors in outcome studies seemed more optimistic since they offered clues as to which treatment components were associated with better results (Costello, 1975a, b). Yet these approaches fail to deal with the heterogeneous nature of alcoholism. The recognition (known by some clinicians for decades) that alcoholics are different and they respond differently to different treatment styles and methods, has been encapsulated in Glaser's 'core shell hypothesis' (Glaser, 1980). Glaser's principal aim is to research different treatments within a large treatment system and attempt to match treatment methods to the actual types of drinking problem. This involves offering as wide a range of treatment as possible, urging that everyone tries everything, the individual with advice from the helper subsequently modifying or rejecting whatever seems relatively useless after trial.

It seems possible that 'perhaps the crucial ingredients in treatment success is not really the treatment at all but rather the personal decision to seek treatment and remain in it' (Armor, Polich, and Stambul, 1977). From the helper's viewpoint, treatment can be seen as involving this, but also a second stage concerned with providing encouragement of, advice about, and reinforcement for, the acquisition of more appropriate coping skills. This latter approach focuses upon the recognition of and responses to drinking cues, strategies of self-control and self-monitoring, and the overall philosophy of self-determination as a key to alcoholism recovery and survival. Treatment is a long-term process and it would seem appropriate therefore to accept the need for long-term support or follow-up. When drinking has ceased or is under control, the alcoholic still has to live with and adjust to the often painful consequences of his or her past pathological drinking. Help from family, especially the spouse, is invariably necessary. Initial rewards usually lose their force within weeks or months. Congratulation from others quickly disappears. There is sometimes a dangerous vacuum to be filled as future plans have yet to bear fruit and past misdemeanours return to haunt the individual. Throughout this period long-established and dangerous habits have yet to begin their slow decay to ultimate extinction. Hence, helpers should remain potentially available for as long as they are needed.

This is also important because relapses are common. The danger is that such an event is construed as failure. Many therapists react as if it were, and the personal sensitivity and attitudes of the therapist are crucial. Avoidance of endorsement coupled with encouragement to use the event as a learning experience would appear essential, yet such golden opportunities are often missed. The drinker construes the relapse as failure, fears censure, and can readily justify continued drinking. The family, often holding on to medical and moralistic models against a personal background of long-suffering despair and disappointment, unwittingly perpetuate the drinking by inappropriate responses. The therapist, if granted access to the alcoholic at this point, may express personal disappointment, even personal annoyance at having failed. This may be conveyed to the alcoholic by actions, words, or deeds, or such beliefs are attributed to the helper when none actually exist. The common statement 'I've let you down doctor', not only serves to reflect feelings of personal failure, but subtly shifts responsibility for drinking from the drinker to the helper. In reality, drinkers can let down nobody but themselves.

REFERENCES

Alcohol Education Centre (1977) *The Lederman Curve*. Report of a Conference, London.

Armor, D. J., Polich, J. M., and Stambul, H. B. (1976) *Alcoholism and Treatment*. Santa Monica, California: The Rand Corporation.

Armor, D. J., Polich, J. M., and Stambul, H. B. (1978) *Alcoholism and Treatment*. New York: Wiley.

British Medical Journal (1980) Alcoholism: an inherited disease? **281**, 1301-2.

Cahalan, D., Cissin, I. H., and Crossley, H. M. (1969) American drinking practices: a national study of drinking behaviour and attitudes. Monograph No. 6. Rutgers Centre for Alcohol Studies, New Brunswick.

Costello, R. M. (1975a) Alcoholism treatment and evaluation: In search of methods. 2. *International Journal of the Addictions*, **10**(2), 251-75.

Costello, R. M. (1975b) Alcoholism treatment and evaluations: In search of methods. II Collation of two year follow-up studies. *International Journal of the Addictions*. **10**(5), 857-67.

DHSS (1978) The pattern and range of services for problem drinkers. *Report by the Advisory Committee on Alcoholism*. London: HMSO.

Davies, D. L. (1976) Definitional issues in alcoholism. In Tartar, R. E., and Sugarman, A. A. (Eds), *Alcoholism: Interdisciplinary Approaches to an Enduring Problem*. Mass.: Addison-Wesley.

Davies, J., and Stacey, B. (1972) *Teenagers and Alcohol: A developmental study in Glasgow*, Vol.1. London: HMSO.

Edwards, G., and Gross, M. M. (1976) Alcohol dependence: provisional description of a clinical syndrome. *Brit. Med. J.*, **1**, 1058-61.

Futterman, S. (1953) Personality trends in wives of alcoholics. *J. Psychiat. Soc. Work*, **23**, 37-41.

Glaser, F. B. (1980) Anybody got a match? Treatment research and matching hypothesis. In Edwards, G., and Grant, M. (Eds), *Alcoholism Treatment in Transition*. London: Croom Helm.

Hayman, F. (1967) The myth of social drinking. *Psychiatric Spectator*, **8**, 3.

Hawker, A. (1978) *Adolescents and Alcohol*. London: Edsall.

Hodgson, R. J. (1980) Treatment strategies for early problem drinkers. In Edwards, G. and Grant, H. (Eds), *Alcoholism Treatment in Transition*. London: Croom Helm.

Hodgson, R., Stockwell, T., Rankin, H., and Edwards, G. (1978) Alcohol dependence: the concept, its utility and measurement. *Brit. J. of Addiction*, **73**, 339-42.

Hunter, G. (1963) Alcoholism and the family agency. *Quart. J. Stud. Alc.*, **24**, 61-79.

Jahoda, G., and Cramond, J. (1972) *Children and Alcohol: A developmental study in Glasgow*, Vol. 1. London: HMSO.

Kammeier, M. L., Hoffman, H., and Loper, R. G. (1973) Personality of alcoholics as college freshmen and at the time of treatment. *Quart. J. Stud. Alc.*, **34**, 390-9.

Kessel, N., and Walton, H. (1969) *Alcoholism*. London: Penguin.

Lederman, S. (1956) *Alcool, Alcoolisme, Alcoolisation*. Institut National d'Etudes Demographiques Cahiers No. 29. Paris: Presses Universitaries de France.

Lishman, A. (1980) Personal communication.

MacAndrew, C. and Egerton, R. B. (1970) *Drunken Comportment: A Social Explanation*. London: Nelson.

O'Connor, J. (1978) *The Young Drinkers*. London: Tavistock.

Orford, J. (1980) Understanding treatment: controlled trials and other strategies. In *Alcoholism Treatment in Transition* (edited by Edwards, G., and Grant, M.). London: Croom Helm.

Orford, J., and Edwards, G. (1977) *Alcoholism: A Comparison of Treatment and Advice with a Study of the Influence of Marriage*. Oxford: University Press.

Pattison, E. M. (1968) A critique of abstinence criteria in the treatment of alcoholism. *Int. J. Soc. Psychiat.*, **14**, 268-76.

Pattison, E. M. (1976) Non abstinent drinking goals in the treatment of alcoholism. *Arch. Gen. Psychiat.*, **33**, 923-31.

Plant, M. A. (1979) Learning to drink. In *Alcoholism in Perspective* (edited by Grant, M.). London: Croom Helm.

Polich, J. M., Armor, D. J., and Braiker, H. B. (1979) *The Course of Alcoholism: Four Years after Treatment*. Santa Monica: The Rand Corp.

Robinson, D. (1977) Factors influencing alcohol consumption. In Edwards, G., and Grant, M. (Eds), *Alcoholism: New Knowledge and New Responses*. London: Croom Helm.

Stockwell, T., Hodgson, R., Edwards, G., and Rankin, H. (1979) The development of a questionnaire to measure severity of alcohol dependence. *Brit. J. Addition*, **74**, 79-87.

Walen, R. (1953) Wives of alcoholics: four types observed in a family service agency. *Quart. J. Stud. Alc.*, **14**, 632-41.

World Health Organization (1974) Expert Committee on Drug Dependence: Twentieth Report, WHO Tech. Rep. Ser. No. 55.

Personal Meanings
Edited by Eric Shepherd and J. P. Watson
© 1982 John Wiley & Sons Ltd.

Personal meanings and alcoholism survival: translating subjective experience into empirical data

Gloria K. Litman

One of the few statements that can safely be made about alcoholism is that it is a condition characterized by relapse. Treatment may be effective in the short term, but it is the high rate of relapse that is of ultimate concern. Depending on the criteria for outcome, the fact that at least 33 per cent, and more likely 66 per cent, of patients will relapse after treatment, is well recognized. Yet, as an area of research, this phenomenon has been surprisingly neglected until recently.

This chapter will focus on two themes. The first is to show how the politics of alcoholism, the 'collective frame of reference' as it were, acted not only to inhibit research into one of the most important and least understood phenomena of alcoholism, but was also incorporated into the subjective experience of relapse of alcoholics themselves. The second focus of this chapter will be on the process through which my colleagues and I attempted to translate personal meanings into empirical data in an attempt to build up a more general conceptual framework of how individuals treated for alcoholism relapse or survive.

E. M. Jellinek is widely recognized as one of the great pioneers of research into alcoholism. What is not so widely recognized is that many of his major statements about alcoholism as a disease and the phenomena of loss of control were actually obtained from a questionnaire designed by members of Alcoholics Anonymous (AA) and circulated through their official organ. Based on the 98 responses he received, Jellinek concluded:

Loss of control means that as soon as a small quantity of alcohol enters the organism a demand for more alcohol is set up which is felt as a physical demand by the drinker. The drinker has lost the ability to control the quantity once he has started. (Jellinek, 1952)

Loss of control was seen as the 'critical symptom of alcohol addiction' and it was thus that the disease model of alcoholism and the notion that relapse is inevitable once alcohol is ingested in any amount became irrevocably entwined. From Jellinek's point of view, 'loss of control' was a clear-cut model where the first drink acts as a signal to the metabolism of nervous tissue cells so that a strong and compulsive desire is set up for more alcohol. This implies that there is no volition on the part of the alcoholic. Once this metabolic triggering has been set off, relapse is automatic, inevitable, and beyond control. Having collected his data from members of Alcoholics Anonymous, Jellinek thus proceeded to rationalize the AA point of view into what appeared to be scientific findings.

Before I discuss the implications of this notion of loss of control, there is another concept that needs to be examined, and that is the concept of 'craving'.

In 1954, The World Health Organization set up a meeting of experts to discuss physical dependence on alcohol. In this meeting, the concept of craving was stressed as a crucial factor. The experts postulated that there were essentially two types of craving. First, there was physical craving which occurs in alcoholics who have consumed large amounts of alcohol over a protracted period of time. This physical, or 'non-symbolic' craving is manifested by certain symptoms when alcohol is withdrawn. However, a second type of craving was postulated, 'symbolic' craving which was psychological in origin and conceptualized in such terms as an 'urgent and overpowering desire' or 'irresistible urge' to account for relapse after a period of abstinence (Isbell, 1955; Mardones, 1955).

With these two notions, 'loss of control' and 'symbolic' craving, the concept in which alcoholic relapse was conceptualized became petrified. 'Craving' became reified to explain relapse as 'willpower' became reified to explain abstinence. The scientific naïveté of this approach is regrettable. However, there were two important consequences of this kind of thinking. First of all, the stage was set for the political or collective frame of reference to be incorporated into the patients' personal frame of reference, so that they were given a quasi-scientific rationale for construing their world to account for their behaviour. The 'one drink, one drunk' notion became a self-fulfilling prophecy. Once alcohol passed their lips in any form or in any quantity, alcoholics were then doomed to continue drinking without choice or volition. The second consequence of the notions of 'loss of control' and 'symbolic craving' was that there was no need to investigate the phenomenon of relapse. If craving explains the first drink and if 'loss of control' is the explanation for subsequent drinking, then alcohologists could readily persuade themselves that they already understood what was happening and therefore relapse was not a pressing subject for systematic investigation. Therefore, it is not surprising that this crucial area was neglected until fairly recently.

However, in the 1960s, Mendelson and Mello (Mendelson, Mello, and Soloman, 1968) pioneered studies of the use of alcohol by alcoholics in an experimental setting. As a result of their findings, other workers began to question the traditional concepts of alcohol problems and we now have an impressive body of work that challenges some of the most widely held and cherished beliefs about craving, loss of control, and the irreversibility of alcoholism (Sobell and Sobell, 1972).

With this new evidence came the opportunity to question the traditional beliefs about the causes of relapse. In 1976, my colleagues and I began a continuing study of the phenomena involved in relapse. Since it was an uncharted area, we began first with in-depth interviews with patients who had come back to hospital for further treatment. At first, we did not even have a hidden agenda, but we put no time limit on the interviews and there was ample latitude for the patients to cover a wide range of experiences, particularly about coming off drink and then the circumstances and situations which led them to relapse again — and for many patients again and again and again. We were particularly interested as the interviews progressed in how the patients themselves saw the underlying causes of their relapse and to what they themselves attributed the precipitating cause.

What resulted from these interviews was a mass of transcripts containing very personal perceptions, beliefs, experience, and attitudes which somehow we had to translate into empirical research. The emphasis on empirical research is particularly important in the field of alcoholism. For too long, our theories about alcohol problems were 'folk science', i.e. we had a compendium of beliefs, values and ideologies which constituted a body of purported and widely accepted knowledge which had been developed to meet humanitarian and sociopolitical needs, but little had been done to synthesize scientific findings.

From the transcripts of these interviews, we constructed a sentence-completion questionnaire which contained open-ended questions designed to elicit information about:

1. Situations which made it difficult to stay off drink.
2. Situations which were particularly dangerous in that they might precipitate relapse.
3. Social and interpersonal situations prior to relapse.
4. Attitudes, perceptions, and cognitions just prior to relapse.
5. Any coping strategies they may have used in order to avoid relapse.

We sent these questionnaires to 65 patients and former patients of the Maudsley and Bethlem Royal Hospitals. We were surprised to find that people had filled in the questionnaires in such detail. Many continued their answers on the backs of the questionnaires and some even appended additional sheets.

From the interviews and the sentence-completion questionnaires, we developed a more formal questionnaire. Here again, we tried to balance the need to maintain a personal frame of reference with the requirements of larger-scale empirical research. When we designed the formal questionnaire, we incorporated as far as possible the areas, the information, and particularly the language which people had used both in the interviews and the sentence-completion questionnaires.

The formal questionnaire was designed to elicit information on situations which were most dangerous in precipitating relapse; the coping strategies and behaviours which were available to the individual; how effective they perceived these coping behaviours to be; and how dependent on alcohol individuals saw themselves. In order to get as wide a sampling as possible, these questionnaires were given individually to out-patients at the Maudsley Hospital and Withington Hospital in Manchester, and to in-patients at the Bethlem Royal Hospital and Warlingham Park Hospital. We also sent questionnaires to former patients who were definitely known to have abstained from drink for at least six months or more.

At this point we formulated a model of alcoholic relapse which hypothesized that there is an interaction among: (1) situations which are dangerous for the individual in that they may precipitate relapse; (2) the available coping strategies within the individual's repertoire to deal with these situations; (3) the perceived effectiveness of the coping behaviours; and (4) the individual's self-perception and self-esteem and the degree of 'learned helplessness' with which the person views the situation. For example, if a person regards themselves as a helpless victim of their feeling, situation, or personality, they will be less likely to take appropriate and effective action to avoid relapse. On the other hand, if a person learns effective behaviours and coping strategies, this may lead to positive changes in self-perception and self-esteem. Concurrent with these changes is feedback from the social environment. Therefore, the process of altering self-esteem and self-perception is generated from external as well as internal sources.

The analyses of the questionnaires indicated that relapse precipitants or dangerous situations could be summarized by four factors: unpleasant affect, external events, social anxiety, and lessened cognitive vigilance. Coping behaviours could also be summarized into: positive thinking, distraction/substitution, avoidance, and negative thinking. Effectiveness of coping behaviours could be summarized by cognitive control (which included both positive and negative thinking), avoidance, and distraction/substitution. The relapse precipitants were associated with certain styles of coping, with varying degrees of effectiveness (Litman *et al.*, 1977).

When we analysed the differences between relapsers and survivors, we found that there were interesting differences in terms of situations seen to be dangerous, the flexibility of coping behaviour, and the use of cognitive control as an effective coping strategy (Litman *et al.*, 1979).

At this point, we had some information about how people relapse, but we wanted to know much more about how people survive. Therefore, we decided to consult the experts in survival. We interviewed 25 patients who had been successful either in abstaining or controlling their drinking.

This time, we did have a 'hidden agenda', in that we asked about dangerous situations and coping behaviours. However, as before, there was no time limit on these interviews and the people we interviewed had ample latitude to tell us about their own experiences and perceptions.

The interviews were tape-recorded and complete transcripts were examined for key concepts, recurring themes, and individual variation. What we have evolved from these transcripts is a 'conceptual framework for alcoholism survival' (Figure 1).

One key concept that seemed to recur throughout the interviews was what we have called the 'critical perceptual shift'—the point at which the individual is confronted with the choice of either a drastic change in drinking habits and life style, or self-destruction. This crisis point was emphasized by each person we interviewed. Since these were retrospective accounts, either this perceptual shift as we have conceptualized it does occur; or equally plausible, when recounting one's story, there is a need to punctuate one's life, so to speak, to pinpoint for oneself and others the moment of change. This seems to be an individual experience and, from the way it has been described, indicates a dramatic shift regarding the consequences of continuing to drink. 'I couldn't hide anymore. There were no corners left for me to hide in. I had used up every excuse. There were none left.'

The event, the turning point which is recounted as the precipitating cause and commitment to change may not even have been a 'new' or unique event. Mr Q. told us how he realized he was an alcoholic and had to change when he was thrown out of his favourite pub, after he had been dried out several times in detoxification centres. On probing, we found that this was not the first time he had been banned from this pub.

MAINTENANCE OF DRINKING

Defences: denial
          distortion
          projection
Inability to utilize
   feedback from
   environment
Exploitation
   of others
Sees self as
   easily influenced
   by others
Seeking 'reasons'
   to drink
Tentative nature
   of help seeking
   behaviour

CRITICAL PERCEPTUAL SHIFT

Dramatic
perceptual
shift of
self-concept
and life
situation
Habitual
defences
shattered
Depression,
'emptiness',
regression

PERCEPTION OF THE 'HELPER'

'Magical'
qualities of the
helper *in loco
parentis, in loco
dei.*

COMMITMENT

Beginnings of
the restruc-
turing of the
self

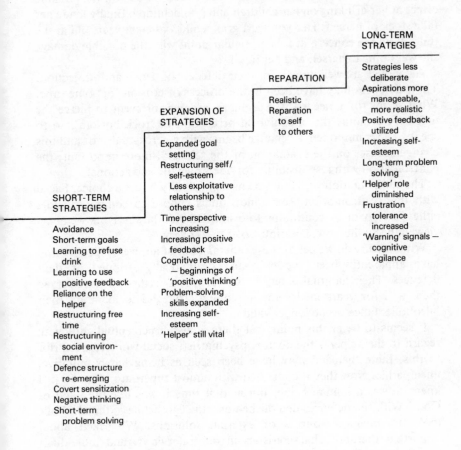

LONG-TERM STRATEGIES

Strategies less
deliberate
Aspirations more
manageable,
more realistic
Positive feedback
utilized
Increasing self-
esteem
Long-term problem
solving
'Helper' role
diminished
Frustration
tolerance
increased
'Warning' signals —
cognitive
vigilance

REPARATION

Realistic
Reparation
to self
to others

EXPANSION OF STRATEGIES

Expanded goal
setting
Restructuring self/
self-esteem
Less exploitative
relationship to
others
Time perspective
increasing
Increasing positive
feedback
Cognitive rehearsal
— beginnings of
'positive thinking'
Problem-solving
skills expanded
Increasing self-
esteem
'Helper' still vital

SHORT-TERM STRATEGIES

Avoidance
Short-term goals
Learning to refuse
drink
Learning to use
positive feedback
Reliance on the
helper
Restructuring free
time
Restructuring
social environ-
ment
Defence structure
re-emerging
Covert sensitization
Negative thinking
Short-term
problem solving

Figure 1   A conceptual framework for alcoholism survival

He had been thrown out of the pub on previous occasions or had left precipitously when he sensed the landlord was about to evict him. Why did this time make an impact on him? Mrs L. recounted how the possible effect of her drinking on her children and grandchildren finally made her take stock of herself. Her youngest grandchild was eight years old at the time. Why the concern at this particular point with the possible damage she was doing to herself and her family?

Alcoholics are well known for their defences of denial and projection. These defences may have been in the process of erosion for some time. What seems to be needed is a dramatic moment or event to pierce the defensive armour, the unequivocal perception of 'rock bottom', so to speak. The commitment to change begins with a perceptual shift and this change focuses on the evaluation of the self and, more important, the confrontation with responsibility for one's own life and actions.

The confrontation with one's own responsibility forces a choice. Faced with this confrontation, some individuals choose to commit suicide, either literally or by continuing to drink. Others, the survivors we interviewed, begin the slow, laborious road to recovery.

What picture do we get of these others? First of all, we see people who have apparently been suddenly and dramatically stripped of their defences. Their habitual defensive styles, which seemed to have served them well for years in developing coping strategies to maintain their 'alcoholic stance', is no longer valid.

It seems to be at this point that there is also a perceptual shift with regard to the helper—the doctor, psychiatrist, social worker, etc. Prior to this, these 'helpers' may have been seen as being harsh, punitive, unempathic. Now they are invested with almost supernatural powers: 'I knew he was a human being, but at that time it was like the hand of God.' With the defences demolished and the ego helpless, the alcoholic looks for magical sources of external solutions. We asked about important therapist characteristics in our interviews, and individuals supplied us with various descriptions—'strong', 'caring', 'someone I respected'. In retrospect, we think these may be irrelevant. It is the patient's investment in the therapist that is most significant. Perhaps this would explain why, given the same 'helper' or series of helpers through relapse after relapse, the help that is sought is finally effective. The therapeutic skill of the 'helper' may not have changed—it is the patient's perception that has changed. The helper is no longer seen as the agent of denial—the person who is asking them to give up their obsession with drink—but as a powerful ally in achieving what has now become *their* goal.

The major short-term coping strategy seemed to be avoidance—

particularly avoidance of external circumstances which were formerly associated with drinking. Some individuals mapped out circuitous routes to avoid passing the pub and avoided all social occasion where drink might be served. Where these occasions could not be avoided, they developed elaborate and lengthy explanations for refusing drink. Avoidance of former drinking companions was another facet of this strategy. Paradoxically, for some patients, the out-patient clinics presented a major threat, since it was there that they were in danger of meeting former drinking companions who were not yet committed to sobriety. This was a particularly dissonant situation since their reliance on the helper was crucial at that time.

Concomitant with avoidance was the need to restructure their lives to fill their leisure time. Since so much of their time had been spent in drinking, many individuals found that free time was a threat to avoiding relapse.

Some individuals developed for themselves sophisticated methods of dealing with strong craving. One coping strategy was what we have called 'negative thinking', i.e. consciously recalling in explicit detail the negative and destructive consequences of their drinking. A form of covert sensitization was another coping strategy used. Some people developed the capacity for reliving somatically withdrawal symptoms, nausea, and vomiting to the point where they actually experienced tremor and nausea.

A few individuals we interviewed seemed to stop at this point and, at least to us, their adaptation seemed fragile, although they had been 'dry' for some years. Others, however, seemed to progress into a further stage where longer-term goals involving career, personal relationships, and so on, were set. Self-esteem seemed to increase and they were able to utilize positive feedback from their environment as a standard by which to evaluate themselves. Concomitantly, a more positive coping strategy seemed to develop, whereby alongside reminders of the negative consequences of their alcoholic drinking, they could now bring in the positive gains of their sobriety. The role of the helper was still seen as important at this stage—both as a reminder of their alcoholic past and as reinforcement for their present.

After several months, or even years, a newer concept seemed to enter into the perceptual scheme: reparation. Realistic reparation involved the acceptance that there were past deeds which simply cannot be undone or changed and that efforts to restore damage must be made in areas where successful reparation is possible: bad debts, relationships with family, friends, and employers who had not dismissed them altogether.

Finally, coping strategies seemed to become less deliberate and more intrinsic. Avoidance of drinking situations became less threatening. Where at an earlier stage elaborate explanations were produced to refuse drink, a simple 'No, thank you' suffices. Tolerance to frustration appears to increase. Long-term goals become more manageable and more realistic. The role of the helper is diminished. Where once they were seen as 'the hand of God', now they are no longer needed. The ability to use and appreciate positive feedback increases, as does self-esteem. At this later stage, negative thinking seemed to be converted into a form of cognitive vigilance. The negative consequences of past alcoholic behaviour are recalled only sporadically and only as reminders 'not to get too cocky'; warnings to prevent regression rather than responses to craving.

The conceptual framework for alcoholism survival is the way we summarized the material we obtained from the interviews. The key concepts emphasized were 'critical perceptual shift', the perception of the helper, the shift in locus of responsibility, and the hypothesis that there may be a gradient of coping strategies that are slowly developed over time. Some of these concepts challenged my own beliefs as a clinician. There were two that were particularly startling. One was the use of avoidance as an effective coping strategy, which challenged my own ideas of confrontation. The second was the 'magical' qualities of the helper. However, I think this may often be the case—that when one assumes the dual roles of clinician and researcher, there may be conflict between one's personal beliefs and one's objectivity.

Once again, we were faced with the task of translating the richness of individual experience into large-scale empirical research. We developed and piloted questionnaires designed to measure the concepts we felt to be most central to the phenomena of relapse and survival. Insofar as possible, we used the information and the language obtained from the interviews. For each key concept, we also included at least one open question, asking about personal experience.

We are now in the process of collecting data in a prospective study to test our hypotheses. The power of our formulation will be tested in three ways. First, it will be tested in terms of how well it predicts behaviour in a prospective study. Second, we hope to know a great deal more about the processes and mechanisms underlying relapse and survival. Third, and perhaps most important, we hope to use our findings to modify our own thinking. Psychologists have hurled charges of petrification and reification at the medical profession for their views on craving and loss of control. Unless we are willing to specify, test and modify our own psychological concepts, we will be equally culpable.

ACKNOWLEDGEMENT

Grateful acknowledgement is made to the Nuffield Foundation for their generous grant which supported part of this work.

REFERENCES

Isbell, H. (1955) Craving for alcohol. *Quarterly Journal of Studies on Alcohol,* **16**, 38–42.

Jellinek, E. M. (1952) The phases of alcohol addiction. *Quarterly Journal of Studies on Alcohol,* **13**, 673–84.

Litman, G. K., Eiser, J. R., Rawson, N. S. B., and Oppenheim, A. N. (1977) Towards a typology of relapse: a preliminary report. *Drug and Alcohol Dependence,* **2**, 157–62.

Litman, G. K., Eiser, J. R., Rawson, N. S. B., and Oppenheim, A. N. (1979) Differences in relapse precipitants and coping behaviours between alcoholic relapsers and survivors. *Behaviour Research and Therapy,* **17**, 89–94.

Mardones, R. J. (1955) 'Craving' for alcohol. *Quarterly Journal of Studies on Alcohol,* **16**, 51–3.

Mendelson, J. H., Mello, N. K., and Soloman, P. (1968) Small group drinking behaviour: an experimental study of chronic alcoholics. In A. Wikler (Ed.), *The Addictive States.* Proceedings of the Association for Research in Nervous and Mental Disease.

Sobell, M. B., and Sobell, L. C. (1972) *Behavioural Treatment of Alcohol Problems.* New York: Plenum Press.

Personal Meanings
Edited by Eric Shepherd and J. P. Watson
© 1982 John Wiley & Sons Ltd.

Personal meanings in cancer

Rosalind C. S. Furlong

Previous contributions to this volume have discussed aspects of the link between personal meanings and effective communication. The accurate perception of personal meanings is of fundamental relevance to communication and, more broadly, to interpersonal relationships. This paper presents the diversity of personal meanings in cancer sufferers and examines some particular barriers to communication which exist. Before doing this, however, let us first consider why it is of importance to understand personal meanings of cancer patients.

RELEVANCE OF PERSONAL MEANINGS IN CANCER

Firstly, understanding and being understood by those in close contact with the cancer patient are means by which his potential social isolation can be reduced. The literature abounds with poignant descriptions of the alienating effect which cancer can have on the sufferer, and a number of studies have found social isolation to be an important factor in the quality of survival. Cobliner (1977) studied factors determining the quality of adjustment in 300 women with gynaecological and breast malignancies. Of the ten factors he suggested which influence adjustment, four could be regarded as social support factors. In particular, inability to confide in key relatives has been identified as a predictor of psychosocial morbidity in studies by Weisman and Worden (1976) and Thomas and Maguire (1980). One study has implicated psychosocial aspects in affecting survival duration also. Weisman and Worden (1975), as part of the comprehensive Omega research project, correlated various psychosocial variables with longevity (in relation to established life expectation for tumour stage and type). They found that among the most significant negative correlations with longevity were hostility towards staff and social withdrawal, both of which could be reduced by greater interpersonal understanding.

Secondly, understaning personal meanings is of importance in clinical management. It is a necessary prerequisite to the assessment of symptoms requiring treatment. An example of this is the description of pain. One person who claims 'I am only troubled by it now and then' may mean that, although severe, most of the time the pain is bearable and they do not want to have to take more pills. Another saying the same words could mean that they only occasionally have pain but worry about it. They would like something to take for it though they hesitate to ask because of its trivial nature. Understanding the true meaning of the remark would give the clinician scope to meet the patient's needs and to treat him effectively and appropriately.

Thirdly, accurate comprehension of personal meanings is vital in cancer research. Investigations of psychological attitudes to cancer in relation to response to treatment or psychosocial morbidity obviously depend upon effective communication of personal meanings. However, apparently objective research on treatment methods can be invalidated if personal meanings are not taken into account. Such therapeutic trials require accurate assessment, and documentation of side-effects which often limit the use of new drugs because of their unpleasant and sometimes deleterious nature. Invalid ratings can occur if the individual variation in meanings is not taken into account. Research methods which rely on self-report questionnaires are prone to inaccuracy in quantification of symptoms as exemplified in the preceding paragraph, while interviewer-rated methods are subject not only to observer bias but to other barriers to staff/patient communication.

Personal meanings of cancer patients, therefore, are not only an important humanitarian consideration but are of relevance to clinical practice and cancer research.

MEANING OF 'CANCER'

The personal meaning which cancer has for any individual depends on a composite of his past experiences and present knowledge of illness in general and cancer in particular, and the way in which his illness threatens valued objects or goals. These personal factors are superimposed on the background of cultural beliefs and are modified by the attitudes of those around him, communicated verbally and non-verbally.

Cultural meaning

Interest is often focused on the meaning of cancer in our society. It still remains synonymous with a death sentence in the minds of the majority of doctors and lay people and death is a universally feared, taboo subject. Death contains elements of both the sacred and the sinister. 'Death, disease and corruption, sin and error, tend to flow together and create an untouchable symbol of life's negation. For almost everyone, the meaning of death is that it is a universal negative, repudiating and nullifying the objectives so sought after in life.' (Weisman, 1972). Death also reflects man's helplessness. What is more, in his own death he effectively experiences the death of all around him and the loss of all that he values. It is, therefore, amazing that adjustment to dying can and does occur, being well documented by Rees (1972) and Kübler-Ross (1973), and that people learn to cope with the dual realities of living and dying.

There are ways, however, in which present-day society views cancer with more dread than death from other causes. It stands out as the prototype of a disease that demands an explanation in more than just medical terms, as though the patient had been singled out for some special misfortune. This is reflected even in medical views as, in a study by Crary and Crary (1974), staff rated cancer as worse, less happy, and more worthless than death. This could be because death itself is a paradox, the conscious mind being unable to conceive of its own negation, and therefore death itself is less distressing in practice than the thought of a prolonged period of dying. This would agree with Hackett and Weisman's findings (1969) in a study comparing patients with heart disease and cancer, all of whom were on the danger list. Both groups had a similar degree of denial and hope for the future, but the cancer group had a higher incidence of psychological morbidity, poorer and more demanding relationships with the medical staff, and a greater need for medication. However, there are other possible reasons for this besides the different ways in which death threatened; for example, it could simply be a response to the chronic progressive illness of cancer compared to the episodic nature of cardiac disease. Whatever the cause, it provides evidence of the distressing effect of being seriously ill with cancer compared with another disease which commonly causes death.

Cancer remains a disease over which medicine still has little control, in contrast with heart disease. The need to find some point of personal influence or control over an illness often supersedes the desire to be objective. This is exemplified in the bargaining phase described by Kübler-Ross (1973) and the way in which, in the absence of aetiological medical explanation, irrational ideas abound. People look for meaning in illness and ask 'Why me?', attributing it to a variety of previous actions, for example eating the wrong sorts of food, or because of some harmful experience like the upheaval of moving house or being hurt by a friend. Bard and Dyk (1956) interviewed 100 patients with cancer and other serious diseases and found that nearly half spontaneously verbalized beliefs about the cause of their illness in such terms of projection of blame or self-blame. Occasionally these beliefs are based on reality; for example, heavy smokers feeling responsible for having lung cancer, but mostly they had no such logical basis. These personal rationalizations can be constructive, giving a sense of security through control of the illness, but may result in personal recriminations, guilt, or unhelpful bitterness.

The other aspect of medical control thought to be lacking in cancer is pain relief. The picture conjured up in many people's minds is of cancer leading inevitably to a painful, lingering death. Although such suffering is no longer necessary with modern methods of pain relief, it will take time before this image is dispelled.

There are some particular ways in which the disease process of cancer takes on a sinister significance. Not only do external growths cause disfigurements, but with internal growths people are seen to be wasting away. Even some treatments for the disease are known to have disturbing visible effects like going bald or becoming hirsute. Disfigurement can lead to a degree of psychic alienation in which the cancer sufferer repudiates identity with his distorted body. It is further increased by feelings of rejection towards the body which is letting him down by wearing out prematurely and, what is more, nourishing its own destructive growth. Such associations make 'cancer' take on a fearful and disturbing meaning in our society.

Individual meaning

For the individual cancer patient, the relevance of cultural concepts of cancer will vary enormously. First and foremost, if he has no idea of the nature of his illness, concepts of cancer will have little bearing on his life other than as a vague threat in the background. Secondly, for those who have had personal contact with a cancer sufferer, this direct experience is likely to take precedence over the indirect collective concepts of society.

Past experiences

The impact of first-hand experiences of cancer varies enormously with the individual. Sometimes it inspires a brave, realistic approach to the illness while in others the association promotes fear and denial. An example of this was the response of a middle-aged electrician with lung cancer whom I saw recently. His mother had died of cancer a few years previously. He described how she had stoically coped with various unpleasant experiences during her decline, remaining a cheerful source of encouragement to her family and dying with dignity. His determination to emulate her gave him a positive aim which sustained him through difficult periods of his illness. In contrast, his wife who also spoke very fondly of her mother-in-law and had coped well with nursing her through the terminal stages, found the reawakening of memories very distressing and could find nothing positive in her past experience from which to draw strength. To the patient, his previous experience of cancer provided him with an example of how to overcome difficulties, while for his wife the same events had left her with a sense of helplessness. Thus one cannot make assumptions about the type of impact that a previous experience will have made on a person from the characteristics of that experience. It is a subjective matter strongly influenced by the personality and attitude of the onlooker.

General experience of illness in the past can accentuate the specific impact of cancer. Unhappy previous encounters with doctors or hospitals cast an unpleasant shadow of apprehension over present medical contact. On the other hand, some people with previous health problems have experienced illness very differently, enjoying being the focus of medical attention or the warmth and security of being looked after. Likewise, a successful outcome to a medical treatment in the past breeds therapeutic optimism for the present condition.

A review of the literature on the influence of past experiences on psychosocial adjustment to cancer yields a wealth of clinical reports but a lack of significant research findings. This contrasts with the variety of studies which show personality characteristics to be potential predictors of psychosocial adjustment, e.g. Morris, Greer, and White (1977), Schonfield (1972), Weisman (1976). It is not surprising, considering the extent to which personality variables will affect the meaning and impact of past events. Furthermore, methodological difficulties of research in this area are considerable (Brown, 1974) and will jeopardize the likelihood of positive findings.

Current experience

The most conclusively researched areas of current experiences of cancer patients have been the unpleasant physical effects of cancer and its treatment. Depression and anxiety are prevalent when physical problems such as pain, nausea, and breathlessness persist (Hinton, 1963). Furthermore, therapy with cytotoxic drugs is associated with psychological morbidity (Cooper et al., 1979) as is radiotherapy (Peck and Boland, 1977) and various surgical procedures (Maguire et al., 1978;

Devlin, Plant, and Griffin, 1971). Some research into personal meanings has been conducted in this latter area of the after-effects of surgery which we will be considering later.

In addition to these distressing physical experiences, being ill with cancer necessitates certain changes which can be understood in terms of potential and actual losses. Marris (1974) developed the idea that any change, even though it might be desirable, has the characteristics of a loss. It creates an internal conflict the expression and resolution of which is akin to the working out of grief in the mourning process. A very simple example of this would be that of acquiring some new clothing; wearing it involves both projecting a new identity and setting aside familiar garments which have been integrated into one's existing self-percept. Thus, any change involving disruption of the familiar pattern of life, however minor, brings with it some degree of loss of security. There ensues a struggle to repair the essential thread of continuity, which consolidates our interpretation of life and re-establishes the predictable pattern on which our security depends. For most people, the onset of illness with cancer represents a major change in life pattern, disrupting their psychosocial equilibrium. Obviously, each patient experiences different degrees of practical change in each area of his life; but also the personal meaning of these changes is unique to the individual, affecting the amount of personal disruption caused by the change and hence the degree of loss and depth of grief.

Marris analysed the types of change into three groups. Firstly, a change can represent a continuity in which the patterns of expectation remain the same. The change involves an increase or a substitution and does not threaten the continuity of outlook or attitude to life. Secondly, a change can be one of growth in which past perspectives are put aside for the new ones, but this process does not necessitate a change of direction or a sense of discontinuity. Finally, a change can represent a loss when a fundamental assumption is shaken or an important object is lost and a new start has to be made in reintegrating life expectations. These three types of change provide a framework for understanding individual meanings of cancer and the concerns which patients express.

Weisman (1979) clarified seven areas of predominant concern: health, self-appraisal, work and finances, family and significant relationships, religion, friends and associates, and existential. Of these, he found that existential concerns were uppermost, i.e. those to do with making sense of life and coping with the unpredictability of its duration. The usual experience is for health deterioration and the existential threat of cancer to represent a loss-type of change in which there is a discontinuity of direction in life. Most people assume that their state of health will remain static and live in the anticipation of life continuing indefinitely. Obviously, contracting a serious illness constitutes a change which demands mourning the loss of a supposedly healthy, secure future. Sometimes for the elderly, neither existential nor health concerns are problematic because developing cancer does little to disrupt the pattern of life. It is seen as one of an increasing number of health problems, consolidating a pattern of steady decline. Death has come to represent a release from suffering and a consummation of relationships, e.g. joining loved ones beyond the grave. In this way, the change can take on the constructive 'growth' form described above and the loss of physical well-being is counteracted by a desired progression. In other age groups it is unusual to see this picture except in the late stages of cancer, when adaptation has enabled dying to be incorporated into the cognitive framework. It is possible that the lack of control for duration of illness, previous health and the personal meaning of health decline explains the range of research findings on age as a factor affecting psychosocial adjustment. One study found it to be better in younger women (Winick and Robbins, 1977); several studies found the opposite (Kent, 1975; Plumb and Holland, 1977); while others failed to find a significant correlation between age and poor adjustment (Schonfield, 1972; Morris, Greer, and White, 1977).

Religious views can modify the appraisal of existential and health concerns. People with a strong belief may view physical suffering as a challenge and death as a necessary step towards a more fulfilled life in the next world. This is borne out by Weisman's (1976) and Hinton's (1975) research findings, that active religious practice correlated positively with lack of distress/depression in cancer patients. It is of interest that in Hinton's study this only applied to those with strong Christian beliefs. Those who professed uncertain beliefs had the highest psychological disturbance, while atheists were intermediate.

There are two ways in which the other areas of predominant concern outlined by Weisman are generated. First, they cover areas in which practical consequences of cancer cause unwelcome changes. For example, giving up work can result in loss of contact with friends and social isolation as well as financial difficulties. Being unwell often deprives people of their independence in practical ways, and can put a strain on close relationships with family and friends. However, adjustment to changes and increased interdependance do furnish opportunities for relationships to grow. In a study by Hinton (1973) the majority of patients with terminal cancer of various types reported that they had been drawn closer to their spouses through the experience.

Ultimately, the extent to which cancer threatens people will depend on what valued activities they have to sacrifice.

The second way in which concerns are generated is through self-esteem and role change. Here again, the personal meaning of the change is of paramount importance. For the person who has always taken the responsibility for decision making at home, the reversal of roles which illness can necessiate results in a major change with discontinuity of life-pattern, while for the naturally dependent person the change is one of increase and no continuity is lost. Giving up work prematurely can occasionally be a growth-type change when retirement is imminent and eagerly anticipated. However, all too often the thought of being unemployable de⁻ls a hard blow to self-esteem. The loss is felt far deeper than the practical consequences when being workless is equated with being worthless.

Another area in which practical difficulties are compounded by ones of self-appraisal is in relation to sexuality. Attention has been focused on this area by Maguire (1978). Up to a third of women with breast cancer were found to develop sexual problems after mastectomy and similar sexual difficulties were found by Krumm (1976) in women treated for cancer of the cervix, and by Devlin, Plant, and Griffin (1971) in men treated surgically for cancer of the rectum. In the latter group of men with colostomies, sexual problems are likely to be due to nerve damage in many instances, but there is also a 23 per cent incidence of moderately severe or severe psychiatric problems indicating the difficulty of adjusting to the change of having a colostomy compared with other types of cancer. The adverse effect of mastectomy on self-esteem has been studied in more detail and illustrates the personal variation in the impact of disfigurement. Sutherland (1967) observed that mastectomy was found to be most devastating for women whose self-esteem was based on beauty and shapeliness, while Woods (1975) noted that the intensity of a woman's reaction to mastectomy depends on her perception of the importance of the breast, with a very large or very small breast size resulting in greater sensitivity. The reaction of the women's partners (McIntosh, 1974) can further contribute to adverse effects on the marital relationships. The result of all these strains is reflected in the findings of Morris et al. (1977), that deterioration in marital relationship after mastectomy was more common (11 per cent) than an improvement in relationship (6 per cent), the opposite of Hinton's findings mentioned above (Hinton, 1973).

There remains a need for the development of counselling services for cancer patients and their families which could maximize the potential for 'growth' changes and facilitate adaptation to the changes of continuity of life-patterns and the loss of valued objects and activities.

COMMUNICATION OF PERSONAL MEANINGS

There can be little doubt that tacit understanding of the personal meanings and experiences of a cancer patient is desirable. To what extent open communication should be an aim, however, remains a matter for debate. Undoubtedly some open exchange of personal meanings is necessary to begin to understand another person. However, people vary considerably in what they choose to talk about and it appears that most cancer sufferers avoid the topic of their illness and prognosis. For example, in Hinton's (1973) study of patients with terminal cancer and their partners mentioned previously, in which the majority reported being drawn closer together and had intimated to Hinton that they knew the diagnosis and the outlook, less than a quarter of the couples had talked about this together. When a situation of open awareness exists, in which all involved share the same information, there is no need to make continual reference to it nor does conversation have to be based within the practical limits that are imposed by the prognosis.

Much of the medical literature on communication in cancer focuses on what doctors tell patients (McIntosh, 1974). Communication between doctor and patient is sometimes viewed as a one-way process, with the doctor discharging his medical responsibilities by dispensing information to the patient. This model may have a place in some impersonal areas of medical practice, but gives a misleadingly inadequate view of the communication potential between staff and patients with malignant illness. Communication involves more than transmitting factual information. An inherent part of it is the expression of feelings and attitudes which reflect relationships between people.

Non-verbal cues are often very expressive and have more impact than the spoken word. Facial movement, eye contact, and the tone of voice all reflect the meaning that a situation holds for a person. In this way relatives and medical staff can either inspire hope and confidence in a cancer sufferer, or impart confusion, anxiety, or suspicion. Particularly the latter situation pertains when there is discordance between optimistic verbal and pessimistic non-verbal cues. There is also a wealth of practical activity that contributes to the cancer patient's understanding of his situation, for example, the urgency with which he was asked to come into hospital, private discussions between the staff and his relatives, his position on the ward, changes of relatives' or doctors' visiting patterns, and evasion of questions (Wilson, 1975). Patients also communicate in a powerful way by non-verbal cues, ranging from the obvious ones of facial expression to possible indirect ones like avoiding making plans for the future.

BARRIERS TO EFFECTIVE COMMUNICATION

Misinterpretation

Non-verbal exchange of personal meanings is non-specific, so that misunderstanding can arise. A patient's frustration expressed as anger can be wrongly interpreted as personal antagonism, while staff's acceptance of his physical deterioration can lead the patient to assume that they are incompetent or uncaring. Silence can indicate reluctance to talk openly on the one hand or fear of offence by broaching the subject on the other. Similarly, if a cancer sufferer is quiet it may indicate the peaceful serenity of acceptance or depressive apathy.

The other way in which misunderstanding can arise is through disparity of medical knowledge. Not only the vocabulary of medicine but the whole concept of normal body function and pathological processes remains a mystery to many non-medical people. Information which is meant to reassure can cause alarm, and conversely the gentle breaking of bad news can be interpreted with false optimism. Specific terminology may assume a wide variety of meanings and lead to a breakdown in effective communication. Furthermore, differences in the past experiences and background of patient, relatives, and medical staff mean that they approach one another with different frames of reference through which to interpret what is expressed. Thus subtle misinterpretations are commonplace.

Practical

Communication does not occur in a vacuum: the practical considerations of time and place play a significant part in limiting or facilitating communication. The lack of privacy in a hospital ward can erect intangible but very real barriers between a patient and his relatives. Emotive subjects are often avoided for fear of becoming tearful in public, while distractions and unpredictable interruptions make it very difficult to talk about things in depth. There are similar constraints on open communication between medical staff and the patient. Ideally there should be scope for private, unhurried interviews but so often, patient contact takes place in a busy outpatient clinic or on a daunting ward round.

The medical hierarchy also imposes a barrier. The team structure is often such that the most senior doctor or nurse with least personal contact with the patient, has the task of giving him information, while those in junior positions who have more opportunity to talk and get to know the patient are restricted in what they can talk about. Even for nursing staff, who may be working in close proximity to the patient throughout the day or night, there can be limits imposed on communication in the form of preoccupation with practical tasks. Sometimes the clinical workload does monopolize staff time, but more often it is the nurses' perception of their role as being just to provide physical care which prevents them giving time to mental and emotional needs.

Emotional

Emotional barriers can reinforce these practical ones in a variety of ways. One obvious emotional pressure on the medical staff is the unpleasantness of being in possession of unwelcome information, particularly if the disease is progressing. In this situation the patient may emotionally cut off from the medical staff also, either feeling let down by the staff for not making him better or somehow feeling that he is failing the staff by not 'doing well' and improving. He may hide or play down a new symptom or not report a poor response to therapy through fear that this may jeopardize his relationship with the staff.

Treating cancer often confronts the doctor with the inadequacies of medical science and thwarts his drive to successfully fight disease. His own fear of death may act as a disincentive to talk openly about such issues as prognosis. Studies have indicated that doctors appear to be more afraid of death than control groups, suggesting that some physicians enter medicine partly because of their need to overcome these fears (Feifel *et al.*, 1967). Whether this is so or not, fear of death is strong in most people, and the doctor's emotional defence may be by holding an unreasonably optimistic view. An example of subconscious forces influencing the physician is given in a study by Brennan (1970). He found a considerable delay in diagnosis and induction of treatment of patients with cancer compared with other conditions presenting with similar symptoms. The physician was more responsible for this than the patient. Brennan concluded that some doctors subconsciously avoid making the diagnosis of cancer, which he attributed to staff reluctance to cope with high-density care needs over long periods of time (although he did not say why other emotional deterrents were not responsible).

Anticipation of the patient's emotional response to frank discussion about the illness may present a further disincentive to open communication.

Staff may feel unable to respond to any emotional needs they discover or unleash. Likewise, the patient may sense staff reluctance or inadequacy to cope with his true thoughts and feelings and hold back from sharing them. This frequently happens between patients and their relatives too. The core reactions that all share are grief and fear. The prospect of separation, both physical and mental, potentially culminating in loss of all contact through death, is inevitably distressing and evokes a wide range of fears, conscious and subconscious. It can lead to withdrawal from close contact not only of staff from patient but of relatives and friends too.

Ethical

Ethical considerations may influence the medical staff's attitude to communication of clinical information of a diagnostic and prognostic type. Views range from one extreme expressed by Henderson (1935), who adheres to the maxim 'do no harm', applying it to mean that patients should never be informed about cancer because the truth might be hurtful. The other extreme, prevalent in the USA where unrestricted communication is usual, is expounded by Wangensteen (1950) and more recently by Wright (1973). The latter focuses on the question 'Have we the right to withhold diagnostic information from adults?', and points out the risks of concealing the truth from patients. This argument could be counteracted by regarding diagnostic information as belonging to the doctor, who therefore has the right to impart it as he sees fit, while the patient's rights pertain to his claim for treatment. The moral error of lying to a patient who asks a direct question is emphasized by Lindahl (1973), and others feel that not giving all the information available is denying the patient the opportunity to make realistic plans both for his material and spiritual wellbeing (Hinton, 1967). Weisman (1972) points out that according to our knowledge of psychological processes, we should share the truth about the serious nature of a diagnosis with an adult because this encourages continuation of viable responsiveness between patient and doctor and fortifies rather than undermines. He eloquently qualifies this, saying 'Truth is not so bitter that it has to be downed in a single gulp or so poisonous that we must avoid it completely.'

Another interesting point is the ethical incongruity of giving diagnostic information to the relatives while withholding it from the patient. Justification for this common practice is usually made on the grounds of having a duty to inform, but considering that it would not be in the patient's best interest to know the information. The influences of the emotional barriers to telling the patient described previously may strongly reinforce ethical considerations combined with a need to involve relatives in the responsibility of information-sharing.

Denial

Denial can serve to separate the patient from those around him, acting as an insurmountable barrier to sharing thoughts and feelings openly. This psychological mechanism is frequently used in adjusting to life-threatening illness. It was observed to be the first of five phases in Kübler-Ross's classical study of emotional reactions to terminal illness (Kübler-Ross, 1973), though in the context of malignant illness these phases are not so clearly defined nor sequential (Glaser and Strauss, 1965). Denial is a means by which a painful portion of reality can be repudiated and reinterpreted. It has been described by Anna Freud (1948) as the final common pathway of other ego defence mechanisms.

Denial has a therapeutic potential in that it can help the person put aside problems which cannot be changed, freeing him to concentrate on those which he can influence. However, Weisman (1972) points out that it can rarely be fully effective as a tension-reducing defence because it is difficult to maintain unless reality-testing is relinquished. He points out that hope can only be achieved through self-acceptance and realistic aspirations. Obviously extensive denial could lead to refusing treatment, avoiding or fearing hospital because of confrontation with the realities of illness or delay in seeking treatment for new symptoms. The usefulness of denial will, therefore, depend on how it is applied.

There are three levels to which denial can pertain: the facts of the disease's existence, the disease implications for the present and future, and the underlying threat of extinction. Denial of the last can be the means of continuing a full life while denial of the first could be life-threatening in its consequences. The variation in effects of denial when applied at different levels could be one cause for the conflicting research findings on the relationship between denial and adaptation to illness. Weisman (1976), in a study of 163 cancer patients, found denial to be a vulnerability factor. In particular, patients who fluctuated between acceptance and denial were more distressed than either persistent deniers or non-deniers. In contrast, Bard and Waxenburg (1957) demonstrated that women after a radical mastectomy who denied that they had been treated for a tumour or cancer, had less post-operative psychogenic invalidism than those who acknowledged it. A recent study by Greer, Morris, and Pettingale (1979) in which psychological response to the diagnosis of cancer at three months post-operatively was related to outcome five years later, found that recurrent-free survival was significantly more common among patients who had initially reacted to cancer by denial or who had a fighting spirit, than among those with attitudes of stoic acceptance or helplessness and hopelessness. The study by Gottheil, McGurn, and Pollak (1979) of cancer patients, some of whom clearly knew their diagnosis and others who were unaware, found that those who did not appear to know (i.e. were potential deniers) lived longer only if they were disengaged, i.e. were not actively involved in the world around them; if they were engaged and did not know, they died sooner. The converse was found among those who were known to be aware that they had cancer.

Another possible cause of these varied results is the difficulty of effectively measuring denial. Firstly, denial is often a fluctuating phenomenon, alternating with periods of acceptance. This was taken into account in both Weisman's and Gottheil's work, but Greer's study relied on a one-off interview. Secondly, the personal interaction between those assessing denial and the patient adds a further complication. It is not uncommon for a patient to exhibit denial of cancer to medical staff while openly acknowledging it to an uninvolved stranger or a close friend and confidant. Moreover, people who value their privacy highly may choose not to disclose the extent of their awareness to anyone else.

Finally, the question of denial of illness is complicated by the dynamic of affirmation of health. This is fascinatingly expounded by Beisser (1979) using a four-cell paradigm.

	Affirm	Deny
Health		
Illness		

He points out the way in which the medical profession is orientated towards the illness dimension and tends to ignore that of health. The patient's illness is the point of encounter with medical staff and therefore assumes a degree of importance to them that may not be shared by the cancer sufferer. From the patient's perspective, life may be focused on his ability to engage in worthwhile activities and fulfil valued roles, and affirmation of health assumes greater significance than affirmation of illness. When indifference to illness and positive attitudes to health are interpreted as denial, an oversimplification is made which gives a false picture of the underlying psychological mechanism; thus a fundamental failure in the sharing of personal meanings can result in confusing research findings and misunderstandings between cancer patients and their 'health' professionals.

CONCLUSION

Confrontations with disease and death are fundamental aspects of our human existence. They present us with a profound challenge in that they undermine the very substance of our lives. Our response to this challenge can be one of retreat ending in withdrawal from life, or one of surmounting the difficulties encountered, giving a sense of achievement and fulfilment. Suffering from cancer can bring life into a new perspective, in which superficial things pale into insignificance and the more profound aspects of life are highlighted. Thus it can provide a stimulus to channel energy into more worthwhile directions and can lead to a period of life which is fulfilling and satisfying. The effects of these fresh insights into life and sharing them with others can be enriching for both the cancer sufferer and those around him, furnishing opportunities for drawing closer to others through the giving and receiving of help and encouragement. This scope for developing and deepening relationships is dependent on the spoken or unspoken sharing of experiences, for which understanding personal meanings provides the key.

The extent of the potential barriers to sharing personal meanings between the cancer patient and those around him are considerable, and yet there are few which cannot be overcome. If priority is given to listening to one another and thinking about the implications of words and actions, mutual understanding comes within reach. Furthermore, facing the emotions generated and sharing them honestly can provide the necessary strength and support to cope with close contact with each other and come to terms with our own experience of cancer.

REFERENCES

Bard, M., and Dyk, R. B. (1956) The psychodynamic significance of beliefs regarding the cause of serious illness. *Psychoanalytical Review*, **43**, 146–62.

Bard, M., and Waxenberg, S. E. (1957) Relationship of Cornell Medical Index responses to postsurgical invalidism. *Journal of Clinical Psychology*, **13**, 151–3.

Beisser, A. R. (1979) Denial and affirmation in illness and health. *American Journal of Psychiatry*, **136**(8), 1026–30.

Brennan, M. J. (1970) The cancer gestalt. *Geriatrics*, **25**, 96–101.

Brown, G. W. (1974) Meaning, measurement and stress of life events. In Dohrenwend, B. S., and Dohrenwend, B. P. (Eds), *Stressful Life Events, Their Nature and Effects*. New York: John Wiley & Sons, pp.217–43.

Cobliner, W. G. (1977) Psychosocial factors in gynaecological or breast malignancies. *Hospital Physician*, **10**, 38.

Cooper, A. F., McArdle, C. S., Russell, A. R., and Smith, D. C. (1979) Psychiatric morbidity associated with adjuvant chemotherapy following mastectomy for breast cancer. *British Journal of Surgery*, **66**, 362.

Crary, W. G., and Crary, G. C. (1974) Emotional crises and cancer. *Cancer*, **24**, 36–9.

Devlin, B. H., Plant, J. A., and Griffin, M. (1971) Aftermath of surgery for anorectal cancer. *British Medical Journal*, **3**, 413–18.

Feifel, H., Hanson, S., Jones, R., and Edwards, L. (1967) Physicians consider death. *Proceedings of 75th Annual Convention of American Psychological Association*, **2**, 201–2.

Freud, A. (1948) *The Ego and the Mechanisms of Defence* (trans. Bains, C.). London: Hogarth Press.

Glaser, B. G., and Strauss, A. L. (1965) *Awareness of Dying*. Chicago: Aldine Publishing Co.

Gottheil, E., McGurn, W. C., and Pollak, O. (1979) Awareness and disengagement in cancer patients. *American Journal of Psychiatry*, **136**, 632–6.

Greer, S., Morris, T., and Pettingale, K. W. (1979) Psychological response to breast cancer: effect on outcome. *Lancet*, **1**, 931–2.

Hackett, T. P., and Weisman, A. D. (1969) Denial as a factor in patients with heart disease and cancer. *Annals of the New York Academy of Sciences*, **164**, 802–17.

Henderson, L. J. (1935) Physician and patient. *New England Journal of Medicine*, **212**, 819–23.

Hinton, J. M. (1963) The physical and mental distress of dying. *Quarterly Journal of Medicine*, **32**, 1–21.

Hinton, J. (1967) *Dying*. Aylesbury, England: Penguin Books.

Hinton, J. M. (1973) Bearing cancer. *British Journal of Medical Psychology*, **46**, 105–13.

Hinton, J. M. (1975) The influence of previous personality on reaction to having terminal cancer. *Omega*, **6**, 95–111.

Kent, S. (1975) Coping with sexual identity crises after mastectomy. *Geriatrics*, **30**, 145–6.

Krumm, S. K. (1976) Changes in sexual behaviour following radiation therapy for carcinoma of the cervix. Unpublished thesis, University of Missouri.

Kübler-Ross, E. (1973) *On Death and Dying*. New York: Macmillan.

Lindahl, J. W. S. (1973) Letter, *British Medical Journal*, **4**, 297.

Maguire, P. (1978) The psychological effects of cancers and their treatments. In *Oncology for Nurses and Health Care Professionals. 2* (Ed. Tiffany, R.). London: George Allen and Unwin, Ch. 1, pp.13–41.

Maguire, G. P., Lee, E. G., Bevington, D. J., Kuchemann, C. S., Crabtree, R. J., and Cornell, C. E. (1978) Psychiatric problems in the first year after mastectomy. *British Medical Journal*, **1**, 963–5.

Marris, P. (1974) Loss and change. *Reports of the Institute of Community Studies*. London: Routledge & Kegan Paul.

McIntosh, J. (1974) Processes of communication, information seeking and control associated with cancer: a selective review of the literature. *Social Science and Medicine*, **8**, 167–87.

Morris, T., Greer, H. S., and White, P. (1977) Psychological and social adjustment to mastectomy. *Cancer*, **40**, 2381–7.

Peck, A., and Boland, J. (1977) Emotional reactions to radiation treatment. *Cancer*, **40**, 180–4.

Plumb, Marjorie M., and Holland, J. (1977) Comparative studies of psychological function in patients with advanced cancer. I. Self-reported depressive symptoms. *Psychosomatic Medicine*, **39**, 264–76.

Rees, W. Dewi (1972) The distress of dying. *British Medical Journal*, **3**, 105–7.

Schonfield, J. (1972) Psychological factors related to a delayed return to an earlier life-style in successfully treated cancer patients. *Journal of Psychosomatic Research*, **16**, 41–7.

Sutherland, A. M. (1967) Psychological observations in cancer patients. *International Psychiatry Clinics*, **4**, 75–92.

Thomas, C., and Maguire, P. (1980) Markers of psychiatric morbidity after mastectomy. (In preparation)

Wangensteen, O. H. (1950) Should patients be told they have cancer? *Surgery*, **27**, 944–7.

Weisman, A. D. (1972) *On Dying and Denying*. New York: Behavioral Publications.

Weisman, A. D. (1976) Early diagnosis of vulnerability in cancer patients. *American Journal of Medical Sciences*, **27**, 187–96.

Weisman, A. D. (1979) *Coping with Cancer*. New York: McGraw-Hill.

Weisman, A. D., and Worden, J. W. (1975) Psychosocial analysis of cancer deaths. *Omega*, **6**, 61–75.

Weisman, A. D., and Worden, J. W. (1976) The existential plight in cancer: significance of the first 100 days. *International Journal of Psychiatry in Medicine*, **7**, 1–15.

Wilson, J. M. (1975) Communicating with the dying. *Journal of Medical Ethics*, **1**, 18–72.

Winick, L., and Robbins, G. F. (1977) Physical and psychologic readjustment after mastectomy. *Cancer*, **39**, 478–86.

Woods, N. F. (1975) Influences on sexual adaptation to mastectomy. *Journal of Obstetric, Gynaecologic and Neonatal Nursing*, **4**, 33–7.

Wright, C. (1973) Personal view. *British Medical Journal*, **4**, 45.

Personal Meanings
Edited by Eric Shepherd and J. P. Watson
© 1982 John Wiley & Sons Ltd.

Life with artificial organs: renal dialysis and transplantation

R. M. Rosser

INTRODUCTION

Yea, the darkness hideth not from thee; but the night shineth as the day: the darkness and the light are both alike to thee.
For thou has possessed my reins [kidneys]: thou hast covered me in my mother's womb.
I will praise thee; for I am fearfully and wonderfully made . . .
(Psalm 139), Verses 12, 13, and 14. Authorized Version.)

Readers of the Old and New Testaments and the Talmud will be familiar with the Hebraic concept of the kidneys as containers of passion, identity, and wisdom (Preuss, 1978). The Chinese believed that the kidneys controlled the spittle, the bones, and the will and were the enemy of the heart, which controlled the spirit.

Renal surgery was particularly dreaded on rational grounds. Hippocrates rejected it as unethical because of the high risk. In 1474, the successful operation took place on the archer Bagnadette, who agreed to surgery for his renal calculus to secure his release from the sentence of hanging (Herman, 1973). A recent practice has been the removal of non-functioning kidneys prior to transplantation, particularly in the presence of chronic infection or hypertension. This practice has now been called into question (Bennett, 1976), but it was striking that some patients resisted this intervention despite cogent arguments by their physicians and lack of rational counter-arguments. To speak to our patients, we need to understand their apparently irrational feelings about the importance of their non-functional organs.

Adaptation to renal failure confronts the patient and the medical team with many of the problems discussed in this collection of papers on Personal Meanings. Barriers to understanding between patients and staff have caused concern (Werztel *et al.*, 1977). The patient who lives with renal failure, like the patient who lives with cancer, confronts a

159

life-threatening illness. Suicide and the decision to withdraw from treatment have taxed nephrologists and some argue that all patients should be told from the beginning that they will be helped to an easeful death should they wish to withdraw from treatment; a form of passive euthanasia.

Two methodological issues are central to a study of personal meanings. Firstly, can we devise a notation which disentangles the subject's and the observer's inner worlds and represents the subject's system of meaning succinctly and accurately? Secondly, whether or not we have such a notation, can we aggregate personal meanings so that we can make quantified generalizations with minimal loss of information about the individual? In nephrology, little attention has been paid to the first issue, and my descriptions of cases are therefore purely clinical. The second issue of aggregation *has* been examined, and is discussed in the later section of this paper.

PSYCHIATRIC ASPECTS OF RENAL DIALYSIS AND TRANSPLANTATION

The literature has been reviewed comprehensively by Czackes and De Nour (1978) and condensed by Salmons (1980). Data are difficult to evaluate because sampling methods are rarely described and comparisons with patients with other chronic illnesses and their families are almost non-existent. Furthermore, there is no consensus on many important issues. I describe below the normal processes of treatment and adaptation, and some forms of maladaptation.

Dialysis

Most patients on long-term dialysis have renal failure, although the treatment has been suggested for many other conditions (Kolff, 1978). I shall confine my observations to chronic renal failure since only this condition leads to permanent machine-dependence. Its prevalence may be as high as 19 per 100 000, and of each 19, 4 people might need dialysis (McCormick and Navarrow, 1973). The UK is low in the international league for providing this, and despite the diminution of explicit rationing, some patients remain untreated. Some suddenly find themselves on long-term dialysis, whereas others start this treatment after many years of chronic renal failure, during which they have developed fantasies and fears about it. Dialysis occurs for a period of roughly 20 hours in two or three sessions per week. Patients begin in a hospital unit, but in the UK, they or their relatives are usually trained

to maintain and run the machine at home and rehousing may be
needed.

Adaptation to dialysis

Normal adaptation. There has been much concern about the quality of
life on dialysis (*B.M.J.* Editorial, 1980) and discussion about who should
be dialysed (Moore, 1971). The new entrant to the dialysis unit has
negotiated selection hurdles but now confronts the certainty of life-long
imperfect health, reduced life expectancy, physical deprivations, and
emotional demands. The normal response is a transient period of denial,
following by depression and anxiety. If these do not occur in the first six
months, maladjustment may follow. In spite of the practical rearranging
and psychological work involved, in most patients despair is rapidly
replaced by a more coherent sense of loss of physical health,
independence, and familiar social roles. This can be worked through and
lead to constructive plans and cautious optimism. In only some 30 per
cent of patients do psychiatric symptoms persist (Farmer, Snowden, and
Parsons, 1979), although they may recur from time to time. Conflicting
demands that the patient should depend on the machine and the staff and
yet become sufficiently competent to dialyse himself and return to work
are often discussed in the literature, but many patients seem to
understand this dilemma and resolve it. Such dependency conflicts are
often invoked as causes of psychosexual dysfunction in addition to the
feeling that the body has been mutilated. Libido is also diminished by
debility and metabolic and endocrine disturbances, but it is notable that
psychosexual problems are also common in the healthy spouse.
Friendships between patients on the dialysis unit tend to be cautiously
distant and psychic withdrawal may facilitate survival (Foster, Cohn,
and McKegney, 1973): therefore it is not obvious that attempts at group
therapy are well-advised (Lubell, 1976). The syndrome of survivor guilt
has been described in patients on home dialysis, but in my experience the
intense depersonalization which characterized the survivors at Hiroshima
(Lifton, 1967) does not occur.

It is the relatives rather than the patients who seek one another's
support, for example through fund-raising activities which assuage
their feelings of helplessness. Many of the families of dialysis patients
seem to adapt in similar stages to those seen in the patient. However, relatively little is known since families commonly resist enquiry about their emotional well-being. Children seem to adapt and
to function better at school if they are encouraged to help with
dialysis.

Knowledge of the cause of renal failure can contribute to individual and family stress. Analgesic nephropathy, for example, may be completely denied, or may evoke intense self-blame. Polycystic disease, transmitted by an autosomal dominant gene, may be denied by the family, whilst the patient may feel guilt or anger and become depressed (Maryinay and McKegney, 1978).

Maladjustment to dialysis. Some patients fail to reformulate their lives in a meaningful way, generally because of previously fragile adjustment. Chronic or recurring depression is the commonest symptom of maladjustment, accompanied either by loss of purpose and volition and mild depersonalization, or by suicidal ideas. Other symptoms include aggression and violence towards the family or the machine; psychological dependence, commonly on prescribed analgesics and tranquillizers; failure to comply with diet or other aspects of treatment including dialysis itself; or serious requests to withdraw from treatment or suicide attempts.

Abram, Moore, and Westervelt (1971), in a questionnaire survey of American dialysis centres, estimated that the suicide rate was 400 times that of the normal population. High rates have recently been reported in Europe and the UK (Haenel, Brunner, and Battegay, 1980; Gomez, 1980). In Abram's study, active suicide, withdrawal from dialysis, 'accidental' haemorrhage, and failure to comply with diet and fluid restriction were considered together. I think this is a mistake since these behaviours reflect different mental phenomena. Active suicide seems to be much less common than accident proneness, and non-compliance is almost universal at some stage. Many patients refuse to dialyse from time to time, fail to take medication, or infringe dietary rules, often denying objective evidence of their behaviour. Whereas active suicide tends to be either depressive or apparently rational behaviour, self-injury is explicitly irrational and commonly reflects premorbid personality traits.

As a group, dialysis patients have been shown to have more idealized concepts of how they would like to be than have normal controls (Clarke, Hailstone, and Slade, 1979). Non-compliance has been attributed to the patient's belief that his actions do not affect his mental condition, as indicated by external orientation revealed by measures of locus of control (Goldstein and Reznikoff, 1971). It has been suggested that psychotherapy, if possible with such patients, should aim to increase their internal orientation, so that they search within themselves for meaning and cause. Whether they should be confronted with the option of withdrawing from dialysis remains contentious (McKegney and

Lange, 1971). Poll and De Nour (1980) found no correlation between locus of control and duration of dialysis, and therefore suggested that a shift from internal to external locus of control occurs prior to dialysis, during the stage of resignation to chronic renal failure. Of their sample, 48 per cent abused diet and 44 per cent achieved poor work adjustment. Locus of control was negatively correlated with compliance with diet, vocational rehabilitation, and acceptance of disability. Another predictor of poor adjustment and survival is formal psychiatric illness (Farmer *et al.*, 1979).

Transplantation

Policy varies, but the question of transplantation is raised by most patients or their doctors. With a successful transplant, patients can return to a normal diet, and have greater freedom to travel, but the price includes immunosuppressive drugs, which are disfiguring and increase the risks of infectious and malignant diseases and psychoses. These patients tend to be in generally better health and may be less anaemic and uraemic, with fewer psychosexual problems and improved fertility (Procci, Hoffman, and Chatterjee, 1978), but the transplant may fail at once, suddenly at a later stage, or chronically and intermittently. In Europe, the average immediate mortality is 25 per cent, which compares unfavourably with survival on home dialysis.

Adaptation to transplantation

Normal and abnormal adaptation to transplantation have not been systematically described. Psychiatric assessment of entrants to dialysis is common and patients on hospital-unit dialysis provide the researcher's ideal population: alert, trained in compliance and confined to the unit for many hours per week. Completing psychosocial questionnaires is almost a feature of adjustment to dialysis! By contrast, transplantation occurs hastily, sometimes after a series of 'false alarms', outside routine hours, on patients who may have passed out of the hands of researchers and psychiatrists. Typically, the patient has been tolerating dialysis for years in the hope of a transplant, which comes to represent a panacea, although a few are transplanted as a last hope, because they failed to adapt to dialysis. Family members may have volunteered or been approached. The family will have produced its short-list of candidates from which the medical team selects a donor primarily on immunological and other medical criteria. If no living donor is available, the patient waits in the queue for a cadaver kidney. Post-operatively he may be barrier-nursed in a special ward with restricted access by visitors and placed on steroids and other immunosuppressives.

The well-adjusted patient tolerates the social and sensory deprivation, and his Cushingoid appearance. He returns gratefully to his welcoming family, unquestioningly confident that the right donor volunteered for the right reasons. He returns to work and reports improvements in his marriage. This capacity for coping seems surprisingly common.

Some 20 per cent of patients may be diagnosed as having a neurotic illness following transplantation. More notably, some 10 per cent may develop psychotic illness in which steroids may be a more important causative factor than psychological conflicts (Penn *et al.*, 1971). The new kidney lies superficially in the groin and almost all patients are preoccupied at first with its survival and the risks of trauma to it.

Muskin (1971), in a thoughtful paper, described stages in the patient's reaction to the 'emotional transplant'. These were: the foreign-body stage, the stage of partial incorporation, the stage of complete incorporation, and a fourth stage of regression to a foreign-body reaction. In the first stage, patients feel the new organ to be odd and in need of protection; a few patients isolate themselves from this and all other emotional responses. Gradually, less energy is consumed in involvement with the new organ and it seems to be completely integrated with the internal images of the patient's body and self. A procedure such as a biopsy may precipitate regression to a sense of isolation from the kidney. The new kidney is commonly fantasized as the patient's baby, in need of protection. Identification with the live donor, or even with the fantasized cadaver donor, is sometimes manifest in transformations of the patient's personality, and in sexual and moral conflicts. The potentially symbiotic relationship with the donor may be accepted with gratitude, but can also be denied, resented, or struggled against, particularly by the adolescent recipient. Religious and 'psychic' experiences are common: Viederman (1974) saw internal representation of the body image as relatively unimportant, but emphasized the need for changes in many aspects of the patient's representational world.

The family's decision to donate a kidney is often precipitous (Fellner and Marshall, 1970) and communication within the family may be poor (Summers and Klein, 1972). The donor and other relatives may therefore be insufficiently adjusted to support the recipient, especially if the transplant fails. Chapman and Cox (1977) studied patterns of pain, anxiety, and depression pre- and post-operatively in abdominal surgery and in donors and recipients in renal transplantation. Donors showed a surprising lack of correlation between trait anxiety and other psychological variables, suggesting substantial changes in the personality of the donor as a consequence of the decision and act. This was not found in recipients, but both donors and recipients showed more extreme pain responses than abdominal surgery patients.

Child dialysis and transplant patients have to contend with extra stresses, including impaired growth and delayed sexual maturation. Even more than adults, they may acquire the status of family and community heroes and have difficulty in accepting a more mundane role later. The chances of physical survival are high, but severe emotional reactions, and social withdrawal, are reported to be common (Bernstein, 1971; Khan, Herndon, and Ahmadin, 1971).

ONTOLOGICAL DILEMMAS

Psychosocial work devoted to patients on dialysis and transplantation programmes seems disproportionately high compared with the prevalence of psychiatric morbidity. One reason for this may be the nature of the difficulties these patients describe. Some present with crises of meaning, which confront the medical team with questions of the kind discussed in this book. Thoughtful and sophisticated patients may lose all sense of meaning and volition. Others are confused by new richness of meaning, and find dialysis a maturing, changing experience. The machine may be invested with good or bad meanings. It may become meaningless and invisible and hence be ignored to the point of danger or it may be felt to drain the patient of vitality. From a collection of some 50 such cases seen over the past five years, I have selected seven whose relationship with the dialysis machine or the transplanted kidney provoked a dilemma of being.

CASE HISTORIES

I The machine as persecutor

It is not surprising that the machine commonly becomes a container of projected persecutory internal objects.

A married man, an Indian Mauritian factory worker aged 50, with five teenage children, was referred after attempting to smash a dialysis machine in the hospital unit. He experienced dialysis as yet another example of life-long discrimination against him as a member of a minority group, a feeling which was reinforced by the news that his tissue-type was rare and he probably faced a long wait for a transplant.

He felt that dialysis undermined his role as head of the household. He punished his 13-year-old daughter's normal rebelliousness with beatings so severe that she was taken into the care of the local authority. He was depressed, but improved sufficiently on medication to endure several years of dialysis. He continued to experience the machine as a persecutor, but eventually he received a cadaver transplant which was internalized as a good object. He adapted well, returned to work, and resumed his role as head of a traditional Indian household.

II   The machine as a good mother

A housewife aged 28 had been dialysing at home for seven years, with occasional admissions to the unit on medical grounds. She said she had no children, 'just the dog'. A quiet but attractive and flirtatious woman, she had few complaints, had never been depressed, and seemed well adjusted to dialysis. She was an orphan and an only child, brought up in straitened circumstances by a strict aunt. She was referred to me as an emergency on the morning after her transplant. I was asked to come at once as 'she had gone quite mad and must be psychotic'. She was wandering round the ward, staring into the distance and seemed to be in a fugue state. The picture was one of hysterical dissociation. She was incapable of the gratitude which is deemed proper in the recipient of a long-awaited and well functioning transplant.

Fortunately, I had chatted to her in the past and she responded in the next few days to comments about how much she and the dog were missing one another. She became depressed and eventually began the work of mourning the loss of her kidney machine, the close links with the unit, and all that the life on dialysis entailed. For her, the medical attention and her status of invalid had 'legalized' the enactment of her craving for unconditional love and dependency. A supportive husband and caring village community helped to give her the parenting and child role she had missed.

The machine had played a variety of benevolent roles in her life. As a life source, she depended on its as a child on its mother, and she felt severed from it by the transplant. The machine had always been there, and was felt to share and understand her feelings; but she also had to care for it and continued to do so after the transplant, visiting it daily, sitting by it and mourning the lost bond, as if it had become an ageing parent. She was an obsessional person, and had adhered to diet and medication. The discipline of practical self-care seemed to have served as a lesson in care and acceptance of the psychic self.

All these good meanings of what had apparently been a terrible ordeal became obvious as she faced and worked through the loss of the machine. Only then could the kidney be experienced and incorporated and a meaningful new life built up. The kidney was experienced as a good object and the new life soon focused on a baby daughter. I feel that she was probably better equipped for the role of mother because of the maturing experience of dialysis.

In formerly well-adjusted patients, depression may be precipitated by removal of the machine from the home. They then present with atypical grief reactions. In other more intractable cases, the problem is loss of the sick role, as described in the next case history.

III   The machine as a sickness certificate

This patient was referred as an emergency, with palpitations occurring three months after the successful transplantation of a kidney from one of his brothers. Aged 31, he had been married for nine years and had no children. He was a secretive man, depressed and anxious. It emerged that he had decided to have a transplant after four years of excellent adjustment to dialysis, because he had heard this led to increased fertility. Three months later, he was ostensibly bitter that his wife had not conceived. Unfortunately, the principal cause of the couple's infertility was his spina bifida, which had led to retention of urine, recurrent renal infection and hence renal failure, but also to retrograde ejaculation and feelings of sexual inadequacy. Although the eldest son, he had been fostered in his teens, because his family could not tolerate his urinary incontinence. Receiving a kidney from a younger brother was an intolerable symbol of dependency and impotence. Physically better, he found himself unable to continue his job as a painter and decorator. He looked back wistfully on his years on dialysis as 'the best time in my life'. The machine had been a palpable symbol of his entitlement to the permanent sick role, his family had been sympathetic, and he coped magnificently. His brother's sacrifice ruined all this and for the first time in his life, he was expected to be well. Surgeons and psychiatrists were naïvely optimistic about their abilities to help with the infertility. His wife felt she could give up work. The patient passively failed to co-operate. However, his wife, to her delight, did become pregnant. The patient's anxiety was replaced by lethargy, and through an alcoholic haze, he gloomily anticipated the role of father, for which he was so ill-prepared. The hope that keeps him going is for the rejection of his transplant and a return to the 'good life' on the machine.

IV   The magic machine

This patient, aged 32, was a married woman with two young children. She was referred because she ignored her fluid restrictions and was eventually admitted to hospital, hypertensive and in heart failure. She denied overdrinking, went home and returned in coma following a cerebral haemorrhage. For her, the artificial kidney was a wish-fulfilling machine, exempting her from all adult responsibilities and she became more convinced of this when she made a full recovery from the stroke. A member of a large and delinquent family, she had drifted through life never recognizing the consequences of her own actions. The likelihood of her survival on dialysis seemed minimal and with reluctance, the decision was taken to transplant her. Her brother, awaiting trial on a charge of grievous bodily harm, was granted bail to act as donor.

Then a remarkable change occurred. After the operation, the patient was alone for the first time in her life. Such solitude taxes the most reclusive patient; for this gregarious extrovert it was a revelation. I sat with her from time to time as she became depressed, but also thoughtful, even contemplative. All the mourning of her loss of health, previously denied, was worked through now. I had feared that the new kidney would be expected to survive by magic, but this did not happen. She complied with the strict post-operative regime, took her steroids and became a 'good' patient. The new concept of herself as an individual, with an identity apart from her family and neighbours intrigued her, and she adapted to her Cushingoid appearance, saying 'it suits me to be fat; I'm a comfortable sort of person'. Despite maturity and psychodynamic change, she returned home to renewed marital contentment. But the family did not change. The donor told the judge about his sacrifice. The judge took this courageous act as evidence that he had changed for the better and his sentence was suspended! The donor thought justice had been done. He explained to me 'I'm not a bad man really; I only rob from the rich.'

V   The invisible machine: the escape from psychic reality

A librarian, married to a school-teacher, was the slightly built father of three girls. He had been treated with fair success for severe diabetic retinopathy, but then needed dialysis. Soon after this, his youngest daughter was found to be diabetic. A kind, humble, and scholarly man, he none the less made the nurses feel inferior, by attempting to draw them into intellectual debate. In discussion with me, he focused on my research, suggested obscure references and classical allusions, and fended off my emotional contact.

This intelligent man behaved very stupidly. It proved impossible to train him to dialyse himself because he showed no interest or sense of responsibility and made the most elementary mistakes. He even accidentally walked into the machine and knocked it over, seeming selectively blind to it. The nurses and his family seemed to function as containers of his split-off emotions, but he identified with the machine which remained devoid of identity like himself. He never adjusted to dialysis and was unable to work again. He gradually became more withdrawn, and semi-stupor, probably depressive, preceded death.

VI The machine as a threat to autonomy

A 46-year-old mother of five unruly young men was a state registered nurse and, since the onset of her kidney disease, she had worked in a renal unit. The cause of renal failure was analgesic nephropathy, i.e. it was a consequence of prolonged self-medication for minor discomfort. This never came up in discussion. An orphan, reared in a convent, she was married to a quick-tempered but reasonably supportive Irish man. She did not believe she needed dialysis and would sometimes refuse to go on the machine. Reality played into her fantasies, since her residual renal function fluctuated and she managed without dialysis for some months.

She became accident prone, subject to frequent falls and clotting or bleeding from her shunt. She abused dietary and fluid restrictions, demanded to be discharged from hospital, took high doses of tranquillizers, and exceeded the prescribed dose of anti-depressives. During dialysis one day, she developed blindness which was probably hysterical and from which she recovered. Soon after this she developed the rare form of pseudo-dementia described by Ganser (1898) in which she described visual hallucinations and gave approximate answers.

Eventually she coped by selling her small, easily run home near the hospital and buying a decaying mansion 70 miles away, to convert into a nursing home where she and her staff nurses would care for elderly and infirm patients. She drove to the hospital twice per week for dialysis. Some months later she became exhausted and distressed, took a little extra diazepam, fell, developed a subdural haematoma and died.

Complex organic factors contributed to her mental state. In psychodynamic terms, her life can be seen as a desperate and inadequate attempt to mother herself in her children and patients, coupled with true self-neglect and injury, consequent on her early emotional deprivation. Dependence on the machine was intolerable to her, and she could only contemplate it by moving far away from the hospital and taking on burdens which were almost bound to lead to catastrophe.

VII   The machine as a missing link

A 23-year-old unmarried woman worked as hospital laboratory technician. The donor of her transplant was her unmarried mother, her only close relative. This functioned poorly. She was maintained on high doses of steroids and frequently admitted to hospital with threatened rejection, sometimes needing dialysis. She was intensely self-conscious about her Cushingoid appearance and led an isolated life. I saw her weekly, but she became anxious about the exclusion of her mother, who started to sit outside the room during her sessions. Then the patient suggested I see the mother instead: 'She needs you more than I do.' The patient left therapy when she felt the bond between us was becoming as close as that between her and her mother. She said 'nobody can understand the bond between people who share a kidney. No one can come between them.' She had no doubt that the recurrent rejection episodes reflected, rather than preceded, her ambivalence towards her mother and her wish for autonomy. Father was imagined as irresponsible and callous, but she had a feeling that if he were to turn up, his kidneys would be a better antigenic match, he would give one to her, and she could lead a normal life. These fantasies of the search for and the return of her father coincided with returning to dialysis. She used to protest about this, yet on the machine she would be sullen but uncomplaining, and I never quite understood what she was experiencing. When she stopped seeing me, she experienced a total rejection of the transplant, returned to long-term dialysis, became withdrawn and depressed, developed medical complications and died.

I describe this patient last because I found her the most perplexing, and felt that my sense of something not understood in her reflected her own experience of an obvious enigma in her life. This was extremely difficult to handle in the transference. At times I felt I was experienced as the father who was equated with the dialysis machine, and with the part of the patient which rejected the kidney. At other times I was experienced as the transplanted kidney which was equated with the mother. The patient thus experienced me as alternately attacking the transplanted kidney and, in defence, being rejected by her as she rejected the kidney. If I were to consider working with another patient in this situation, I would take a more supportive and less analytic approach, and would work first on problems of symbolization before taking up material about the transplant.

MEASUREMENT AND AGGREGATION OF VALUE

These detailed psychiatric accounts are of relevance primarily to clinicians. I turn now to the perspective of the planner who, in

determining Health Service policies, is obliged to make broad generalizations about the states of patients. Machines and organs, so richly
endowed with meaning, clearly have a value. Economists and
operational researchers have set aside the nuances of meaning discussed
above and embarked on estimates of how much the average person
thinks the average life on renal dialysis is worth. The economic value of
preventing death implied by various public and medical decisions is very
variable (Mooney, 1977). The real cost of maintaining patients on home
dialysis is about £6000 per annum, and on hospital dialysis, about
£11 000. Successful transplants cost over £1000 initially and £4250 per
annum to maintain. The 40 per cent which are unsuccessful cost about
£5000 (Laing, 1978).

These costs are so high that rationing has to occur. On what basis
could this be formalized? Pliskin and Beck (1976) devised a health index
which incorporated doctors' judgements about the characteristics of
patients which should influence the decision about whether to offer
treatment to a particular patient, and their valuations of the relative
importance of combinations of differing degrees of these circumstances,
e.g. presence or absence of more or less severe psychological problems.

Torrance, Thomas, and Sackett (1972), working in the field of global
measures of illness (Rosser, 1976), were concerned with the views of a
wider sample of the population. Using psychometric methods such as the
standard gamble (von Neumann and Morgenstern, 1947), they obtained
a scale of people's preferences for a typical life of dialysis or with a
transplant. Examples of his descriptions of typical lives are shown in
Figure 1. His results are shown in Table 1. The subjective benefits of the
various treatments are inversely related to their costs and in this example,
it is not difficult to choose the most cost-effective kidney programme.
The choice would become more difficult if the relative costs of home
dialysis and transplantation were to change.

Hospital dialysis

Two or three times/week you must travel to the hospital and spend about 8 hours hooked up to a dialysis
machine. Working men generally go overnight; others go during the day. You're very anaemic and this
may limit your activity. You're on a restricted diet (only 3 cups of fluid per day). There is a permanent
shunt imbedded in your arm or leg which restricts your physical activities some — no swimming. You're
geographically bound to your machine — vacations are difficult. There is no severe pain but chronic
discomfort and for some people, emotional depression. You should be able to work full-time but not on a
physical job.

Kidney transplant

You have received a successful kidney transplant. Your anaemia from the kidney disease is better, and
there are only minor restrictions on your diet and activities. You must take drugs against rejection which
makes you more susceptible to infections and other diseases. In addition the drugs will produce side-
effects such as a strikingly Cushingoid appearance, and possibly other major effects (e.g. diabetes).

Figure 1   Typical 'scenarios' (Torrance *et al.*, 1972)

Table 1   Utility of life during various treatments (*Source:* Torrance *et al.*, 1972)

State	Utility
Healthy	1.00
Kidney transplant	0.83
Home dialysis	0.66
Confinement to home with TB	0.56
Hospital dialysis	0.53
Confinement to sanatorium with TB	0.34
Dead	0.00

The question of the value of life with end-stage renal failure becomes more complex when the decision must be made between funds for dialysis, and for treatments for other conditions such as cancer or tuberculosis. Torrance's data for tuberculosis are also shown in Table 1. This scale implies that life with tuberculosis treated at home is marginally better than life on hospital dialysis, but less tolerable than life on home dialysis. Other things being equal, funds would therefore be allocated preferentially to home dialysis.

This average scale conceals large differences in the opinions of individuals. The mathematical validity of aggregating such data is contentious (Arrow, 1963; Whitmore, 1972). The reader is invited to reflect on the validity of this attempt to translate the shades of meaning discussed earlier into the concept of an average subjective value and to question whether this approach to the thorny problem of planning costly treatments is likely to be fruitful. Information about the individual's state is lost at each of the three stages of description, scaling, and aggregation. None the less, it may be helpful to have some notion of an average set of values against which to view the feelings of an individual.

REFERENCES

Abram, H. S., Moore, G. L., and Westervelt, G. V. (1971) Suicidal behaviour in chronic dialysis patients. *Am. J. Psychiat.*, **129**, 119–23.

Arrow, K. J. (1973) *Social Choice and Individual Values* (2nd edn), Cowles Commission Monograph 12. New York: Wiley.

Bennett, W. M. (1976) Cost benefit ratio of pretransplant bilateral nephrectomy. *Journal of the American Medical Association*, **235**, 1703.

Bernstein, D. M. (1971) After transplantation—the child's emotional reactions. *Am. J. Psychiat.*, **127**, 109–13.

Chapman, C. R., and Cox, G. V. (1977) Anxiety, pain and depression surrounding elective surgery: a multivariate comparison of abdominal surgery patients with kidney donors and recipients. *J. Psychosomat. Res.*, **21**, 7–15.

Clarke, R., Hailstone, J. D., and Slade, P. D. (1979) Psychological aspects of dialysis: a semantic differential study. *Psychological Med.*, **9**, 55–62.

Czackes, J. W., and De Nour, A. K. (1978) *Chronic Haemodialysis as a Way of Life*. New York: Brunner-Mazel.

B.M.J. Editorial (1980) Quality of life in renal failure, *BMJ*, **2**, 97–8.

Farmer, C. J., Snowden, S. A., and Parsons, V. (1979) The prevalence of psychiatric illness among patients on home haemodialysis. *Psychological Med.*, **9**, 509–14.

Farmer, C. J., Bewick, M., Parsons, V., and Snowden, S. A. (1979) Survival on home haemodialysis: its relationship with physical symptomatology, psychosocial background and psychiatric morbidity. *Psychological Med.*, **9**, 515–23.

Fellner, C. H., and Marshall, J. R. (1970) Kidney donors—the myth of an informed consent. *Am. J. Psychiat.*, **126**, 1245–51.

Foster, F. G., Cohn, G. L., and McKegney, F. P. (1973) Psychobiologic factors and individual survival in chronic renal haemodialysis—a two year follow up. *Psychosomatic Med.*, **35**, 64–80.

Ganser, S. J. M. (1898) *A Peculiar Hysterical State*. Translated by C. E. Shorer and reprinted in Hirsch, S. R., and Shepherd, M. (1974), *Themes and Variations in European Psychiatry*. Bristol: John Wright and Sons.

Goldstein, A. M., and Reznikoff, M. (1971) Suicide in chronic haemodialysis patients from an external locus of control framework. *Am. J. Psychiat.*, **127**, 1204–7.

Gomez, J. (1980) Paper to Conference on Psychiatric Aspects of Chronic Renal Failure, University of Birmingham.

Haenel, T., Brunner, F., and Battegay, R. (1980) Renal dialysis and suicide: occurrence in Switzerland and in Europe. *Comprehensive Psychiatry*, **21**(2), 140–45.

Herman, J. R. (1973) *Urology: a View Through the Retroscope*. Harper and Row.

Khan, A. V., Herndon, D. H., and Ahmadin, S. Y. (1971) Social and emotional adaptations of children with transplanted kidneys and chronic haemodialysis. *Am. J. Psychiat.*, **127**, 114–18.

Kolff, W. J. (1978) Dialysis of Schizophrenics. *Artificial Organs*, **2**, 277–83.

Laing, W. (1978) *Renal Failure, a Priority in Health?* Office of Health Economics.

Lifton, R. J. (1967) *Death in Life. Survivors of Hiroshima*. New York: Random House.

Lubell, D. (1976) Group work with patients on peritoneal dialysis. *Health and Social Work*, **1**, 159–77.

McCormick, M., and Navarrow, V. (1973) Prevalence of chronic renal failure and access to dialysis. *Int. J. Epidemiology*, **1**, 247–55.

McKegney, F. P., and Lange, P. (1971) The decision to no longer live on chronic haemodialysis. *Am. J. Psychiat.*, **128**, 47–53.

Maryinay, M. D., and McKegney, F. P. (1978) Individual and family coping with polycystic kidney disease: the onset of denial. *Int. J. Psychiat.*, **9**, 19–31.

Mooney, G. H. (1977) *The Valuation of Human Life*. London: MacMillan.

Moore, G. L. (1971) Who should be dialysed? *Am. J. Psychiat.*, **127**(9), 1208–9.

Muskin, H. L. (1971) On acquiring a kidney. *Am. J. Psychiat.*, **129**, 105–9.

von Neumann, J., and Morgenstern, O. (1947) *Theory of Games and Economic Behaviour* (2nd edn). Princeton University Press.

Parkin, D. M. (1977) The economics of treating chronic renal failure. In Anderton, J. L., Parsons, F. M., and Jones, D. E., *Living with Renal Failure*, MTP Press.

Penn, U., Bunch, D., Olenik, D., *et al.* (1971) Psychiatric experience with patients receiving renal and hepatic transplants. *Sem. in Psychiat.*, **3**, 144-7.

Pliskin, J. S., and Beck, D. H. (1976) A health index for patient selection: a value function approach with application to chronic renal failure patients. *Management Science*, **22**, 1009-21.

Poll, I. B., and De Nour, A. K. (1980) Locus of control and adjustment to chronic haemodialysis. *Psychological Med.*, **10**, 153-7.

Preuss, J. (1978) *Biblical and Talmudic Medicine* (trans. Rosner, F.). New York: Sanhedrin Press, p.107.

Procci, W. R., Hoffman, K. I., and Chatterjee, S. (1978) Sexual functioning of renal transplant recipients. *J. Ner. Ment. Dis.*, **166**, 402-6.

Rosser, R. M. (1976) Recent studies using a global approach to measuring illness. *Medical Care Supplement*, **14**(5), 138-47.

Salmons, P. H. (1980) Psychosocial aspects of chronic renal failure. *Brit. J. of Hospital Med.*, June 1980, 617-22.

Summers, R. G., and Klein, S. D. (1972) Family non-communication: the search for kidney donors. *Am. J. Psychiat.*, **129**, 687-92.

Torrance, G. W., Thomas, W. H., and Sackett, D. L. (1972) A utility of maximization model for evaluation of health care programs. *Health Services Research*, **7**, 118-33.

Viederman, M. (1974) The search for meaning in renal transplantation. *Psychiatry*, **37**, 283-90.

Wertzel, H., *et al.* (1977) Analysis of patient-nurse interaction in hemodialysis units. *Journal of Psychosomatic Research*, **21**, 359-66.

Whitmore, G. A. (1972) Health state references and the social choice. In Berg, R. L., *Health Status Indexes*. Chicago: Hospital Research and Educational Trust.

Personal Meanings
Edited by Eric Shepherd and J. P. Watson
© 1982 John Wiley & Sons Ltd.

Aspects of personal meaning in schizophrenia

J. P. Watson

INTRODUCTION

I recently received the following letter:

Dear Proffessor,
   I find the toll of modecate injections and modecate tablets too much for me. Every Thursday I go to . . . hospital for them. And have been going for them for the past two years. I find unbearable pain in my leg and back. I have been nearly killed in three or four hospitals . . ., . . ., . . ., and . . . where they have been unkind to me and are being unkind to me in . . . hospital. Dr . . . is a foreiner and is not a Christian whom I have no faith in. Since I have been nearly killed in those hospitals, they have made me mentally handicapped.
   I was Joseph of Nazareth in a previous life. Our good Father God came to me in the month of July 1977, and looked down to me from the sky. And said, I know what they are doing to you my sons. When my Son our Lord Jesus Christ Descends to me, as it is written in the 'New Testament' I shall, and only I know when He shall descend to me. Tell Him all those who have been unkind to me, or if you can let me go to my GP for the Disipal tablets twice a day, I shall forget them.

J. . . .

The aim of this paper is to clarify a difficulty which may arise when one attempts to understand a person with schizophrenia who uses religious language. My patient's letter provides a convenient starting point.

Ordinarily, reading a letter involves trying to understand *what* the writer has to say. If understanding proves difficult, as with J's letter, the reader is likely to attend to the writer's use of language, *how* he has attempted to communicate. Accordingly, in this instance we may notice that while sentences are constructed more or less normally, concepts and personal pronouns are used in such a way, especially in the letter's second paragraph, as to suggest to the clinician the presence of schizophrenic thought disorder in the writer.

175

It is helpful to distinguish between form and content; roughly 'form' refers to 'how', and 'content' to 'what'. 'Form' has a broad meaning which is, following Jaspers (1963, p.59), 'the particular modes of existence in which content is presented'. Schizophrenic thought disorder is one of the forms in which the content of schizophrenia may be manifest.

The same content may be experienced in quick succession in different phenomenological forms (Koehler, 1979), and the reader might infer from J's letter that he had experienced delusions (e.g. 'I was Joseph of Nazareth in a previous life') or hallucinations (e.g. our good Father God came to me . . . and said . . .) as well as disturbed form of thought. Whether or not it is appropriate to infer the presence of delusions or hallucinations, or manifestations of schizophrenia, from statements such as these, either written or spoken, is the question of this paper.

Some might not see any problem here. After all, it could be said that schizophrenic processes disrupt thinking and lead the sufferer to misidentify fancy as fact and dream or vision as reality. However, it is certainly legitimate to attempt to construe my patient's letter in terms of communication, before we discard it as the meaningless meanderings of a lunatic, because writing, addressing, and posting a letter form a sequence of goal-directed acts which may be intended to serve some communicative purpose. Of course, 'schizophrenic thought disorder' impairs many aspects of the communicative process and must be taken into account if we are to understand the meanings being communicated; but the response of impaired communication processes does not mean that the subject has nothing to communicate. This is as true of schizophrenia as it is of aphasia, deafness, Parkinsonism, or the numerous other illnesses wherein aspects of communication processes may be impaired.

We can clarify the matter by attempting to paraphrase the letter:

Dear Professor,
  I am very unhappy about my current treatment. I have been receiving modecate injections for two years and am still having them every week. I am very disheartened by this. I have severe pain in leg and back which I think is somehow connected with the treatment. I keep remembering frightening experiences in other hospitals and keep feeling that the . . . staff are being unkind to me. I have lost confidence in Dr . . . who does not share my cultural and religious views. I worry about the treatment making me worse.

This revised first paragraph includes explicit references to emotional aspects of experience, suggested by my attempts to understand the sender of the letter by putting myself in what I imagine his situation to have been and guessing what I would have felt if I had been him in that situation. My idea was that the writer experienced some of these feelings but was either unable to articulate them or chose not to do so. It is possible that it would have been adaptive for the letter writer to have experienced the feelings mentioned in the paraphrase, but that he did not do so because his illness had impaired his capacity for emotional experiences. It is also possible that I was simply not successful in my attempts to understand the patient; there are many experiences I do not understand and my capacity to put myself in another's shoes is, like everyone else's, limited. Not understanding a communication may as well derive from the receiver as from the sender of the message.

This applies also to the letter's second paragraph. 'I was Joseph of Nazareth in a previous life' may not be understandable to me, but that would not imply that it has no meaning. We can acknowledge but for present purposes ignore the possibility that our example demonstrates the way schizophrenic patients sometimes repeat the same utterances in a stereotyped way which does not serve to communicate meaning. Alternatively, the patient might be trying through the use of metaphor or other stylistic device, to put into words an experience singularly difficult to share with another. This, especially in the presence of formal thought disorder, might contribute to my inability to paraphrase the letter's second paragraph.

However, the point to be made here is that any meaning contained in this second paragraph can only be discerned using criteria different in kind from those applicable to the first paragraph. Paraphrasing the first paragraph involves clarifying the empirical referents (Ogden and Richards, 1949, p.11) of the statements. Religious and metaphysical statements are non-empirical and hence cannot be judged on empirical grounds.

In trying to decide what to make of the religious utterances of schizophrenic individuals, especially hallucinatory experiences, we find it convenient to discuss the nature of delusion and of some religious experiences. We shall ask ourselves if non-empirical statements of schizophrenics and of non-schizophrenics can be dealt with in much the same way. Finally, we shall see if the discussion has any implications for our views of the nature of schizophrenia.

DELUSION

Textbook definitions of delusion usually refer to unshakeable false beliefs out of cultural context. Thus (Leff and Isaacs, 1978):

A delusion is a false belief, firmly held by the patient, which is not consistent with the information available to him and with the beliefs of his social group, and which cannot be dispelled by argument or proof to the contrary.

In rather more detail, Mullen (1979) indicates that delusions are abnormal beliefs held with absolute conviction; experienced as self-evident truths usually of great personal significance; not amenable to reason or modification by experience; whose content is often fantastic or at best inherently unlikely; and which are not shared by those of a common social and cultural background. Mullen goes on to state that these characteristics do not entirely separate delusions as a class of phenomena from non-pathological beliefs and convictions.

Kräupl-Taylor (1966) gives a helpful discussion of the matter, beginning by defining delusion as 'an absolute and incontrovertible conviction of the truth of a proposition'. 'Conviction' implies absolute certitude; and delusions are false convictions. Kräupl-Taylor suggests that 'false' implies 'irrational', but that we should be cautious in judging beliefs to be irrational. This is because 'irrationality' may mean no more than an inability to see how certain propositions can be right; and our inability may arise from the fact that the propositions are derived from convictions that are culturally conditioned and which we ourselves do not share (Kräupl-Taylor, 1966, p.126).

Delusions are false convictions but not all false convictions are delusions. Kräupl-Taylor notes (p.115) that there are 'in every social group, collective convictions which were once regarded as absolutely true, but have gradually come to be recognised as absolutely false'. This is true within medicine: for example, earlier beliefs previously held with conviction about the harmful effects of excessive masturbation or the advantages of colectomy are now regarded as false. At the present day, some groups of individuals interested in schizophrenia hold contrasting and incompatible views of the nature of schizophrenia which amount to beliefs held with absolute conviction. Thus Horrobin (1981) refers to the 'multifactorial concepts of the establishment' in contrast with the ideas of organizations which have come out 'unequivocally in favour of the view that schizophrenia is a disease which has a biochemical cause'. In the mental-health field, every professional has an ideology whether explicit or not (Watson, 1979); and some aspects of the currently popular somatic, psychological, and sociological ideologies are logically incompatible with one another. Some professionals adhere to their ideologies with complete conviction. Holding false beliefs, even with conviction, does not alone and of itself indicate psychiatric disorder.

In addition to being false convictions, psychotic delusions are ego-involved, incorrigible, and have great preoccupying power. The term 'ego-involved' refers to beliefs which matter personally to the individual; they affect and become part of the person's fundamental view of self and of the world. Every adult has deeply held beliefs about self and the world, sometimes referred to as forming part of personal identity. Some of these ideas amount to ego-involved beliefs held with conviction. They may be false, as in highly intelligent people who believe firmly that they are unintelligent, and in liked people who believe themselves to be disliked, unattractive, or unloved. Self-beliefs which seem to observers to be false sometimes occur in psychiatric disorders other than schizophrenia; examples are the body-image belief which occurs in anorexia nervosa and the gender beliefs of the transsexual. False ego-involved convictions are not necessarily delusions.

Incorrigibility is a feature of many ego-involved beliefs as well as of schizophrenic delusions. Anorexic individuals continue to believe themselves to be fat and gender-reassigning persons to believe themselves to be of the anatomically discordant gender, despite evidence to the contrary. Also, incorrigibility is a characteristic of the beliefs of martyrs and heroes as well as of lunatics; persuasion and evidence can increase the intensity with which beliefs are held rather than lead to their modification. No one sanely achieved anything of substance against odds without being preoccupied with his aims and involved in his beliefs. John Bunyan's 'Pilgrim' experienced a set of private beliefs of great preoccupying power. No saint did otherwise.

So it is not just psychotic delusions which are false convictions, ego-involved, incorrigible, and preoccupying. Beliefs with all these characteristics may be found in non-psychotic psychiatric patients and also in individuals both religious and non-religious who are without psychiatric disorder. Observation suggests that novelty contributes to the identification of an incorrigible false conviction as a delusion. Beliefs which are new for the individual and represent a change in self-view, or view for the observer or in society, are particularly likely to be thought delusional. Traditional psychiatric teaching is that psychotic delusions have an unshared or idiosyncratic quality, an idea which acknowledges the social importance of people's beliefs, particularly those concerned with fundamental questions about the nature of the world, life, man's destiny, the afterlife, and so on. Thus,

it becomes a psychotic delusion only if the patient belongs to a social and cultural milieu in which there is no overt belief in—for example—witchcraft as a pathogenic cause of disease. (Kräupl-Taylor, 1966, p.126).

Societies need myths (Eliade, 1968); yet a metaphysical conviction incompatible with a local myth is not thereby declared to be a delusion, for in the field of non-empirical propositions majorities can be as readily mistaken—deluded—as individuals. This idea has helped to sustain many persecuted saints. The fact that the herald of a novel belief system is often thought by his fellows to be 'mad' is a social-psychological phenomenon reflecting processes governing the interaction of people with contrasting belief systems, and says nothing about the truth or otherwise of the new beliefs.

Psychotic delusions are false convictions, ego-involved, incorrigible, and preoccupying; but not all beliefs with these characteristics are psychotic delusions. To emphasize that delusions 'are not shared by those of a common social and cultural background' (Mullen, 1979) or 'it becomes a psychotic delusion only if the patient belongs to a social and cultural milieu' (Kräupl-Taylor, 1966) is to make two points. Firstly, as already noted, beliefs which are delusions have no unique qualities which distinguish them from non-delusional beliefs. Secondly, people derive their beliefs from socio-cultural as well as intrapersonal sources, a belief system being the possible resultant of several different processes. Schizophrenic individuals who may have delusions generated by intrapersonal processes will tend to be found among people with idiosyncratic beliefs. This group also includes innovators, visionaries, and messiahs who, as already noted, are not infrequently regarded by society as mad.

Our initial concern was with religious or metaphysical utterances of schizophrenics. Consideration of belief problems found in schizophrenia suggests similarities with the beliefs of non-schizophrenics. We can now approach the topic from the religious standpoint.

ASPECTS OF THEOLOGY

Theology refers to the 'science of (especially the Christian) religion' (*Concise Oxford Dictionary*); the 'contents and implications of the revelation in Christ' (*Encyclopaedia Brittanica*, 14th edn) or 'a structure of thought about God' (Selby, 1976, p.163). Selby's statement is convenient for present purposes. I take theology to refer to 'God-related statements and their meaning'.

In the Christian tradition, theology is based upon revelation through the natural order, the Bible, Christ, and the Church. Experiences of particular kinds, which might be called 'religious', are a ground out of which a person's individual theological system may grow. There is the expectation that a person's theology will in turn affect his experiences and his actions (in the biblical words, 'by their fruits ye shall know them').

The individual Christian is likely to be taught that the 'evidence' for God-related statements is to be sought in historically based revelation informed by 'faith', which was defined by the author of the Epistle to the Hebrews (chapter II, verse 1) as 'the evidence of things not seen'. For millions over many centuries, 'faith' has implied knowledge and certitude concerning the objects of faith.

The knowledge implied by faith is not knowledge 'in the same sense that rational science is knowledge' (*Encyclopaedia Britannica* on 'theology'). As Martin (1966) has noted, statements like 'I had a direct experience of God' are not empirical statements and there is no checking procedure applicable to them. Likewise, there can be no empirical tests to distinguish genuine from false 'God' experiences. To try and judge knowledge of non-empirical kinds by empirical criteria seems to be to make a mistake of category (Ryle, 1946).

Martin also points out that psychological statements like 'I feel as if an unseen person were interested in my welfare' can claim only that the speaker has the complex feelings to which the statement refers, nothing else (such as that God exists) following deductively. It appears that theological statements are one kind of statement which people may make when they wish to account to themselves or others for experiences which seem to require explanation. Theological statements may help speaker or hearer make sense of experience.

This kind of meaning sometimes emerges from experiences which provide a self-authenticating sense of certainty to ideas which emerge from them. Such experiences, authoritative to the subject, include some which could be termed 'mystical'. According to William James (1892, pp.366–8), mystical states characteristically cannot adequately be described, yet seem to be states of knowledge; are relatively short-lived; and are accompanied by a sense that the will is in abeyance as if the individual is 'grasped and held by a superior power'.

Many less spectacular experiences provide individuals with support for their non-empirical belief systems. Included here are many experiences of a religious nature. However, 'religious' is a somewhat loose term in this context, and differing answers have been given by those seeking the defining characteristics of 'religious' experience. For William James (1892, p.50) the term religious refers to 'the feelings, acts, and experiences of individual men in their solitude, so far as they apprehend themselves to stand in relation to whatever they may consider the divine'. While beliefs may seem to emerge from religious experiences which validate the beliefs for the experiencing individual, this does not validate the beliefs for others. We have noted that non-empirical beliefs cannot be validated empirically. Also, William James and more recently

Christie-Murray (1978) are among many indicating that no particular religious experience is associated with the genesis of any particular set of beliefs. Indeed, a 'religious' experience can generate a long-lasting belief in atheistic doctrine. So if religious beliefs are not to be judged on empirical grounds, or (except for the subject) in terms of the experiences from which they emerge, how are they to be validated?

William James is again helpful here. He says (p.38) that religious opinions must be judged by 'immediate luminousness, philosophical reasonableness, and moral helpfulness', not by any accompanying experiences. This implies that religious sentiments should be judged by the actions which issue from them. Ramsey (1967) suggests one way in which this happens, a specifically religious attitude meaning among other things that a person will attempt quite deliberately to achieve goals against very long odds in situations discerned as requiring intentional action, because of commitment to ideals, values, principles, or persons. Ramsey's emphasis upon the will is of interest in the present context because it suggests a contrast between intentional goal-directed activity informed by religious experience, and the difficulties which so many schizophrenic people have in formulating and working deliberately towards long-term goals.

It would seem then that we might seek to evaluate beliefs by their consequences for action. As James points out (p.38 and elsewhere), beliefs should not be judged by their origins: genius, theological and moral insights, creative acts, and scientific discoveries may all derive from all kinds of doubtful beginnings including neurotic, psychotic, eccentric, religious, and mystical experiences. Extremes of the human condition, insanity included, may provide insights hidden from those whose experiences are more ordinary. It would follow that we may have difficulties in understanding schizophrenics whose experiences are unfamiliar to us, but that we should make every effort to understand people who may be able to teach us much. We should most certainly not assume that because a person is schizophrenic he has nothing insightful to tell us.

NOTE ON DEFINITIONS OF SCHIZOPHRENIA

The emphasis in this paper is upon similarities between some schizophrenic and some non-schizophrenic experiences. To inform the discussion we shall indicate some current views of the concept of schizophrenia.

Diagnostic criteria for schizophrenia have varied widely from time to time and from place to place within different psychiatric traditions and are not agreed within the psychiatric community. Ten current definitions were compared by Brockington, Kendell, and Leff (1978), who obtained estimates of concordance between such definitions of 0.29 and 0.59 in two sets of patients. The former figure rose somewhat (to 0.54) if some very strict definitions were excluded, but this is a very low level of agreement about whether 'schizophrenia' is present or not.

However, it is important to note that disagreement about the presence of schizophrenia using the definitions compared by Brockington and his colleagues need not be due to doubt about symptoms being present or absent. Trained observers can do this reliably using standardized interview methods such as the 'Present State Examination' of Wing, Cooper, and Sartorius (1974) which informed the International Study of Schizoprehnia conducted by the World Health Organization (WHO, 1979).

Current definitions of schizophrenia all begin with symptoms but vary in the extent to which other sorts of information (such as social state, family history, age) are utilized with symptoms in making diagnostic decisions, and in the fixity or chronicity which the symptoms must have for schizophrenia to be judged present. The criteria of Feighner et al. (1972), for example, include 'chronicity with at least six months of symptoms before index evaluation' as well as 'delusions or hallucinations without significant perplexity or disorientation' and 'verbal production . . . (which lacks) . . . logical or understandable organization'. Such a definition excludes from study individuals who have particular experiences which are relatively transient. This group of people might include both 'early schizophrenics'—people with schizophrenia who would be recognized as such once the symptoms had been present long enough to meet the diagnostic criteria—and people without schizophrenia but who have short-lived experiences which would meet the diagnostic criteria for schizophrenia if they continued long enough. Defining schizophrenia in terms of chronicity makes it difficult to investigate any indistinct boundaries which may exist between schizophrenic and non-schizophrenic experiences. Defining schizophrenia in terms of chronocity also ensures that schizophrenia is regarded as a category even if a dimensional view would be more appropriate (which it may not be). (Thus people 6 feet or more in height are obviously 'tall' compared with 'short' people less than 4 feet tall; more adequate observation would disclose that height is a continuous variable).

All definitions of schizophrenia in current use naturally include reference to symptoms, notably hallucinations, delusions, and formal thought disorder. The 'first rank' symptoms of Schneider (1959) have provided the basis for one list of phenomena found in many acute patients and a smaller proportion of chronic ones (Mellor, 1970; Bland and Orn, 1980) even though definitions of the first-rank symptoms have sometimes varied (Koehler, 1979). Koehler includes three continua among the first-rank symptoms, namely delusional and passivity experiences and sense deceptions, each continuum including several distinct phenomena. In this paper we have not discussed these systematically or comprehensively but have only focused upon some aspects of delusion. It should be remembered that experiences of different form not infrequently coexist in schizophrenia (hallucinations and delusions, for example) and that one form of experience may contribute to the genesis of another.

RELIGIOUS AND SCHIZOPHRENIC EXPERIENCES

As previously noted, most definitions of schizophrenia emphasize delusions, hallucinations, and passivity experiences among symptoms of diagnostic significance. We have alluded to possible similarities between religious and schizophrenic experiences, without attempting a systematic comparison or considering whether or not the similarities are superficial rather than deep, more apparent than real.

Again, William James has considered the matter. He says (1892, p.410):

Delusional insanity . . . the same sense of ineffable importance in the smallest events, the same texts and words coming with new meanings, the same voices and visions and leadings and missions, the same controlling by extraneous powers . . .

It is of interest to consider this paragraph in terms of the Present State Examination (PSE) previously mentioned (Wing *et al.*, 1974). Using numbers in brackets to refer to symptoms as ordered in the PSE, we may suppose that James might be referring to delusional mood (49); verbal hallucinations (61 or 63); visual hallucinations (66 or 67); delusions of control (71), of reference (72), of assistance (75), or of grandiose ability (76); and religious (78) or primary (82) delusions. Very many of the 'symptoms' which may occur in schizophrenia are reminiscent (to put it no stronger) of some religious experiences.

The PSE definition of religious delusions (78) is instructive:

Both a religious identification on the part of a subject (he is a saint or has special spiritual powers) and an explanation in religious terms of other abnormal experiences (e.g. auditory hallucinations) should be included . . . Partial delusions are expressed with doubt, as a possibility which the subject is prepared to entertain but is not certain about . . .

The concept of partial delusion enshrines the idea that beliefs may arise from the individual's attempts to account for extraordinary experiences, rather than from some underlying disorder of thinking. Maher (1974) has elaborated the view that schizophrenics suffer an impairment of sensory input processing which distorts the evidence from which the individual derives his judgements about occurrences in self and the world. The schizophrenic experiences eccentric perceptions requiring explanation. The religious tradition has many individuals who interpreted unexpected experiences as indicating the direct intervention of God in their lives; James (1892) and Christie-Murray (1978) provide varied examples.

On the other hand, there seems no need to doubt that unusual beliefs sometimes derive from disturbed thinking. For example, Arieti (1974) indicates how Von Domarus' principle can illuminate schizophrenic beliefs. This principle concerns 'palaeologic' thought processes, supposed to occur—though not exclusively—in schizophrenia; it states that whereas the normal person accepts identity on the basis of identical subjects, the palaeologician accepts identity based on identical predicates. Thus: 'Our Lady was a virgin, I am a virgin, therefore I am the Virgin Mary.' It is, however, not at all certain that logical howlers occur more frequently in the speech of schizophrenics than in the speech of others. The logical status of much ordinary, political, even pro-fessional and 'scientific' talk scarcely bears examination. Language, which philosophers tell us is meaningless, can nevertheless serve to transmit meaning in real life.

James suggests guidelines for distinguishing the phenomena of 'delusional insanity' from their congeners in religious experience. He says (1892, p.410):

The emotion is pessimistic: instead of consolations, we have desolations; the meanings are dreadful; and the powers are enemies to life.

This does not seem satisfactory. Religious conversion is not in-frequently associated with desolation and dread, perhaps relieved when the commitment to God is made. 'Insane' individuals are not always pessimistic, desolated, filled with dread; and the dread of 'delusional mood' may dissipate when the delusional explanation 'crystallizes out' (Hamilton, 1976, p.41).

This experience, the dread of delusional mood lifting with the development of delusional idea, is one of the numerous schizophrenic phenomena with a possible parallel in religious experience. Thus there are passivity experiences to compare with the sense of personal leading and guidance experienced as from God, reported by many religious individuals. Hallucinations in schizophrenia contrast with speaking in tongues or visions of saints, or conversations with them. The aspiring clergyman is required to learn and then to demonstrate that he has a vocation — and so on. It is not possible here to pursue these comparisons further. Two points are to be made. The first is that there may be no experiences qualitatively unique to schizophrenia. Secondly, we re-emphasize that it is not possible to judge a metaphysical belief, stated in a correctly constructed proposition, as true or false on empirical grounds. Such beliefs are true or false to the believer, and evidenced by faith; a person is certainly not mad *simply because* he believes God spoke to him, or appeared to him, or that he was Joseph of Nazareth in a previous life.

The frequency of religious content in schizophrenia doubtless varies between cultures but is substantial; 'religious delusions' were reported in 18 per cent of male and 24 per cent of female schizophrenics in one series (Granville-Grossman, 1971). The development of religious interest with the emergence of a schizophrenic disorder may derive from the fact that the schizophrenic process somehow draws the subject's attention to fundamental life issues: a religious quest grapples with these issues also. Religious conversions not infrequently occur in a setting of an urgent crisis experience wherein the subject acts to avert personal disaster, the commitment of faith sometimes being associated with a vast surge of relief.

In addition, we have already indicated that religious opinions may perhaps be evaluated in terms of their effects on action rather than on the basis of their origins or phenomena. Two classical examples come to mind. Saul of Tarsus, after conversion, became the missionary Paul who founded new churches, and so on. Joan of Arc, after her visions, collected armies and defeated the English. There seems no reason to doubt that many would apply terms like delusion and hallucination to any St Joans and St Pauls who appeared today. The activity of these saints contrasts with the experience of the patient who informed me on admission to hospital that God had told him to disrobe and remain motionless in the men's room of a railway station. It is not that the metaphysical proportion, properly stated, can be judged true or false on empirical criteria — it cannot; the point is that the effects of the experience on the person's life are problematic, or distressing, or constraining. That is not to deny difficulties in borderline instances, particularly when elevated mood seems evident.

The practical outcome of all this is that the clinician should remember that he is trying to assess and to help the person as a functioning whole in an environment. He should not overemphasize individual symptoms, which may mislead. Schizophrenia is thus a whole-person diagnosis. This is close to an espousal of Bleuler's (1950) concept of schizophrenia, with its emphasis upon disturbed connections between part functions of the whole person, except that we must not underemphasize individual symptoms, which has happened in the past and unfortunately discredited Bleuler's concept. Current clinical practice sometimes emphasizes symptomatic forms rather than the experiencing person, and physical treatment possibilities rather than communications and personal meanings. The letter writer with whom I began this paper clearly indicated that he wished to be understood as well as treated.

Finally, we may indicate again that beginning to compare religious and schizophrenic experiences has led us to begin to doubt the traditional psychiatric idea that schizophrenia involves experiences qualitatively different from normal. Starting from a quite different origin, Slade and Cooper (1979) have proposed a cognate hypothesis. Their idea is that schizophrenia is a manifestation of a set of random, independent phenomena (signs and symptoms) which appear to coexist simply as a result of selection factors. This is compatible with recent emphases within psychology (Frith, 1979) and phenomenology (Scharfetter, 1980) upon processes subserving consciousness in schizophrenia. Frith's idea is that in schizophrenia much activity concerned with information processing of which the subject is usually unaware, becomes conscious. It seems possible that religious experiences may have similar effects, and that similar mechanisms may be activated at other times, for instance at times of crisis, especially during adolescence. Some psychobiological adaptational advantage might be based upon the capacity to explore the bounds of conscious awareness. This could be akin to the presumed though still mysterious biological functions of dreaming. In any event, it does seem that religious and other experiences of the kind discussed here are almost invariably relatively short-lived, in contrast with their duration in schizophrenia. If it is in fact true that the phenomena of schizophrenia are not in themselves abnormal, then there follows the possibility that in schizophrenia the problem is not that the experiences happen, but that they do not stop happening.

REFERENCES

Arieti, S. (1974) *Interpretation of Schizophrenia* (2nd edn). New York: Basic Books.

Bland, R. C., and Orn, H. (1980) Schizophrenia: Schneider's first rank symptoms and outcome. *British Journal of Psychiatry*, **137**, 63–8.

Bleuler, E. (1950) *Dementia Praecox or the Group of Schizophrenias* (trans. J. Zinkin). New York: International Universities Press.

Brockington, I. F., Kendell, R. E., and Leff, J. P. (1978) Definitions of schizophrenia: concordance and prediction of outcome. *Psychological Medicine*, **8**, 387–98.

Christie-Murray, D. (1978) *Voices from the Gods*. London: Routledge and Kegan Paul.

Eliade, M. (1968) *Myths, Dreams and Mysteries*. London: Collins.

Feighner, J. P., Robins, E., Guse, R. B., Woodruff, R. A., Winokur, G., and Munos, R. (1972) Diagnostic criteria for use in psychiatric research. *Archives of General Psychiatry*, **26**, 57–63.

Frith, C. D. (1979) Consciousness, information processing and schizophrenia. *British Journal of Psychiatry*, **134**, 225–35.

Granville-Grossman, K. (1971) Diagnosis of schizophrenia. In K. Granville-Crossman (Ed.), *Recent Advances in Clinical Psychiatry*. Edinburgh: Churchill-Livingstone.

Hamilton, M. (1976) *Fish's Schizophrenia*, 2nd edn. Bristol: Wright.

Horrobin, D. F. (1981) What should be done about schizophrenia. *Journal of the Royal Society of Medicine*, **74**, 180–2.

James, W. (1892) *The Varieties of Religious Experiences*. Collins, Fontana Library Edition, 1960.

Jaspers, K. (1963) *General Psychopathology* (trans. J. Hoeing and M. W. Hamilton). Manchester: University Press.

Koehler, K. (1979) First rank symptoms of schizophrenia: questions concerning clinical boundaries. *British Journal of Psychiatry*, **134**, 236–48.

Kräupl-Taylor, F. (1966) *Psychopathology. Its Causes and Symptoms*. London: Butterworth.

Leff, J., and Isaacs, A. D. (1978) *Psychiatric Examination in Clinical Practice*. Oxford: Blackwell.

Maher, B. A. (1974) Delusional thinking and perceptual disorder. *Journal of Individual Psychology*, **30**, 98–113.

Martin, C. B. (1966) A religious way of knowing. In A. Flew and A. MacIntyre (Eds), *New Essays in Philosophical Theology*. London: SCM Press.

Mellor, C. S. (1970) First rank symptoms of schizophrenia. *British Journal of Psychiatry*, **117**, 15–23.

Mullen, P. (1979) The phenomenology of disordered mental function. In *Essentials of Postgraduate Psychiatry*. London: Academic Press.

Ogden, C. K., and Richards, I. A. (1949) *The Meaning of Meaning*. London: Routledge and Kegan Paul.

Ramsey, I. T. (1967) *Religious Language*. London: SCM Press.

Ryle, G. (1946) *The Concept of Mind*. London: Hutchinson.

Scharfetter, C. (1980) *General Psychopathology* (trans. H. Marshall). Cambridge: University Press.

Schneider, K. (1959) *Clinical Psychopathology*. New York: Grune and Stratton.

Selby, P. (1976) *Look for the Living*. London: SCM Press.

Slade, P., and Cooper, R. (1979) Some conceptual difficulties with the term 'schizophrenia'. An alternative model. *British Journal of Social and Clinical Psychology*, **18**, 309–17.

Watson, J. P. (1979) Psychiatric ideologies. In R. N. Gaind and B. L. Hudson (Eds.), *Current Themes in Psychiatry*, vol. 2, London: Macmillan.

Wing, J. K., Cooper, J. E., and Sartorius, N. (1974) *The Measurement and Classification of Psychiatric Symptoms*. Cambridge: University Press.

WHO (1979) *Schizophrenia. An International Follow-up Study*. Chichester: Wiley.

Author index

Abram, H. S., 162
Adams, J., 34, 35
Adelstein, A., 105
Ahmadin, S. Y., 165
Alarcon, J., 105
Alcohol Education Centre, 115
Alliance Building Society Housing Research Unit, 80
Antaki, C., 71
Aries, P., 24
Arieti, S., 185
Armor, D. J., 124, 125
Arrow, K. J., 172
Austin, J. L., 13

Bakan, D., 39
Bancroft, J. H. J., 104, 105, 107, 108, 109, 112
Bannister, D., 48
Bard, M., 143, 153
Battegay, R., 162
Beck, A. T., 110
Beck, D. H., 171
Beisser, A. R., 154
Bennett, W. M., 159
Berenson, F. M., 39
Berger, P. L., 34
Bernstein, D. M., 165
Bevington, D. J., 145
Bewick, M., 161, 163
Birtchnell, J., 105
Bland, R. C., 184
Bleich, D., 44
Bleuler, E., 187
Bloombaum, M., 72
Boland, J., 145
Borg, I., 74
Braiker, H. B., 124
Brandon, D., 95

Breaux, J. J., 80
Brennan, M. J., 151
Brenner, M., 38, 40, 41, 71
Brentano, F., 25
British Medical Journal, 119
British Medical Journal Editorial, 161
Brockington, I. F., 183
Brown, G. W., 145
Brown, J., 71, 75, 79, 80, 88
Browne, K., 35
Brunner, F., 162
Buber, M., 38, 39, 43
Bunch, D., 164

Cahalan, D., 118
Canter, D., 80
Card, W. I., 65
Casson, J., 109
Chapman, C. R., 164
Chatterjee, S., 163
Chowdhury, B., 113
Christie-Murray, D., 182, 185
Cissin, I. H., 118
Clark, J., 105
Clarke, R., 162
Claxton, G., 29
Cobliner, W. G., 141
Cohen, S., 72
Cohn, G. L., 161
Cole, D., 112
Connelly, J., 97
Cook, N. G., 96, 110
Cooper, A. F., 145
Cooper, J. E., 183, 184
Cooper, R., 187
Cornell, C. E., 145
Costello, R. M., 124
Coulter, J., 10
Cox, G. V., 164

Crabtree, R. J., 145
Cramond, J., 116
Crary, G. C., 143
Crary, W. G., 143
Crean, G. P., 65
Crossley, H. M., 118
Cumming, C., 105, 107
Czackes, J. W., 160

Davies, D. L., 119
Davies, J., 116
Department of Health and Social Security, 122
Devlin, B. H., 146, 148
Diggory, J., 98, 99
Duck, S., 71
Durkheim, E., 97
Dyk, R. B., 143

Edwards, C., 124
Edwards, G., 119, 124
Edwards, L., 151
Egerton, R. B., 115
Eisenberg, L., 38
Eiser, J. R., 133
Eliade, M., 180
Elizur, D., 84
Epictetus, 93
Evans, C. R., 65

Fagg, J., 105, 109
Farmer, C. J., 161, 163
Feifel, H., 151
Feighner, J. P., 183
Fellner, C. H., 164
Fienberg, S. E., 82
Forgas, J. P., 71, 72, 73, 74, 87
Foster, F. G., 161
Fransella, F., 48, 51
Freeling, P., 35
Freud, A., 153
Friedman, M., 39
Frith, C. D., 187
Futterman, S., 115

Gaines, B. R., 65, 69
Ganser, S. J. M., 169
Gauld, A., 23, 30
Geertz, C., 24
Gilmour, R., 71
Ginsberg, G. P., 104

Ginsburg, G. P., 71, 72
Glaser, B. G., 153
Glaser, F. B., 125
Goffman, E., 19
Goldstein, A. M., 162
Gomez, J., 162
Gottheil, E., 154
Granville-Grossman, K., 186
Green, P., 94
Greer, H. S., 145, 147, 148, 153
Griffin, M., 146, 148
Gross, M. M., 119
Guse, R. B., 183

Hackett, T. P., 143
Haenel, T., 162
Hailstone, J. D., 162
Hamilton, M., 185
Hammond, K. R., 43
Hanson, S., 151
Harré, R., 13, 23, 42, 71, 73
Harvard-Watts, O., 109
Hawker, A., 117
Hawton, K., 105, 107, 109, 112
Hayman, F., 120
Henderson, L. J., 152
Herman, J. R., 159
Herndon, D. H., 165
Hillman, J., 98
Hinkle, D., 49, 50, 52
Hinton, J. M., 145, 147, 148, 149, 152
Hirsch, E. D., 44
Hodgson, R. J., 119
Hoffman, H., 115
Hoffman, K. I., 163
Holding, T. A., 113
Holland, J., 147
Hollis, M., 19
Holy Bible, 45, 93, 100, 159, 181
Hopson, B., 34, 35
Hora, T., 39
Horrobin, D. F., 178
Hudson, L., 43
Hunter, G., 123

Independent Commission on International Development Issues (The Brandt Report), 100
Ineichen, B., 75
Inge, W. R., 94
Isaacs, A. D., 177

Isbell, H., 130

Jahoda, G., 116
James, W., 181, 182, 184, 185
Jaspers, K., 176
Jellinek, E. M., 129
Jones, R., 151
Jong, E., 28

Kammeier, M. L., 115
Kelly, G. A., 3, 35, 47, 49, 55, 57, 59
Kendell, R. E., 183
Kent, S., 147
Kermode, F., 43
Kessel, N., 115
Khan, A. V., 165
Kinget, G. M., 33
Kingston, B., 105, 107
Klein, S. D., 164
Koehler, K., 176, 184
Kolff, W. J., 160
Kovacs, M., 110
Kräupl-Taylor, F., 178, 179, 180
Kreitman, N., 113
Krumm, S. K., 148
Kübler-Ross, E., 143, 153
Kuchemann, C. S., 145

Laing, R. D., 26
Laing, W., 171
Lange, P., 163
Leach, C., 59, 60
Lederman, S., 115
Lee, E. G., 145
Leff, J., 177, 183
Lenrow, P., 36, 37
Lifton, R. J., 161
Lindahl, J. W. S., 152
Lingoes, J. C., 72, 73, 74
Lishman, A., 121
Litman, G. K., 133
Loper, R. G., 115
Lubell, D., 161
Luckmann, T., 34
Luft, J., 41, 43

MacAndrew, C., 115
MacMurray, J., 24
McArdle, C. S., 145
McCormick, M., 160
McGrath, J. E., 72, 73

McGreal, J. P., 50
McGurn, W. C., 154
McIntosh, J., 148, 149
McKegney, F. P., 161, 162, 163
Magill, F. N., 50
Maguire, G. P., 145
Maguire, P., 141, 148
Maher, B. A., 185
Mardon, C., 105
Mardones, R. J., 130
Margolis, J., 39
Marris, P., 146
Marsack, P., 105, 109
Marsh, P., 71
Marshall, J. R., 164
Martin, C. B., 181
Maryinay, M. D., 162
Mello, N. K., 131
Mellor, C. S., 184
Mendelson, J. H., 131
Michelson, W., 75
Mills, J., 105
Mooney, G. H., 171
Moore, G. L., 161, 162
Morgenstern, O., 171
Morris, J., 34, 35, 44, 209, 211, 213
Morris, T., 145, 147, 148, 153
Mullen, P., 178, 180
Munos, R., 183
Muskin, H. L., 164

Naess, A., 33
Navarrow, V., 160
von Neumann, J., 171
Newson, J., 23
Nicholson, M., 65
North, M., 36
de Nour, A. K., 160, 163

O'Connor, J., 117
Ogden, C. K., 177
O'Grady, J., 112
Olenik, D., 164
Oppenheim, A. N., 133
Orford, J., 121, 124
Orn, H., 184
Ortony, M., 20
Osborne, M., 112
Osgood, C. E., 60

Parsons, V., 161, 163

Pattison, E. M., 123
Peck, A., 145
Penn, U., 164
Pettingale, K. W., 153
Pettit, P., 75
Phenix, P. H., 1
Plant, J. A., 146, 148
Plant, M. A., 117, 118
Pliskin, J. S., 171
Plumb, M. M., 147
Polanyi, M., 3, 7, 54, 57
Polich, J. M., 124, 125
Poll, I. B., 163
Pollak, O., 36, 37, 40, 154
Preuss, J., 159
Pride, J. B., 34
Procci, W. R., 163

Ramon, S., 104, 105, 108
Ramsey, I. T., 182
Rankin, H., 119
Rawson, N. S. B., 133
Rees, W. Dewi, 143
Reynolds, F., 109
Reznikoff, M., 162
Richards, I. A., 21, 177
Richards, M. P. M., 23
Robbins, G. F., 147
Roberts, R., 56
Robins, E., 183
Robinson, D., 116
Rommetveit, R., 26, 34
Rosser, R. M., 171
Russell, A. R., 145
Russell, D., 65
Ryle, G., 181

Sabini, J., 9
Sackett, D. L., 171, 172
Sale, I., 105
Salmons, P. H., 160
Sartorius, N., 183, 184
de Saussure, F., 14
Scharfetter, C., 1, 187
Scheffler, I., 41
Schneider, K., 183
Schonfield, J., 145, 147
Searle, J. R., 25
Secord, P. F., 23
Selby, P., 180
Shapira, Z., 74

Shaw, M. L. G., 39, 61, 65, 66, 69, 70
Shotter, J., 23, 26, 30, 71
Shye, S., 72, 74, 84
Silver, M., 9
Sime, J. D., 71, 75, 80, 88
Simkin, S., 105, 107, 108, 112
Skinner, B. F., 30
Skrimshire, A. M., 104, 105, 108, 109, 112
Slade, P. D., 162, 187
Slater, P., 66
Smith, D. C., 145
Snowden, S. A., 161, 163
Sobell, L. C., 131
Sobell, M. B., 131
Soloman, P., 131
Stacey, B., 116
Stambul, H. B., 124, 125
Stengel, E., 95, 96, 100
Stockwell, T., 119
Strauss, A. L., 153
Suci, G. J., 60
Summerland Fire Commission, 80
Summers, R. G., 164
Sutherland, A. M., 148

Tannenbaum, P. H., 60
Taylor, C., 30, 34
Taylor, L., 72
Teilhard de Chardin, P., 33
Thomas, C., 141
Thomas, W. H., 171, 172
Tiryakian, A. A., 35, 38, 39
Toch, H., 72
Torrance, G. W., 171, 172
Tschudi, F., 50

Vaneigem, R., 33
Vernon, P. E., 36
Viederman, M., 164
Vygotsky, L. S., 15, 42, 44

de Waele, J. P., 71
Walen, R., 115
Walton, H., 115
Wangensteen, O. H., 152
Watkinson, G., 65
Watson, J. P., 178
Watts, F. N., 37
Waxenberg, S. E., 153
Weinstein, E. T. A., 75

Weisman, A. D., 141, 143, 145, 146, 147, 152, 153
Weissman, M. A., 110
Wertzel, H., 159
Westervelt, G. V., 162
Whalen, R., 168
White, P., 145, 147, 148
Whitehurst, G. J., 1
Whitmore, G. A., 172
Whitwell, D., 105, 107
Williams, C. O., 105
Williams, W. J., 75
Wilson, J., 65

Wilson, J. M., 149
Wing, J. K., 183, 184
Winick, L., 147
Winokur, G., 183
Wolff, R. P., 33
Woodruff, R. A., 183
Woods, N. F., 148
Worden, J. W., 141
World Health Organization, 119, 183
Wright, C., 152

Zvelun, E., 74, 78

Subject index

Abstention, 120
Accessibility, 3, 12, 20, 37, 47
Accidents, 13
Accountability, 25
Accounting for actions, 26
Accounts, 3, 4, 71, 72, 133
Act-sequences, 13
Actions, 2, 9, 10, 11, 12, 13, 15, 17, 19,
    20, 23, 24, 26, 27, 30, 43, 48, 59,
    125
Acts, 9, 13, 17, 103, 110, 165, 176
Agency, 1, 3, 9, 10, 17, 38, 39, 40
Agents, conscious, 9
Aggression, 48, 162
Alcoholic personality, 115
Alcohol problems, 5, 115 et seq., 129
    et seq.
Alcoholics Anonymous, 122, 123, 129,
    130
Alienation, 144
Ambivalence, 122, 170
Analysis, 7
    account, 4, 88
    cluster, 66
    content, 42, 72, 80, 107, 131, 133
    factor, 66, 72, 73
    logical entailment, 67
    loglinear, 82
    Multidimensional Scalogram, 77
    partial order scalogram, 81, 84, 87
    principle components, 66
    purposive, 36
    repertory grid, 49 et seq., 65 et seq.
    smallest space, 75
Anger, 150, 162
Anxiety, 48, 118, 149, 161, 164, 167
Apathy, 150
Approaches to research, 8, 73, 74, 130,
    131, 135

Appropriate behaviour, 13, 24, 25, 26,
    36, 95, 98, 99, 116, 117, 118, 119,
    120
ARGUS, 70
Assertion, 51
Asymmetry, 36, 37
Attempted suicide, 91 et seq., 103 et
    seq., 162
Attention, seeking, 92
Attitudes, professional, 5, 6, 7, 96, 97,
    152
Autobiography, 18, 19, 35; see also
    Biography
Autonomy, 170
Awareness, 3, 49, 55, 57, 60; see also
    Consciousness

Being, moral and social, 2; see also
    Existence
Belief, 7, 92, 125, 138, 147, 171, 177,
    178, 179, 181, 182
Bereavement, 92
Bias, 3, 4, 41, 103
Biography, 35, 39, 40
Bitterness, 144
Blame, 144, 162
Body image, 161, 164, 168, 170
Boredom, 118
Breakdown, 35

Cancer, 6, 7, 141 et seq.
Causality, 25, 27
Change, 43, 97, 121, 146, 148; see also
    Continuity and Discontinuity
Characteristics, demand, 41
Cognitive
    control, 133
    functioning, 120, 121

'Collective frame of reference', 6, 129, 130
Common sense, 12, 105, 107
Communication
  barriers to, 141, 142, 148, 149, 150, 151, 152, 153, 154, 159, 160, 177
  channels of, 41
Compulsion, 119
Computer
  applications, 3
  feedback, 3, 64, 65
Confidence, 149
Confusion, 149
Consciousness, 17, 33, 38, 56; see also Self-consciousness
Consequences, 13, 110
Construct space, 66
Constructive Alternativism, 47
Constructs
  bipolarity of, 49, 50
  context, 65
  elicitation of, 60, 61, 64, 67
  examination of, 3
  identification of, 42
  impermeable, 56
  implications of, 49
  injection of, 64
  loosened, 57
  making explicit, 3
  negation of, 3
  preverbal, 55, 57
  range of implications, 52, 54
  reversal of, 66
  role, 35
  submerged, 3, 55, 56, 57
  subordinate, 56
  superordinate, 56
  suspended, 56, 57
  tested of, 47
  transcontextual identity of, 49
Construing, 1, 48, 49
Content, form and, 176
Context, 2, 3, 10, 26, 27, 29, 30, 40, 43, 44, 48, 49, 50, 65
Continuity, 4, 34, 43, 146, 147
Contradiction, 5, 43
Contrast, 43
Control, 2, 6, 25, 31, 34, 38, 48, 49, 119, 120, 123, 125, 129, 130, 138, 143, 144, 147

Conventions, 2, 9, 13, 14, 16
Conversation, 40, 41, 43, 44
  mode, 40
  purposive, 40
Coping, 35, 36, 37, 92, 132, 136, 137, 138, 145, 146, 152, 153, 155, 164
Counselling, 6
Curiosity, 40
Craving, 6, 123, 130, 137, 138
Crisis, 96, 121, 186, 187
Critical Perceptual Shift, 6, 121, 133, 136, 138
'Cry for help', 95, 110
Cylindrex, 74

Death, 6, 92, 121, 142, 143, 147, 151, 152, 155, 170
Decisions, 7, 121, 122, 124, 125, 151, 160, 172
Degradation, 92, 95
Delusions, 176, 177, 179, 180, 183, 184, 186
Denial, 6, 7, 120, 123, 136, 143, 144, 153, 154, 161, 162, 164, 168
Dependence, 5, 160, 161, 162, 166, 169
Depersonalization, 161, 162
Depression, 91, 95, 96, 101, 118, 145, 147, 150, 162, 164, 166, 167, 168, 169, 170
Deprivation, social, 164
Desirability, social, 41
Despair, 91, 125
Detachment, 36
  Development
  of science, 8
  personal, 8, 35; see also Continuity, Discontinuity and Growth
Dialogue, genuine, 44
Dialysis, 7, 159 et seq.
Dignity, 14, 145
Dilemma, implicative, 50, 51
Disappointment, 118, 125
Discontinuity, 34, 97, 146, 147
Discourse, 11, 12
Disfigurement, 144, 145, 146, 148, 161, 163
Display, 11, 17, 19, 21
Dissatisfaction, 119
Dissonance, 119, 137
Distancing, 36, 37, 38
Divorce, 92

Domains of meaning, 11 *et seq.*
Drama, 7, 36, 39
Dramatis personae, 42
Dreaming, 56
Drinking behaviour, 5, 115 *et seq.*, 129
    et seq.
Dying, 143, 145; *see also* Death *and*
    Suicidal behaviour

Ego-involvement, 179
Empathy, 123
Employment, 14, 148
Encounters, 2, 3; *see also* Interaction
ENTAIL, 67
Entailment, 69
Envy, 10
Epistemic access, 20
Equilibrium, 146
Ethics, 152, 152; *see also* Professional
    helping
Euthanasia, 160
Events, speech, 34, 44
Existence, 4, 5, 11, 15, 17, 23, 25, 26,
    30, 38, 95, 147
Experience, 4, 7, 20, 21, 25, 34, 35, 37,
    39, 48, 56, 59, 64, 119, 131, 132,
    133, 138, 142, 143, 144, 145, 146,
    150, 155, 161, 164, 167, 170, 171,
    176, 180, 181, 182, 183, 184, 185,
    187
Expert, 2, 36; *see also* Helper *and*
    Professional
Expressive behaviour, 4, 5, 6, 91 *et
    seq.*, 103 *et seq.*
Expressive order, 13, 17

Facet Theory, 4, 74, 87
Failure, 122
Fantasy, 16
Fate, 92
Fear, 6, 92, 144, 152
Feedback, 3, 4, 60, 61, 64, 65, 132, 137
First person singular, 3, 7, 33, 38, 39,
    45
First person statements, 33
Fit
    mind-to-mind, 25
    mind-to-world, 25, 30
    world-to-mind, 25, 30
Fittedness, 25
Focus, 62

Form, content and, 3, 176
Frame of reference, 1, 2, 4, 6, 129, 130
Frustration, 150
Fugue, 166

Goals, 142
Glosses, normative, 13
Grammar, 11, 15
Grid
    focussing of, 61
    implications, 51
    repertory, 48, 59, 60, 62
Grief, 6, 146, 152, 166, 167; *see also*
    Mourning
Growth, personal, 6, 148, 165, 167
Grudges, 92
Guilt, 48, 96, 144, 161, 162

Hallucinations, 176, 183, 184, 186
Help, 4, 36, 37, 39, 45
Helper
    response of, 37, 39, 45, 122, 123,
        124, 125, 136, 138, 145, 148,
        149, 150, 151, 154
    role of, 2, 36, 136, 138, 148, 149,
        151, 154
Helplessness, 132, 145, 161
Hermeneutics, 13, 17, 30, 43
Hope, 149
Hopelessness, 92, 98
Hostility, 5, 48
Humiliation, 92
Hysteria, 166, 169

'I–it' relationship, 38, 45
'I–thou' relationship, 39
Ideology, 131, 178
Impartiality, 36
Impulse, 112, 119
Incorrigibility, 179
Independence, 147, 148, 161
Individuality, attributes of, 17
Inference, 29
INGRID, 66
Insight, 182
Instrumental behaviour, 2, 4, 5, 6, 98,
    103, 104, 105, 108
Intelligibility, 2, 9, 12, 16, 18, 19, 21
Intentionality, 9, 10, 13, 25, 27, 29, 75,
    104, 107
Interaction, 23, 26, 33, 34, 64, 65

Interdependence, 147
Interpretation, 10, 13, 15, 17, 29, 30,
    42, 43, 47, 62
Intonation, 41
Intuition, 7, 10, 43
Irrationality, 143, 159, 178
Isolation, social, 6, 96, 141, 152, 168,
    170
'It–it' relationship, 39, 45

Jealousy, 10

Knowledge
  asymmetrical, 36
  faith as, 181
  public, 19
  rational science as, 181
  tacit, 54

Language, 11, 12, 41, 132
  meaningless, 185
  natural, 41
  religious, 175
  use of, 175
'Learned helplessness', 132
Lethargy, 167
Lexicon, 10, 12, 15, 19
Listening, 5, 48, 150, 151, 155
Locus of control, 129, 130
Loneliness, 119
Loss, 92, 129, 130, 146, 161, 165, 169
Lying, 152

Machine-dependence, 160, 161, 169
Macro-plan, 37, 40
Macro-proposition, 40
Madness, 16, 21
Maladjustment, 161, 162
Manipulation, 5
Mapping, 74, 78, 81, 84
Maturity, 35; see also Growth
Meaninglessness, 97
Meaning
  collective, 2, 70
  personal, 1, 2, 9, 11, 12, 14, 16, 17,
      18, 19, 21, 23, 27, 28, 38, 40, 42,
      44, 48, 51, 52, 55, 57, 59, 65, 71,
      72, 73, 87, 92, 129, 142, 148,
      155, 165
  private, 2, 16
  public, 2, 12, 17, 19

search for, 163
scientific, 2
social, 2, 12, 16, 17, 19
subjective, 2
taken for granted, 2
Metaphor, 2, 7, 12, 20, 21, 41
Misunderstanding, 48, 150
Moral weakness, 122
Mourning, 146, 166, 167, 168; see also
    Grief
Multidimensional
  scaling, 4, 71
  space, 66
Mystical experience, 164, 181, 182
Myths, 180

Neglect, 169
Non-empirical statements, 177, 181
Nonverbal behaviour, 37, 149, 150,
    155
Novelty, 11, 12, 13, 20, 21

'Object-for-me', 38
Objectification, 36
Objectivity, 2, 138
Objects, semiotic, 11
Oratory, 15
Order
  expressive, 7, 13, 18
  practical, 7, 13, 18

Pain, 142, 144, 164, 165
Palaeologic, 185
Passivity experiences, 184, 186
PEGASUS, 60, 61
Person, 1, 3, 4, 9, 20, 30, 187; see also
    Personhood
Personal meanings, 1, 2, 9, 11, 12, 14,
    16, 17, 18, 19, 21, 23, 27, 28, 38,
    40, 42, 44, 48, 51, 52, 55, 57, 59,
    65, 71, 72, 73, 87, 92, 129, 142,
    148, 155, 165
Personhood, 7, 8, 10, 24, 39, 44
Power, asymmetrical, 36
Prediction, 47, 48, 51
Privacy, 154
Problem drinking; see Alcohol prob-
    lems
Professional
  attitudes, 5, 6, 7, 36, 96, 97, 104,
      122, 123, 143, 151, 152

codes, 123
helping; *see* Helper
pressures upon, 3, 36
role, 2, 5
Profiles, 73, 78, 79, 87
Projection, 100, 120, 136, 144
Proto-interpretation, 34
Pseudo-dementia, 169
'Psychic' experience, 164
Psychosexual problems, 148, 161, 163, 167
Psychosis, 163, 164, 176, 180, 181, 182
Purpose, loss of, 162

Questioning
invitational, style of, 40
objective, style of, 38

Radex, 74
Rationalization, 120, 144
Rationality, 3, 11, 36
Reference, extra-linguistic, 15
Reflectiveness, 33
Rejection, 92
Relapses, 6, 122, 125, 126, 129, 130, 132, 138
Relationships, 10, 92, 95, 109, 112, 113, 118, 137, 147, 148
Religion, language of, 175
Religious
delusions, 186
experience, 164, 181, 182, 187
Renal dialysis and transplantation, 159 *et seq.*
Reparation, 137
Repertory grid, 3, 48 *et seq.*, 59 *et seq.*
Responsibility, 25, 44, 136, 169
Revelation, 180, 181
Right to die, 91, 92, 93, 94, 95
Ritual, 13, 34, 37, 38
Role, 2, 5, 19, 37, 148, 161, 167
Routine, 34, 37, 38
Rules, 13, 23, 26, 116; *see* Appropriate behaviour

Sacrifice, 147
Samaritans, 94, 113
Scalogram, 78
Scapegoating, 100
Schizophrenia, 175 *et seq.*

Science
convention and, 2
development of, 8
language of, 20
personal, 8, 35, 47 *et seq.*, 59 *et seq.*
Self, 2, 4, 5, 6, 7, 23, 31, 33, 34, 35, 38, 39, 40, 41, 51, 56, 103, 125, 137, 144, 148, 162, 166, 169
Self-concept(ion), 33, 35, 132, 136, 146, 162, 164, 168, 179
Self-conscious/consciousness, 2, 36, 52, 56; *see also* Awareness *and* Consciousness
Self-esteem, 120, 132, 137, 148
Self-existential, 36
Self-expression, 6, 7, 38, 40
Self-fulfilling prophesy, 43, 123, 130
Self-image, 161, 164, 168, 170
Self-injury, 162, 169; *see also* Suicidal behaviour
Self-perception, 33, 35, 39, 132, 136, 146, 162, 179
Semantic
differential, 60, 65
field, 14
relations, non-arbitrary, 14
space, 10, 59, 60, 66
system, 14
Semiotic, 12, 21
Separation, 152
Sexuality, 148
Sick role, 167
Significance, 13, 14, 15, 16, 17, 18, 27; *see also* Meaning *and* Personal meaning
Silence, 150
Singularity, 34
Skills
conversational, 41
interviewing, 41
ontological, 24
Social
acts and actions; *see* Acts *and* Actions
deprivation (sensory), 164
desirability, 41
isolation, 6, 96, 141, 152, 168, 170
roles, 161
withdrawal, 141, 165, 170
SOCIOGRIDS, 70
Soliloquy, 11

Solipsism, 44
Solitude, 168
Space
  cartesian, 11
  construct, 66
  multidimensional, 66, 71
  semantic, 10, 59, 60, 61
Speaking with tongues, 186
Speech, 9, 42
Speech-act, 13
Speech event, 34, 44
Splitting, 100
Status, 30, 36, 37
Suicidal behaviour, 4, 91 et seq., 103 et seq., 162
Suspicion, 149
Symbolic actions, 11
Symbolic craving; see Craving

Talk, ordinary, 11
Taxonomies, search for, 72
Tendency, affective-volitional, 44
Terminal illness, 92, 145
Terror, 91
Text, 3, 37, 39, 41, 42, 43
Theme, 41
Therapy
  conjoint, 113
  family, 113

Thought
  analytical, 43
  disorder, 183
  circular, 33
  reflective, 44
Toehold principle, 2, 11
Topic progression, 40
Transition, 34, 35
Transplantation, 7, 159 et seq.
Typification, 39, 72, 74, 152, 178

Unconscious, 55, 57
Unemployment, 14, 148
Uniqueness, 11, 12
Unity, 34

Value, 1, 7, 14, 15, 16, 17, 18, 36, 64, 92, 95, 98, 99, 100, 119, 120, 121, 125, 131, 138, 142, 147, 148, 154, 171
Verbal behaviour, 64, 142, 155; see also Intonation, Speech and Talk
Violence, 162
Volition, 162

Willpower, 130
Withdrawal, 141, 165, 170
Worth, 143, 148